The important thing is not to stop questioning. Curiosity has its own reason for existence. One cannot help but be in awe when he contemplates the mysteries of eternity, of life, of the marvelous structure of reality. It is enough if one tries merely to comprehend a little of this mystery each day.
- Albert Einstein -

"I HEARD OF THAT SOMEWHERE"

A Compendium of Monsters, Mysteries, Phantoms and Phenomena of the Strange

MICHEAL D. WINKLE

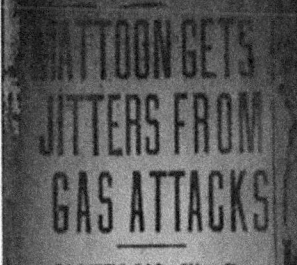

© Copyright 2018 by Michael D. Winkle
Published by American Hauntings Ink
All Rights Reserved, including the right to copy or reproduce this book, or portions thereof, in any form, without express permission from the author and publisher.

Original Cover Artwork Designed by
© Copyright 2018 by April Slaughter & Troy Taylor

This Book is Published By:
American Hauntings Ink
Jacksonville, Illinois | 217.791.7859
http://www.americanhauntingsink.com

First Edition – December 2018
ISBN: 978-1-7324079-3-0

Printed in the United States of America

INTRODUCTION

This book is a compendium of strange stories, some old, some new, some familiar, some obscure. Some are wildly at odds with what we know of science and nature, others are simply amusing, what the news media call "human interest stories."

These accounts include ghost stories, UFO reports, monster sightings, unsolved murders, and experiences with unexplained forces. They come from Hawaii, Texas, the Arctic, New England, Great Britain, and many other areas across the globe. Some accounts are centuries old, while other strange sagas are still ongoing. They were not chosen at random, however. The seeds of this book sprouted from some frustrating interactions I've had with otherwise intelligent people.

Recently, while visiting a friend's house, the conversation turned to the paranormal and thence to mysterious disappearances. The only case anyone could think of was "that boy who went out to the well and vanished." "Didn't people still hear him calling for help afterwards, but they couldn't find him?" "I think so."

This was as close as anyone could come to the tale of Oliver Lerch (or Larch), let alone the short story that account was apparently based on, Ambrose Bierce's "Mysterious Disappearances."

While clicking through a paranormal message board, the subject of "a vortex or portal opening beside a man's bed" came up. Several posters admitted that they had heard of such a story someplace, about a "vortex" almost swallowing a man, but his wife pulled him out in time. No one could bring to mind the 1873 case of Mr. and Mrs. Cumpston, which I always considered one of the top five stories collected in the books of Charles Fort.

A radio talk show devoted to the paranormal had as a guest a policeman-turned-investigator who struck me as thorough and capable. Near the end of the show the host took calls from the listeners.

Again, the subject was mysterious disappearances, and the caller talked about an American colony "around 1700" whose inhabitants had vanished. Neither the radio host nor his guest seemed to have ever heard of such a thing, and the caller could not give any specific details. It took several YouTube commentators to point out that the caller was trying to describe the Roanoke colony.

I myself often stop in the middle of reading or writing, thinking things like: "Didn't I hear about a nine-foot-tall 'spaceman' in a silvery suit who casually walked through a small town – somewhere?" Or: "Didn't I hear about a carload of teenagers who drove out to a cemetery one night and scary things happened to them?"

These unsatisfying incidents convinced me that people have "heard of" many famous paranormal cases, but tales that should be basic knowledge to those interested in the unexplained are remembered only as rumors – things that happened to "somebody somewhere." Even the Internet is of little help in these cases. Search for a subject – "John Keel on strange footprints," for instance – and you receive either the same quote multiplied a dozen times on different sites (a single excerpt from The Mothman Prophecies for the above), or comments that are almost as vague as your own muddled memories.

My idea was to create a lexicon of paranormal and Fortean events – not a dictionary or an encyclopedia, but a volume constructed along the lines of Roget's Thesaurus or Bartlett's Quotations: an index of keywords and key phrases a reader can consult to pinpoint an account only partly remembered.

For young Oliver Lerch, some key phrases might be:

Bierce, Ambrose – "Mysterious Disappearances"
Boy or man's voice still heard after vanishing
Boy or man walking to well vanishes
Indiana: Oliver Lerch disappearance
Man/boy pulled into the sky

As the work progressed, other possibilities presented themselves. The list of themes and phrases came to look more like a random-access generator – a Rorschach pattern of paranormal suggestions. Look up "Coffin, floating/flying," and your eyes will probably sweep down over "Colorado: Dinosaur reports" following, and back up to take in "Clowns, mysterious," before. Or seek out "Toxic dump – creatures seen dwelling in," and you'll find it sandwiched between "Time traveler hit by car" and "Train station, supernatural." You may open this book searching for some specific item and start flipping through it chasing other tantalizing phrases. It doesn't matter, really, how you look through a book of unsolved mysteries. "One measures a circle, beginning anywhere," as Charles Fort wrote in LO!

The spirit of finding long forgotten stories expanded to include a sense of getting back to the basics – trying to give a full account of each subject in a limited space, as well as adding new information that has appeared over the years. I mean, as long as you're here... Thus I have included articles on such well-known subjects as Jack the Ripper, the Vanishing Inuit Village, and Ambrose Bierce's "Mysterious Disappearances."

I have also included stories that are more obscure, but which (in my opinion) should be better known. You may have heard of the theory that some UFOs might be huge, living "space animals" that inhabit the upper atmosphere, but have you ever heard of the aviators who encountered a monstrous, flying-saucer-shaped creature in 1925?

And I admit it: I've included some stories just because I like them. I don't think "The Wazooey Man" or "On the Track of – Bighead?" will really advance the subject of Cryptozoology, but I've always had a fondness for those goofy old monsters.

I think you will, too.

Michael D. Winkle
Fall 2018

- Amelia Earhart – ghost seen
- Earhart, Amelia – predictions made by/apparition of
- Indiana: Amelia Earhart's ghost, Purdue University
- Phantom airplane and pilot, Purdue (IN) University

Amelia Earhart Walks at Purdue

The name of pioneer aviator Amelia Earhart appears frequently in books of unsolved mysteries due to the fact that she sailed off the map during her final flight, never to be seen again. Not content with being the first woman to fly across the Atlantic or break altitude records, she decided with typical Earhart determination to become the first person to fly around the world more-or-less along the equator. A preliminary attempt, traveling west from California to Hawaii, ended with a crash; though unharmed herself, Earhart's plane, a Lockheed Electra model 10-E, was returned to California for repairs. The itinerary was altered so that the trip would be made east around the globe. Although Earhart flew her Lockheed from Oakland to Miami, the flight officially began on June 1, 1937, from Miami, Florida.

Earhart, or AE as she preferred to be known, was accompanied by a navigator, Fred Noonan, who was essentially trapped in the tail section behind enormous gas tanks that held extra fuel. AE and Noonan stopped and started across the globe, from Florida to Puerto Rico to Senegal to India to Australia and many points in between, occasionally held up by bad weather but never by the peoples they met in their journey. On July 2, the Electra lifted off from Lae, Papua New Guinea, its destination a tiny speck of land in the vast Pacific called Howland Island. Aside from radio messages transmitted over the next several hours, that was the last anyone saw or heard of Earhart, Fred Noonan, or the twin-engine plane.

Many theories have been put forward as to what happened that July day in 1937. Earhart might have quite mundanely missed the dot of an atoll called Howland, run out of fuel, and fallen into the sea. Some have it that she and Noonan spent the rest of their lives on a desert island.

Or that she was captured by the Japanese in those days before World War II and executed as a spy (some suggest she really was spying for the U.S. government). Or that she was taken alive to Japan and became the mysterious voice on the radio known as "Tokyo Rose." Some even believe that Earhart returned to America and lived out her life under an assumed name (Amelia Earhart Lives!, (1970), by Joe Klaas, and Amelia Earhart: Beyond the Grave (2016), by W. C. Jameson).

It is fairly obvious from AE's surviving correspondence that she was of a pragmatic, materialist nature; she did not believe in an afterlife. ("You know that I have no faith we'll meet anywhere again, but I wish we might," as she wrote in a letter to be opened in event of her death [Butler, p. 170]). It seems odd, then, that late in her career she believed she had developed psychic abilities.

In 1936, Amelia and her husband, publisher George Palmer Putman, spent the Christmas season with Floyd Odlum and his wife Jacqueline Cochran, another notable female pilot. Cochran's and AE's conversations drifted from aviation to telepathy and ESP. They tried to evoke psychic powers from within themselves.

On December 15, 1936, a Western Air Express plane disappeared. AE called the airline officials, claiming that she had had a vision "in which a trapper had found the wreckage and looted it." Subsequently a trapper near Salt Lake City reported finding the crash site – no word on any looting. On December 27, a United Airlines flight was reported missing. Amelia told the airline officials to search near Saugas, a small community north of Burbank, California. "The wreckage was duly found in the location she had given them."

Finally, about two weeks after this, a Western Express aircraft crashed. Once again Amelia contacted the airline, telling them to search near Newhall, CA. Again, the wreckage was discovered where she said it would be.

After leaving the Odlum/Cochran home, this sequence of visions stopped. Amelia apparently never suffered another psychic experience. Perhaps Jacqueline and Amelia, concentrating together, formed some sort of extrasensory radar. [Lovell, pp. 240-241]

It may be that AE was premature in rejecting notions of an afterlife.

At least, an apparition answering to her description has been reported at Purdue University, West Lafayette, Indiana.

Earhart had no connection with the college until 1934. After giving a talk in New York, she was approached by the president of Purdue, Dr. Edward C. Elliott. Elliott suggested AE teach there. The university provided many aviation courses; the grounds held a sizable airfield and large hangars; and Elliott wanted to attract more female students. Amelia agreed, and in November 1935 she joined the Purdue faculty.

Earhart's position was rather informal. She lectured occasionally, but often she just mingled with the students, giving advice and encouragement.

AE still planned her 'round the world flight, but neither she nor her husband G. P. Putnam could raise the money to buy the airplane she needed. Dr. Elliott suggested promoting the plane as an aerial laboratory, filled with scientific instruments to take various readings. Donations poured in, and soon the Lockheed Electra occupied Hangar One at the Purdue airfield. Amelia worked on it endlessly in the months leading up to her final flight. Perhaps something of her powerful personality rubbed off on that aviation-intensive environment.

Writer Mark Marimen interviewed several people about the university for his book, Haunted Indiana 2. Two women, "Sally Jonas" and "Jane Jonas" (not their real names) told him about several incidents involving their father, Pete.

"My father came to America in the late thirties or early forties," explained Sally. Although an engine mechanic in Dublin, Pete could only get a job as a janitor on the Purdue airfield. One freezing January night, as Pete and other employees drank coffee in cold, drafty Hangar One, a mechanic came charging in so fast he hit one of the workmen and fell to the floor. The frightened young man said that he had been in the tool room looking for a specific wrench. All the time he was there, he felt certain he was being watched. When he finally located the right tool, he found himself confronting a dark figure, "like a person in silhouette, but three dimensional." He threw the wrench at it, but the tool passed through the phantom, which vanished.

The other mechanics told him "It's OK. She won't hurt you. Just shut up and don't tell anybody about it." Pete asked a supervisor about this "she" and learned that the men on the airfield believed the phantom was Amelia Earhart, due to her ties to Purdue and in particular Hangar One.

One evening the following December, Pete entered the break room and found an old mechanic at a table, pale and shaking. The mechanic said he was ready to quit, because "I'm tired of that damn woman pilot coming around and bothering me. I try to ignore her, but she stands there in the corner and watches everything that goes on." As time passed, more and more people told Pete of the lurking figure that resembled the missing Earhart.

During World War II, the U.S. Army commandeered part of the airfield. One night during the military occupation, the mechanics heard several shots being fired. When they felt brave enough to look outside, they found a soldier on guard duty yelling into his radio about an intruder. More soldiers arrived and swept the field with lights. The near-hysterical sentry told the officer in command that he had been walking the perimeter when someone in pilot's gear approached out of the darkness. The figure ignored the soldier's challenges and headed toward Hangar One, a restricted area. The sentry fired warning shots into the air, then he finally shot at the intruder. The figure simply vanished.

A more modern report, found in a newspaper of the late 1970s, is even more spectacular. A student working in a newly-renovated office in Hangar One was about to leave for the afternoon when suddenly the roar of a propeller-driven plane starting up all but deafened her. "It sounded like it was right there in the office with me!" she told a journalist. The student fled the office, and the ear-splitting noise abruptly ceased.

In recent years Earhart's presence has been reported in the dormitory she once occupied, according to Marvis Boscher, a resident hall manager. At least, students have reported windows opening by themselves, cold drafts in Amelia's old quarters, the clatter of a typewriter in an empty room, and sightings of a slightly-built woman with close-cropped hair who vanishes when approached. Ms. Boscher chalks these stories up to typical campus folklore.

Maybe, however, the missing pioneer of the skies returned to the place where she touched the lives of so many young people.

Butler, Susan. East to the Dawn (New York: Da Capo Press, 1999).

Lovell, Mary S. Sound of Wings: The Life of Amelia Earhart (New York: St. Martin's Press, 1989).

Marimen, Mark. Haunted Indiana 2 (Holt, Michigan: Thunder Bay Press, 1999).

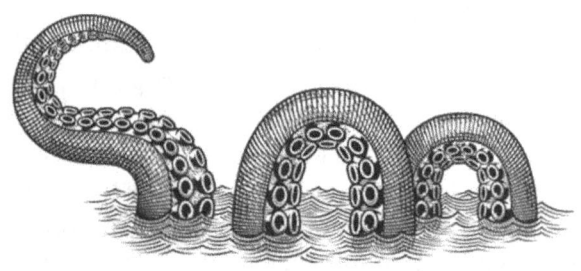

- Ape, phantom
- Gorilla, phantom
- East Sussex, UK: Phantom ape
- Tulpa (thought-form)
- Zooforms (animal-like entities)

The Astonishing Affair of the Accidental Ape

On August 4, 1913, "Miss M. B." (name on file with the Society for Psychical Research) invited her friends Mr. L. C. and Mrs. Isabel G. Powles over to meet James W. Sharpe, who had some reputation for seeing visions or "auras". The Powles lived in Rye, East Sussex, UK, and Miss B. lived about three miles away. That day, unfortunately, Mrs. Powles felt too ill to travel, so Mr. Powles rode off alone.

Mr. Powles himself had only recently recovered from pneumonia, however, and the wind that day was unusually strong and cold for August. Isabel Powles worried about him, so she started reading the latest issue of The Strand Magazine to occupy her mind. She became engrossed in what she described as "a very horrible story of a man disguised as a gorilla who came behind his enemy and broke his neck with his powerful hands."

"I have always had a great horror of gorillas from childhood, and far-fetched as it was, I was made very nervous and oppressed by the story," Mrs. Powles continues.

At Miss B.'s house, meanwhile, tea-time arrived, and the conversation touched upon psychical matters. Mr. Powles asked Sharpe about the "auras" he saw around people, and whether he saw one around him (Powles). At first Sharpe claimed to see nothing, but later he said, ominously, "You asked me to tell you; I do now see something." Sharpe saw two images lurking near Powles. One was a young woman whose description fit Mrs. Powles'. The other, however, was a "dark, non-human, creature behind me with his knotted hands on my shoulder[s]." [Sidgwick, p. 53] The woman was trying to "avert this monster's apparently evil intent."

Sharpe believed the creature to be a "health-warning", a symbol of approaching illness. Mr. Powles returned home that afternoon to hear his wife speak of the strange story she had read and of the "nervous state" it left her in. Their conclusion was that Mr. Sharpe had not only "picked up" Mrs. Powles' appearance but that of the fictional murderer she had become fixated on.

It is rather creepy that Sharpe did not say the woman thought about a hairy creature, but that he saw it with its paws on Mr. Powles' shoulders, as killer and victim were described in the story.

Mr. Powles did not fall ill at any time before writing his account for the Society for Psychical Research, three years later. Rather than a symbolic health-warning, the "gorilla strangler" was a personification of what preyed on Mrs. Powles' imagination.

Mr. Sharpe, from what little is mentioned of him, did not normally have such odd visions, nor did the Powles ordinarily undergo psychic readings. The implication is that the juxtaposition of the psychic reading with Mrs. Powles' story reading created a unique telepathic entity.

This might have been a forgettable incident of parlor-magic had Mrs. Powles' thoughts not been objectified in a form visible to Mr. Sharpe. The concept of a "tulpa" – an entity formed of pure thought – became popularized by the lady explorer Alexandra David-Neel in her 1932 book, Magic and Mystery in Tibet. A "tulpa", however, supposedly takes months to create and shape, while the "gorilla strangler" sprang whole from a single psychic observation.

Paranormal researchers Janet and Colin Bord list hundreds of reports of unknown creatures in their book Alien Animals. After concluding that many such creatures seemed too fantastic to be physical animals, they tackle the problem of what they could be. One possibility "is the idea that the human mind is, by its power of 'image making,' capable of creating a physical being which can then exist as an independent creature." [Bord, p. 191] People might expect to see, or hope to see, or imagine they see a monster, like the hair-covered semi-humans the Bords call BHMs (Big Hairy Monsters). They continue: "So are they solely hallucinatory, taking shape from the archetypal monster image? They might sometimes originate in this way, but then take on an independent existence, feeding by vampirism on whatever energy source is available." [Bord p. 192]

I am fascinated by the part chance played in this account. No one expected to see a "monster". No one tried to create a "tulpa". The gorilla image came about only because 1) Mrs. Powles happened to read that specific story in that specific magazine on that specific day, 2) it had an exceptionally upsetting effect on her, and 3) Mr. Sharpe happened at that time to examine Mr. Powles' "aura". It was truly an accidental ape. It is doubly ironic that it took on a visible existence, since even in Mrs. Powles' work of fiction there was no real ape.

Perhaps if the Powles had told and re-told the story and others dwelt on the idea of the phantasmal gorilla, it might have taken on a life of its own . . . and perhaps something like this has happened elsewhere, because there are legends in Britain of such things as the Hairy Hands of Dartmoor, the Man-Monkey of Staffordshire, and the Big Grey Man of Ben MacDhui.

Bord, Janet and Colin. Alien Animals (Harrisburg, PA: Stackpole Books, 1981).

Sidgwick, Eleanor Mildred, et. al. Phantasms of the Living (New Hyde Park, NY: University Books, 1962 [1886]), pp. 50-53.

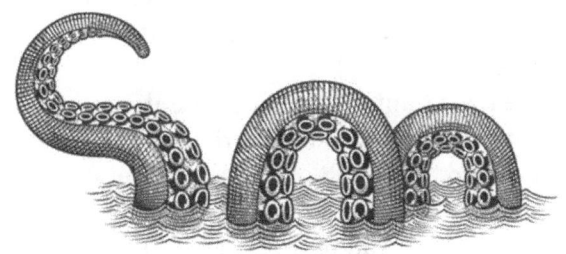

- Flying wolf-headed humanoid
- Mount Rainier: Winged humanoid
- Washington state: Winged wolflike creature
- Winged wolflike creature

Batsquatch

On Saturday night, April 16, 1994, Brian Canfield, 18, was driving his Toyota pickup from his girlfriend's house in Buckley, Washington, to the small rural community of Camp One in the foothills of Mount Rainier. At about 9:30 pm, for no apparent reason, his engine died, and his truck halted abruptly. His headlights still burned. He sat puzzled for a moment in the middle of the gravelly road, surrounded by scrubbrush and grassy fields, then something dropped into view about thirty feet ahead of his pickup.

First, he saw huge, clawed, birdlike feet, then hairy legs and a broad torso. The object landed with a distinct thud that raised dust on the road.

"It" was a muscular, humanoid creature with vast bat-like wings as well as arms, a wolfish head, and pointed ears with lynx-like tufts. It stood approximately nine feet tall and was covered with blue fur. A local newspaper described the color as a conservative gray-blue, but Canfield insisted that it was a quite striking shade, "like the bright blue in the NBC-TV peacock logo." [Benjamin, p. 30]

"Its eyes were yellow and shaped like a piece of pie with pupils like a half-moon. The mouth was pretty big. White teeth. No fangs. The face was like a wolf." [Roberts]

The creature fixed Canfield with a penetrating stare, but it gave off an air of puzzlement as well, as if it were trying to get its bearings. "I didn't feel threatened. I just felt out of place," the witness reported.

The creature stood there for several minutes, "then its fingers twitched, and its wings began to unfold." It turned, its wingspread as wide as the road, and gave Canfield a final look over one shoulder before flapping its wings. The backwash shook the small pickup. The flying beast disappeared slowly into the night, apparently heading for Mt. Rainier.

After a few moments, the pickup started again (it is unclear from the articles whether Brian started it, or if it came to life by itself a la Close Encounter of the Third Kind). He rocketed home, his hair literally standing on end, and roused his parents. His mother made him lie down, but he popped back up after a few minutes and began sketching the creature. The youth then convinced his father and a neighbor to gather gun and camera and accompany him back to the site. There was, unfortunately, nothing to be found on the gravel road five miles from the Canfield house.

Canfield wanted no publicity, but he couldn't resist talking about his encounter at school. Some of his fellow students laughed, but others came up with a name for the creature: "Batsquatch". One student of an artistic bent, Dave Kiele, took Brian's rough sketches and fleshed them out for the local newspaper.

Local journalist C. R. Roberts interviewed Canfield, his family, and his neighbors and came to the conclusion that Brian was an average high school senior "who wasn't into drugs, heavy metal music, nor Dungeons & Dragons." A year later, in an article for The INFO Journal, Phyllis Benjamin was careful to evaluate Roberts as well as Canfield:

The newspaperman impressed her as "committed, decent and thoughtful," and Brian seemed to be down-to-earth and truthful. When told that Fortean writer John Keel doubted the creature's size, Brian responded that he was sure the Batsquatch was about nine feet tall because it was standing next to a tree that served as a local landmark. He added that he was rushing home to get ready for a date, not coming back from one.

"In an interesting aside, Brian mentioned that the Camp One townspeople heard peculiar high-pitched cries several days before and after the sighting." [Benjamin, p. 31]

A unique sighting in 1994, Batsquatch has been joined in recent years by other winged, gargoyle-like beings, like the "Winged Lizard Man" of Highway 13 in Wisconsin, described by Linda Godfrey and others. Perhaps a new class of entity has come into being to join the ranks of the Chupacabras, Shadow People, and other modern bogeymen.

I think it interesting that Ms. Benjamin investigated the previous investigator as well as Canfield. One can't be too careful in the paranormal realm.

A spurious story using the name "Batsquatch" has turned up on the Internet; it concerns a Rodan-sized monstrosity that knocks a logging truck off a mountain. A similarly unlikely photograph found when Googling "Batsquatch" shows a purple something-or-other in the sky.

In recent years reports of "Dogmen" have grown more and more frequent: huge, upright canine creatures with wolflike heads. Many match Batsquatch in height, and, curiously, many witnesses mention the tufted ears, like those of a bobcat or lynx. The bright blue fur and, of course, the wings seem to be Batsquatch's alone.

Roberts, C. R. "Mount Rainier-Area Youth Has Close Encounter," Tacoma News Tribune (Tacoma, WA), May 1, 1994.

Benjamin, Phyllis. "Batsquatch, Flap, Flap," INFO Journal no. 73 (Summer 1995), pp. 29-31.

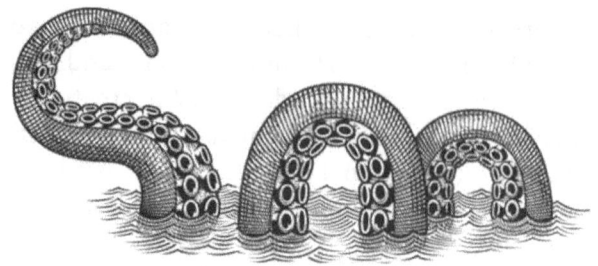

- The Birds (movie) based on real events
- California: Bird attacks
- Hitchcock, Alfred: The Birds based on real events

Behind *The Birds*

Alfred Hitchcock's 1963 thriller The Birds was loosely based on the novella of the same name by English suspense author Daphne du Maurier. Certain events in the early 1960s spurred Hitchcock to translate it to the screen despite the technical difficulties he faced in the special effects area. These bird-related events make rather creepy reading.

Birds started acting strangely beginning on or about April 26, 1960, in La Jolla, California, "where a thousand birds flew down a chimney and ravaged the inside of a house." [1] Soon thereafter: "Residents in a quiet Midwestern town -- the quintessential American Hitchcock setting -- suddenly found themselves under invasion by a covey of barn swallows, who seemed to delight in dive-bombing newsboys . . . sea gulls were reported to be terrorizing fishing ports along Germany's North Sea coast, pilfering piles of fresh fish and attacking fishermen and chimneysweeps." [2]

Several characters in the restaurant scene in The Birds discuss an event that occurred on the night of August 17-18, 1961. The August 18 Santa Cruz Sentinel headlined the story as "Seabird Invasion Hits Coastal Homes." At about 3:00 AM gulls known as sooty shearwaters, numbering supposedly in the millions, "crashed into cars and buildings, broke television aerials and streetlamps, and tried to enter houses when the residents ran out to investigate the noise." [3] The birds "pecked people, smashed into houses and cars, knocked out car headlights, broke windows, chased people around the streets and staggered around vomiting pieces of anchovy." [4] Alfred Hitchcock jumped on the story so quickly, the Sentinel mentions him calling the paper for information that very morning.

Hitchcock officially began work on his film on March 22, 1962, and even this was shadowed by eerie synchronicities. On that day a red-tailed hawk started attacking children in Victoria Park and had to be shot. Cinefantastique magazine mentions that "a Bodega Bay farmer approached Hitchcock during filming to report that he was having trouble with birds pecking out the eyes of his young lambs." [5]

There are probably complicated natural explanations for the pre-Hitchcock "attacks". The Santa Cruz invasion has been blamed on domoic acid in the fish eaten by birds in Monterey Bay. An alga called Pseudo-nitzschia australis produces domoic acid when it is starved of certain nutrients, and this toxin builds up in fish and crustaceans -- and anything that eats them. It can cause erratic behavior, aggressiveness, and, eventually, death. [6]

The brains of birds are constructed differently than those of mammals. Some biologists consider them to be much more intelligent than previously assumed. Even so, they could not plot and carry out large-scale assaults -- could they?

Always be kind to your fine feathered friends, just in case. Toss bread and popcorn to the ducks in the park and spread birdseed around the yard. Maybe they won't peck the hand that feeds them.

    Paglia, Camille. BFI Film Classics: The Birds (London: British Film Institute, 1998), p. 10.
    Counts, Kyle B., and Steve Rubin. "The Making of Alfred Hitchcock's The Birds." Cinefantastique Vol. 10, no. 2 (Fall 1980), p. 26.
    Paglia, pp. 10-11.
    "Deranged by Dodgy Anchovies." Fortean Times no. 83 (Oct.-Nov. 1995), p. 10.
    Counts and Rubin, p. 26.

Fortean Times, op. cit.

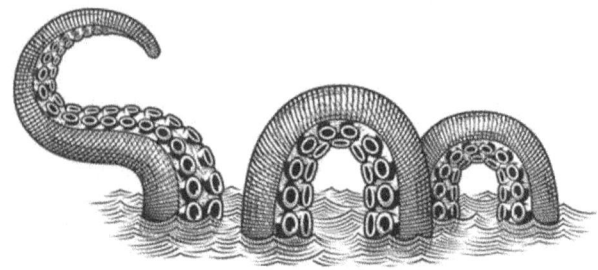

- Body parts, ghostly
- Dartmoor, UK: Hairy Hands
- Eye, disembodied
- Hairy Hands of Dartmoor
- Hand of Glory
- Hands, disembodied.
- Heads, disembodied
- Heartbeats, mysterious
- New York: Haunting
- Sandringham, Norfolk, UK: Poltergeist phenomena

Bits and Pieces

"Not only do bodies without heads appear, but miscellaneous parts of anatomy appear too."
--Louis C. Jones

When I was six or seven, we lived in a house on 27th Street in Tulsa, Oklahoma. My bed sat next to a large window. One night I woke and looked around my dark room. I glanced up at the window, and, through an unshaded pane, a pair of eyes stared back.
The eyes weren't connected to anything. They floated, raw and white, about ten feet off the ground. I shut my own eyes as hard as I

could and didn't even breathe. Eventually – somehow – I fell asleep.

On subsequent nights I not only imagined the eyes returning, I imagined a hairy, half-human Thing searching for its wandering orbs, patting blindly along the neighborhood houses in the middle of the night and sniffing around window sills like a dog. If it couldn't find its own eyes, I reasoned, maybe it would settled for a frightened little boy's. I did not sleep well.

I am fairly certain that the eyes I saw were a dream, but others have reported encountering bits and pieces of bodies floating around as if to make their own way in the world. This category of apparitions is grotesque as well as eerie. It is horrible enough to come across hands, heads, or other pieces torn from a once whole and hearty person; how much more horrible if those parts take on a life of their own? There is the sheer visceral image that gets hold of your thoughts as you envision how a body – even your own – might be mutilated and violated by accident or murderous assault; there is the unnaturalness of such pieces somehow materializing and moving by themselves; there is the thought that such entities could lurk in cupboards or dark shadows, where no human-sized monster or specter could hide; and finally there are uncomfortable spiritual questions – can a "piece" of someone have its own existence? Is that all that's left of someone, or at least all he or she can manifest? Is it possessed by, or an image created by, an outside source?

If some ghosts return as severed heads, and others as headless bodies (see "Here Comes a Chopper..."), could you come back as both at once? Which would be "you"? Or do you control both?

Now images of cartoon characters' chopped-off heads yelling at their bodies rise from memory ("Over here, stupid!"). Before we lose the eerie mood, let us look upon some bits and pieces.

The Drip

A man living near West Chazy, northern New York, decided to go fishing in a small local lake. He cast off in a flat-bottom boat, taking his dog for company. He had no luck for hours, and he finally rowed out to the middle of the lake, hoping that fish might be lurking in the deepest part. His dog started to tremble and whine.

The man's hook became entangled in something, and simultaneously his dog barked and jumped around. The animal would not lay still, even after being threatened and hit. Finally, the fisherman tugged his line free, but to his astonishment the dog sprang into the water and swam to shore.

The man reeled up his line and found what appeared to be a large tangle of human hair caught in his lure. Also caught in the hair was a gold barrette clasp that looked to be quite valuable. He took the mess home and showed it to his wife. The fisherman intended to let the hair dry out so that it would be easier to remove the gold clasp. His wife felt ambivalent about the grotesque discovery, but the barrette was so beautiful she let her husband hang the clump of hair by the fireplace.

The dripping of water from the hair seemed unusually loud to the couple – and it seemed to continue long after the hair should have dried. They left it by the fire, but to their horror, around midnight a woman's voice filled the room. The vocal apparition announced that she, the owner of the barrette, had been murdered and dumped in the lake, and she demanded that her remains be recovered and buried.

The fisherman and his wife could not bring themselves to tell the police, partly because of greed and partly because the story was so unbelievable. The ghostly voice did not speak again, but the sound of water dripping continued. Drip, drip, drip – the noise went on for days. Eventually the couple's nerves broke, and they contacted the authorities. The lake was dragged, and the body recovered.

We are not told whether the couple kept the barrette or not. I'd have given it up.

One of the creepier stories found in Colby's Weirdest People in the World, I assumed "The Drip" was a simple urban legend – until I read Things That Go Bump in the Night by college professor and folklorist Louis Jones. Between 1940 and 1946, Jones encouraged students from the New York State College for Teachers, Albany, to collect local ghost stories. A prosaic line from Jones' book states that "Mrs. John O'Brien of Herkimer [NY] heard about the talking hair from the woman who heard it talk." (!)

Colby, Carroll B. Weirdest People in the World (New York: Popular Library, 1965), pp. 32-33.

Jones, Louis C. Things that Go Bump in the Night (New York: Hill and Wang, 1959), pp. 14, 186.

The Floating Head

Charles Beidle, an employee of the Watervliet arsenal, provided another exceptionally odd story for Things that Go Bump in the Night.

When Charles was a boy in Germany in the early years of the twentieth century, he wandered from farm to farm during harvest time to work at gathering crops. Many other young men did the same. After one long, hard day, Charles and several other youths climbed into a haymow to spend the night.

For a while the group of workers gossiped and joked. For some reason they picked out a gangly Bavarian lad named Ernst to serve as the butt of their jokes. Ernst grew more and more irritated, and young Charles Beidle felt he was about to come to blows with his tormentors, when their little drama was pre-empted by a far more bizarre one.

A light appeared near the ladder that led up to the haymow. Everybody assumed someone was ascending the ladder with a lamp, perhaps to complain about their antics. Instead:

"[T]he group saw a brightly glowing head swim up through the hole in the loft, move swiftly among the men until it hovered above the shaking Ernst. The heavy-lidded eyes looked at him, through him; the voice was clouded and far away: 'Pray, Ernst, pray for your sister's soul, for this day she was drowned.'"

The head then drifted away like a toy balloon and exited a window near the roof. The next day a neighbor visited the farm to inform Ernst that, yes, his sister had died.

Jones, op. cit, pp. 13-14, 186.

Spindizzy

Mere floating isn't enough for some roaming noggins. Lyna Tan, a 14-year-old student from Singapore, wrote to that country's flamboyant ghost-chaser Russell Lee concerning a strange apparition her mother saw a few years earlier.

One night at about 2:00 am, when the whole family was asleep, a strange "twirling" noise woke Lyna's mother. At first, she could not locate the sound, but she finally decided it was coming from outside her window. Parting the curtains, she saw only a dark, spinning object. When she stepped closer however, she realized it was a disembodied human head, whirling like a top!

Understandably, she screamed, rousing the household, but the revolving specter vanished by the time the family gathered. Everyone withdrew to the family altar to pray for protection against – whatever it was.

Editor Lee remarks that very strange things seem to gather around the apartment houses of Singapore at night.

Lee, Russell. True Singapore Ghost Stories 2 (Singapore: Native Communications, 2000), pp. 143-145.

A Horrid Harvest of War

When the Pilgrims arrived in Massachusetts in 1620, their chances for survival looked slim. Fortunately, Massasoit, the great sachem (multi-tribal chief) of the Wampanoag Indians, took an interest in the white visitors and aided them in establishing a colony in North America. Massasoit's people and the Plymouth colony co-existed in peace for the most part, but after the sachem's death relationships deteriorated quickly. By 1675 Massasoit's son Metacom (called King Philip by the English) was engaged in all-out war with the European usurpers.

On June 29 of that year, near what is now Warren, Rhode Island, eight white settlers were slain in the early days of King Philip's War. Their heads were chopped off and set up on wooden stakes in an attempt to demoralize the English colonists. Atrocities of this sort were committed on both sides of this, the worst conflict between the native peoples and the European immigrants in history.

Centuries later, along the wilder sections of the Kickemuit River near Warren, witnesses have reported seeing a frightening reminder of King Philip's War: eight severed human heads, floating over the tops of trees in succession, like some ghastly aerial parade. Others have come across the heads on the ground near the river – or nearly on the ground: they sit atop crude poles or spears driven into the earth. Freelance writer Charles Turek Robinson interviewed ten witnesses of the terrifying visions in 1992. It seems the heads always appear in the same spot near the Kickemuit, usually in the early evening. Once seen, they fade away after a moment. The locals believe the heads represent the spirits of the eight dead colonists, who are making certain the terrible war is not forgotten.

Irving, Washington. Sketch Book (New York: Signet Classic, 1981 [1811]), pp. 283-299.
Robinson, Charles Turek. New England Ghost Files (North Attleborough, MA: Covered Bridge Press, 1994), p. 215.

A Pocket Full of Eye

In 1973, when Michael Melvin Adams was 12, he and his family moved to Irvington, Alabama. One day he and his cousin Tommy (age 10) explored the woods behind the house.

The two came to a clearing and distinctly saw "an old house with a tin roof and an old rocking chair sitting on the front porch." The boys worked their way through the last few feet of brush and found – nothing. The house, which should have been obvious in the empty field before them, was gone (see "Dream Houses" for similar phenomena).

A strange welcome to the area, but Michael forgot the vanishing shack after a couple of months. Then one Saturday morning he started for a female friend's house, or rather barn, where said friend would be tending to her horse. A boy named Bubba joined him.

As they walked, Michael grew aware of a lump in his pants pocket that hadn't been there before, large enough to rub uncomfortably against his leg. The boys stopped; Michael reached into his pocket, and, he writes, "pulled out what looked and felt like a real human eyeball!"

The boys screamed in horror. Michael threw the eye to the ground and stomped it flat (yucch!). The pair ran until they had to stop from sheer exhaustion, then Michael decided they should go back and investigate.

They retraced their steps, literally following their own footprints back to the site of the incident – but there was no sign of the eye, even though the ground ought to have been stained with its vitreous humor. The disturbing event was never repeated. [Warren, pp. 143-144]

Warren, Joshua P. It Was a Dark and Creepy Night (Pompton Plains, New Jersey: Career Press, Inc., 2014).

The Dancing Fingers

It Was a Dark and Creepy Night also contains a short anecdote from Tanjrina Arena, a copywriter/ proofreader from Pennsylvania. In 1995, when Tanjrina was 8 years old, she lived with her grandparents in Evon, PA. One day, with Grandpa and work and Grandma in the living room, she played with her Barbie dolls on the floor in front of her Barbie Dream House.

Suddenly a human hand plopped over the top of the dollhouse. "The hand was much larger than my then child-sized hand," Tanjrina recalled nearly twenty years later. "It was closer to the size of an adult hand."

If the hand had been attached to anyone or anything, the owner was hidden behind the house – which was far too small, however, to conceal a human being. As the young girl watched in horror, the hand "danced" on the dollhouse, scrabbling quickly from one end of the roof to the other. Finally, Tanjrina screamed and ran for her grandmother.

As with Michael Adams' eyeball, this was the one and only

appearance of the dancing hand, so it is inappropriate to call either case a haunting. Tanjrina speculates that it was some sort of "trickster entity," which is as good an explanation as any for such pointless manifestations. [Warren, pp. 122-123]

The Glowing Hand

Horror/fantasy writer F. Paul Wilson, author of Healer, The Keep, the Repairman Jack series, and many other novels and short stories, admits that this true tale comes to him third-hand (if you'll pardon the expression): It happened to his Aunt Margaret, who told it to the former Mary E. Sullivan, Wilson's mother, who frequently, at his request, told it as a bedtime story.

One night, when Margaret's son Billy was 12 years old, Margaret woke in the middle of the night. She noticed a pale white light out in the hall. It seemed to be moving down the hall toward the master bedroom.

Just as she was about to wake her husband (Wilson's Uncle Bill), the source of the light passed across the open doorway. It was a pale, glowing, disembodied hand.

When she could shake off her terror, she woke Bill (and Billy, by accident), and they all searched the house, predictably finding nothing. The next night Margaret woke and saw the floating hand pass by again. This time she forced herself to walk to the door. The hand drifted down the hall to Billy's closed door and faded out. Margaret checked her son, but he was alone and fast asleep.

The third night Margaret waited near the bedroom door, and, sure enough, at about 2:00 am: "[T]here, drifting through the air not two feet from her, was the hand, glowing brighter than ever. But this time – saints preserve us – clutched in its glowing fingers was a long, sharp knife!"

The thing drifted over to Billy's door and passed through the solid barrier. Margaret dashed down the hall and threw open the door just in time to see the hand plunge its knife into the boy's stomach.

Her scream woke Billy and Uncle Bill, but the boy seemed

unharmed. The next day, however, Billy was seized by terrible abdominal pains, requiring an emergency appendectomy.

In the nineteenth century, some members of Britain's Society for Psychical Research theorized that telepathy and clairvoyance might exist, even if the personality did not survive death. Their rather convoluted ideas held that when events brought powerful emotions out in a person – if a family desperately needed to find someone's lost will, for instance, or if a soldier was dying in a foreign land – "super ESP" might kick in and locate the wanted object or person no matter where it was on earth. The thing is, as the subconscious mind communicates through symbol-laden dreams, this "super ESP" creates imagery of its own: The dead person's "ghost" will reveal the whereabouts of his will; the soldier will materialize before loved ones at the moment of his death.

In Aunt Margaret's case, it could be that she sensed something wrong within her son, though he seemed perfectly normal in all respects, and the imaginary hand pinpointed the problem in no uncertain terms. A rather extreme warning, but one that eventually benefited F. Paul Wilson, who many years later used the tale in one of his novels.

Wilson, F. Paul, "The Glowing Hand," in: Jones, Stephen. A Ghostly Cry (New York: Fall River Press, 2009), pp. 316-318.

Hand of Glory

From his wallet drew a human hand,
Shrivell'd, and dry, and black;
And fitting, as he spake,
A taper in his hold,
Pursued: 'A murderer on the stake had died;
I drove the vulture from his limbs, and lopt
The hand that did the murder, and drew up
The tendon strings to close its grasp;
And in the sun and wind

Parch'd it, nine weeks exposed.

Robert Southey, "Thalaba the Destroyer"

Whether or not hands went a-haunting in medieval times, they were important in the manufacture of one famous occult artifact. The Hand of Glory is the hand of a man who has been hanged. It is cut off, emptied of blood, prepared with various compounds and herbs including saltpeter, salt, and pepper, and dried in the sun or even in an oven if time is of the essence. It becomes then a magical tool often used by criminal bands. One places a candle in the Hand's grip (sometimes the candle is supposed to be made of bizarre substances like the fat of the aforementioned hanged man), or one actually lights the fingers like tapers, and upon entering the target building, anyone within who sleeps or lies near sleep will remain unconscious, and anyone awake will remain awake (otherwise it would affect members of the gang). The Hand can also shatter locks, bolts, and wooden bars, and it can lead the user to treasure.

Richard Barham, writing as Thomas Ingoldsby, gives an eerie incantation in his Ingoldsby Legends that sums up the Hand quite well:

Open, lock,
To the Dead Man's knock!
Fly, bolt, and bar, and band!
Nor move, nor swerve,
Joint, muscle, or nerve,
At the spell of the Dead Man's hand!
Sleep, all who sleep! – Wake, all who wake!
But be as the dead for the Dead Man's sake!

Sabine Baring-Gould, in his Curious Myths, reports that "a labouring man in the West Riding of Yorkshire" told him a tale of a Hand of Glory. It seems a poor beggar appeared at the door of an inn, long after closing time, on a stormy night. He was allowed to lie on a mat in the kitchen.

The personnel and guests of the inn all went to bed except for a servant girl. Through a tiny window in the kitchen door, the servant noticed the beggar rising. She watched as he pulled out a mummified human hand and set it up like a candlestick. The beggar then "anointed the fingers, and, applying a match to them, they began to flame." The girl tried to arouse the men of the house, but they could not be awakened.

On checking the kitchen again, she saw that the "thumb light" had gone out, an indication to the beggar that "one of the inmates of the house was not asleep." The intruder did not seem bothered by this; instead he carried the Hand through the rooms, opening locked doors and chests. He set the Hand down as he gathered his loot, and the serving girl tried to put out the flaming fingers of the grotesque artifact. They could not be blown out, and beer poured on them only made them burn brighter. Finally a jug of milk sloshed on the Hand doused it. She then locked the beggar in the room he was ransacking and roused the household. The beggar was captured, and he hanged himself in jail.

Baring-Gould, Sabine. Curious Myths of the Middle Ages (New Hyde Park, NY: University Books, 1967 [1866]), pp. 405-410.
Ingoldsby, Thomas. Ingoldsby Legends (London: MacMillan and Co., 1911 [1840]), pp. 23-30.

Hairy Hands of Dartmoor

Now for the most infamous hands of all:

"As far as I have been able to ascertain," writes Ruth E. St. Leger-Gordon in her book Witchcraft and Folklore of Dartmoor, "there is no mention or hint of the Hairy Hands before the second decade of the present [20th] century." There were an unusual number of cases, however, of horses throwing their riders, wagons and traps overturning, and motorcars crashing, near a village called Postbridge, as far back as 1908.

In June of 1921, Dr. E. H. Helby, Medical Officer of Provincetown

Prison, was riding his motorcycle along the B3212, formerly Carter's Road, between Princetown and Postbridge. He was heading for Postbridge to attend an inquest. In his sidecar rode two young girls, the daughters of the Deputy Governor. Just as they were rolling down a hill into Postbridge, the doctor yelled for the two girls to jump out. They obeyed just as the medical man was flung from his vehicle. He broke his neck, but the girls were relatively unharmed. There seemed to be nothing wrong with the motorcycle.

A few weeks later a motor coach driving up the same hill swerved unexpectedly into the ditch, though no one was injured. On August 26, 1921, a "Captain M." of the British Army – "a very experienced rider" – crashed his motorcycle outside Postbridge, but he survived. Indeed, he had something very interesting to tell journalist T. Gifford, who published his statement in the London Daily Mail of October 17:

"A pair of hairy hands closed over mine. I felt them as plainly as ever I felt anything in my life – large, muscular, hairy hands. I fought them for all I was worth, but they were too strong for me. They forced the machine into the turf at the edge of the road, and I knew no more till I came to myself, lying a few feet away on the face of the turf."

Devonshire folklorist Theo Brown received a letter from Mrs. E. M. Battiscombe (the wife of the doctor who replaced Dr. Helby) in which she mentioned a young man visiting people in Postbridge. He, too, went on an errand on a motorbike, but he returned in less than an hour, "very white and shaken." "He said he had felt his hands gripped by two rough and hairy hands and [they made] every effort to throw him off the machine. He had never got much beyond the clapper bridge." [Brown, p. 97]

The authorities blamed the Postbridge accidents on reckless driving, high speeds, and a poor camber on the curves in that section of the road. Repairs were implemented, but if roadwork drove the Hands from the B3212, they made a spectacular reappearance at the abandoned Powder Mills about half-a-mile north.

Theo Brown and her parents pulled a caravan out of mothballs for a month each summer, hauling it into the country and setting up camp in some rural area. In 1924, as a change from the usual holiday spots,

Mr. Brown decided they should camp at the deserted gunpowder factory. (I'm sure it seemed like a good idea at the time.)

Mrs. Brown, having an artistic bent, produced several sketches of the countryside. Young Theo played with the local farm children. One night, however, while her family slept, Theo's mother encountered something horrible. She did not tell her daughter what happened until many years later.

As mentioned in "The Hole in the Path" (see "Voids"), the young Ms. Brown was expert at getting people to open up about their strange experiences. In 1950 she convinced her mother to write an account of her frightening vision.

"It was a cold moonlit night and I was in my bunk in a caravan on a very lonely part of Dartmoor," Mrs. Brown began. She woke confused, feeling that something menacing and powerful lurked nearby. She looked around, and her gaze fell upon Mr. Brown, whose bed lay at the end of the caravan under a small window.

"I saw something moving, and as I stared, my heart beating fast, I saw it was the fingers and palm of a very large hand with many hairs on the joints and back of it, clawing up and up to the top of the window which was a little open." [Brown, p. 98]

Mrs. Brown felt instinctively that the hand hated them and wanted to do harm to her husband. She also felt that no weapon would stop it. So, being a good Christian, she made the sign of the Cross and prayed. The hand withdrew.

The family remained at the powder works for several weeks, but the hand or hands did not return. However, Mrs. Brown finished, "I did not feel happy in some places not far off and would not for anything have walked alone on the Moor at night."

The prolific fortean writer Nick Redfern uncovered a Hairy Hands encounter – an outright assault, in fact – as recently as 2008. Michael Anthony, a salesman for a large photocopying firm, was in Postbridge on January 16 of that year closing a deal with the proprietor of a new business, who wanted to rent several copiers. It was about 11:00 pm by the time the papers were all signed, and Anthony felt pleased as he started back home to Bristol and his family.

Just outside Postbridge, however, the atmosphere in his car

became oppressive. Anthony felt cold, clammy, and afraid. He actually thought he was having a stroke. Instead, to his horror, a disembodied set of hairy hands or paws clamped over his own hands and tried to steer his vehicle off the road. He fought them off only to have them leap back on the steering wheel and try again. He fought them off a second time, yet they whipped back like a pair of evil bats and grabbed the wheel a third time.

As Anthony struggled against this last assault, a flash of light filled the car, followed by a sulfurous stink. The hands vanished. The salesman roared off and did not stop until he reached a gas station miles away. [Redfern, pp. 54-55]

Michael Williams, author of Supernatural Dartmoor, was enjoying a drink with Rufus Endle, a "thoroughly professional journalist," at a Devonshire men's club. When Williams mentioned he was researching the above-mentioned book, Endle told him of a frightening event that befell him one night as he drove from Chagford to Princetown – a route that took him through Postbridge.

"Suddenly, as I approached the bridge, a pair of hands gripped the driving wheel and I had to fight for control. It was a very scary minute or so. God knows how I didn't crash at the bridge, and the hands went as inexplicably as they came. I never wrote about it in the newspapers, or even told anybody else for fear of ridicule."

Even after this confession Mr. Endle worried about admitting to an experience this strange; he made Williams promise not to print it until after the journalist's death.

Sometimes, Williams points out, the Hands are seen; sometimes they aren't. Sally Jones, collecting material for her own book on Devonshire, told him of a Somerset doctor who was driving through Postbridge in 1977. Although he saw nothing, "he was aware of some powerful force inside his car: 'something quite out of my control...' In his case 'the steering wheel seemed to go wild.'"

Williams may have even uncovered an account of the Hands almost but not quite materializing. In June 1955 a man named Maurice Dart traveled to North Bovey and attended the Fair. "I was cycling home across Dartmoor on the lovely warm sunny Sunday morning, really enjoying the experience," Dart told Williams.

Dart passed through Postbridge and entered a section of road hemmed in by trees and brush. Even a touch of claustrophobia, however, wouldn't explain the feeling of panic that hit him. He continues: "I looked back and upwards over my left shoulder and saw what appeared to be a swirling cloudy mass in the otherwise clear blue sky descending rapidly towards me."

Mr. Dart pedaled for all he was worth, reaching the village of Two Bridges and shooting right through, not stopping until he had topped a hill beyond. There the panic left him. He looked back again "and just glimpsed the fuzzy mass disappearing up into the sky, way behind me." [Williams, p. 20]

Another correspondent wrote to Williams about a "furry paw" causing car accidents, but that he had not heard any reports of it since the Second World War. Ruth St. Leger-Gordon and Theo Brown make similar observations in their books of Dartmoor folktales. However, it seems that, whether you see them or not, the Hairy Hands have not gone away.

Brown, Theo. Devon Ghosts (Norwich: Jarrold & Sons Ltd., 1982).
Fort, Charles. Complete Books (NY: Dover Books, 1974 [1941]), p. 958.
Redfern, Nick. Wildman! The Monstrous and Mysterious Saga of the "British Bigfoot" (Bideford, North Devon: CFZ Press, 2012).
St. Leger-Gordon, Ruth E. Witchcraft and Folklore of Dartmoor (New York: Bell Publishing, 1965).
Williams, Michael. Supernatural Dartmoor (Launceton, Cornwall: Bossiney Books, 2003).

"It is the beating of his hideous heart!"

Edgar Allan Poe might have thought up this next story. In 1900, two brothers, Bob and Emmitt Smith, built a house in Irvington, Kentucky, beside what is now U.S. Highway 60. Eventually Bob married a woman named Gladys Spink, who unfortunately did not like Emmitt at all.

Emmitt had a heart condition and required frequent medication. In December 1939, while Bob had business in town, Gladys removed the medicine from Emmitt's bedroom and locked him in. Emmitt's own struggles to escape brought on a fatal heart attack.

In 1973, young Elbert Cundiff, his parents, and his grandfather rented the former Smith house. The family decided to sleep in the house the very day they moved in, unpacking their bedding while leaving their other possessions boxed up. At about 11:00 pm, as Elbert was getting ready for bed, he heard something:

"I listened and it started off real faint, sounded like a heartbeat. The more I listened to it, the louder it got. Sounded just exactly like a heartbeat." [Montell, p. 47]

Elbert ran to get his parents, but his father couldn't be bothered to get up. Mrs. Cundiff did follow the youth back to his room, and yes, she agreed, the noise did sound like a heart thumping away.

The noise grew louder and louder, practically shaking the house. Elbert thought the building was going to explode, so strong were the pulsations. Unlike Poe's tale, the noise seemed to come from above Elbert's room (Emmitt Smith had lived upstairs).

"Then, all at once it just stopped." Apparently the haunting heart had had its say – so to speak.

Montell, William Lynwood. Ghosts across Kentucky (Lexington, KY: University of Kentucky Press, 2000), pp. 45-47.

Home is Where the Heart is

In 1889, a house was built over a coal mine near Lydney, Gloucestershire, England, in the Forest of Dean. The mine was shut down in 1923, and by the mid-1980s John and Johanna Mizen were living in the century-old domicile. One night in October 1985, at about 3:00 am, a noise like a muffled heartbeat awakened the couple. It could be heard in every room, but not outside, and the four Mizen sons who still lived at home could not hear it. A fifth son, Barry, could hear the "heart" when he came to visit.

Many inexplicable noises or vibrations have been reported in various parts of the world, usually (apparently) pulsing out of the earth. Unlike many of those mystery sounds, the "heartbeat" registered on electronic equipment, specifically that from the Environmental Health Department. The "heart" throbbed "at 31.5 cycles at 38 decibels, a frequency not normally audible to the human ear." The noise was still audible as of that December.

The mention of a coal mine below the house reminds me of John Lymington's Ten Million Years to Friday (1967) and Brian Lumley's The Burrowers Beneath (1974). In both novels cosmically powerful beings sleep beneath the world of tiny mortal men, who build their cities and wage their wars like ant colonies until one day, miners or geologists dig into the earth and hear a loud, impossible heartbeat...

"Haunted by Heartbeats," Fortean Times no. 47 (Autumn 1986), p. 25.

Heartbeat – it's a Love Beat

One Pete Wilson described a "heartbeat" out in the natural world, in an email to the Fortean Times. "About three years ago" (circa 2001), Pete and his wife were walking through Wakerley Woods in Northamptonshire, UK. It was such a nice, sunny day that the Wilsons left the trail and hiked amongst the pine trees. Mrs. Wilson, several yards ahead, suddenly stopped.
"Can you hear that?" she asked.
Pete Wilson heard nothing at first, but gradually he "tuned in" to a dull throb he described as a "chthonic heartbeat."
"It was rhythmical and sensed in a rather unpleasantly visceral way; when you tuned into it you had the sense of it being so massively dispersed that you were almost part of it . . . There was the definite sensation that whatever was producing the vibration was massive, as it seemed to pervade the Earth and air."
Mr. Wilson noted that there were no roads nearby, nor any reports of seismic activity in the local newspapers.

Wilson, Pete, "Cthonic Heartbeat," Fortean Times no. 185 (Aug. 2004), p. 77.

Breathe Deeply . . .

This may be the most bizarre partial entity yet. Peter Underwood, the British ghost hunter, reports that the country house and estate of Sandringham, Norfolk, a favorite retreat of the British royals, is haunted by poltergeistic phenomena. Footsteps, doors opening and closing, light switches flipping on and off, sheets pulled off newly-made beds -- the usual tricks.

The phenomena concentrate on the servants' quarters and are said to begin around Christmas Eve and continue for several weeks. There is something in the manse that gives off a noise of "heavy breathing," and this entity has been seen: "One footman refused to sleep in the room assigned to him after he claimed to have seen something which he described as 'looking like a large paper sack breathing in and out like a grotesque lung.' He also heard heavy and regular breathing apparently emanate from the curious bulging object."

Underwood, Peter. Gazetteer of British, Scottish and Irish Ghosts (New York: Bell Publishing, 1985 [1971]), p. 201.

There are many more tales of partial entities. Some could fill volumes, like stories of the Screaming Skulls of the British Isles. Perhaps we can get to them in a future volume.

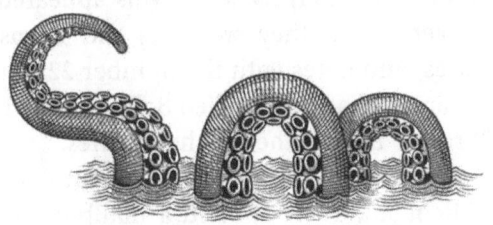

- Clowns, mysterious
- King, Stephen: and fear of clowns
- Michigan: Mysterious clowns
- Numerical coincidences

Bobo and the Lord of 22

During the summer and fall of 2016 a flap – or perhaps flop, as of oversized shoes – of "creepy" or "killer" clowns swept the USA, Great Britain, and Europe. People saw clowns in parks, woodlands, suburban neighborhoods and even on deserted country roads. Most simply wandered around, looking strange and ominous, while others chased innocent citizens, brandished weapons, and assaulted people and even moving vehicles. Numerous photos and videos surfaced of the eerie harlequins, many staged but all rather disturbing to watch. Podcaster Donnie Barnett called it the Clown Apocalypse, after the "Zombie Apocalypse" so beloved of horror movies, while other news sites referred to Clownmaggedon.

The recent wave of bulb-nosed invaders, however, was not the first appearance of strange, baggy-pants apparitions.

Sometime around the beginning of 1980, Bob Tarte directed an amateur Super 8 film entitled "Monsters". One scene featured his friend Bill Holm sitting in a bathtub wearing a clown mask and giant sunglasses. For the next year, an ever-growing quantity of "clown coincidences" intersected their lives. Clowns appeared in ads, on TV and in person everywhere they went, as did license tags, phone numbers, addresses, and dates with the number 22 in them. Jokingly – or not – they invented characters called Bobo and the Lord of Twenty-Two to be the "brains" behind the synchronicities.

In February 1981, while driving in a semi-rural area northeast of Grand Rapids, Michigan, Tarte spotted a mailbox with the name A. CLOWN on the side. On March 25 a "battered white Chevy" with clown faces and the words BOBO THE ROLLER CLOWN painted on it rolled up beside Tarte's Subaru. The driver was "plump" and "grizzled".

After seeing this physically real Bobo the clowns came in a steady stream. Tarte and Holm went to see the Jerry Lewis movie Hardly Working only to discover that Lewis played an unemployed clown named Bobo. Stopping in a store called Toys Ahoy, they found that the last person to sign the register was "MR. BUM THE CLOWN." A glance in the phone book showed that a "K. Bobo" lived only two blocks from Tarte. Driving past this address, they discovered a "Mr. Jolly" ice cream truck, covered with pictures of clowns, parked in front of it. Naturally they crossed paths henceforth with Mr. Jolly trucks wherever they went. One parked all day – illegally – in front of Holm's office at Grand Rapids Magazine.

On June 16 the Detroit Free Press reported that a man in New Orleans had legally changed his name to "LOVE 22." He had been arrested for selling "twenty-two dollar bills" to finance his Presidential campaign. LOVE 22's campaign site, by the way, is still up as of this writing. See: http://www.love22.com/

Tarte and Holm outlined the story of clowns and 22s to several friends. This was unfortunate – for the friends. Dave Bartek of Flint, Michigan, volunteered that he had spotted a clown hitchhiking. A few days later he saw a clown on a bicycle and upon going out to the parking lot found that the car next to his bore the license plate "222".

Bartek moved to Phoenix, Arizona – to N. 22nd Street, of course. He drove to a shopping mall – where clowns happened to be capering that day – and upon returning to this Ford Fairmont discovered two dozen blue and white balloons attached to his vehicle.

Steve Williams of Cloquet, Minnesota, found himself stuck in traffic behind city bus no. 2222 while the theme from the early '70s TV show Room 222 played on the radio ("And how many times do you ever hear that on the radio?" he asked. [Tarte and Holm, pp. 46-47])

Tarte learned that Fortean author Loren Coleman was researching "phantom clowns" (this eventually became a chapter of Coleman's book Mysterious America). He contacted Coleman and outlined the Bobo saga. The clowns and 22s popped up as never before:

"[Holm's] co-worker Bonnie Hanger got a porcelain clown music box from her mother on her 22nd birthday. Holm's boss John Brosky was downtown in Kalamazoo when a golf cart carrying two clowns drove slowly by. They wore name tags. HI, I'M BOBO, said the driver's; HI, I'M JOHNO the passenger's. Then, the following poem from New York was inexplicably submitted for publication: 'A raving beauty/Got into a stew,/She finished a contest/Raving "Oh, 22!"' [Tarte and Holm, p. 47]

Dennis Keller, a local cartoonist, invited Tarte to his house to meet his lady friend, Arlene "Sam" Samrick. Tarte started in on the clown story for Sam when suddenly she interrupted: "Oh, Bobo the Roller Clown. He lives on Four Mile by the Stop 'N' Go."

Tarte and Holm investigated. The area was close to where Tarte had seen the A. CLOWN mailbox. The duo parked at the Stop 'N' Go and walked to a nearby row of mailboxes. There indeed stood a box with the word BOBO painted in 2-inch-high letters, accompanied by the legend "Leo Torpey." As if this second discovery of the "real" Bobo were some sort of signal, the clowns and 22s began fading away.

Even as Fortean Times no. 38, containing the story of Bobo, hit the newsstands, Bob Tarte learned that Leo Torpey, aka Bobo T. Clown, had died in Grand Rapids. As if in honor of Torpey's passing, a final round of synchronicity hit, having to do with the name Tartal (relatives of Torpey – "too close to my own for comfort"), the word "turtle", the number 22, and the name Kim.

"I received a $1 dollar bill with the legend 'Kim 22' written on it. Natch, there had been a spate of wrong numbers on the telephone here and at work asking for Kim . . . last week, while at a friend's house, the babysitter for his children arrived, a teenager named Kim Tuttle." (Rickard, p. 27)

Perhaps Tarte and Holm strung together unrelated events into an apparent conspiracy. "Synchronicity" was Carl Jung's term for "meaningful coincidences," but what is the meaning of Bobo?

According to folklorist Gertrude Jobes, the number 22 symbolizes "arrogance, catastrophe, error, folly . . . one who gambles, is ostentatious, philanthropic, has wanderlust." [Jobes, p. 1614] Bobo himself might represent a new version of the ancient Trickster archetype, known in mythologies worldwide.

Many Fortean and paranormal writers, after trying to make sense of ghosts, UFOs, sea-monsters, crop circles and the like, have finally thrown up their hands and suggested that a "Cosmic Clown" creates these phenomena just to have fun at our expense. That may be as good an explanation as any. As Bob Tarte put it, "Only a figure as stupid as Bobo would make me long for an intelligent deity."

Did Stephen King know the story of Bobo? King's monumental novel IT features a being from beyond our universe that haunts the small town of Derry, Maine. It takes on a variety of forms, but Its favorite is that of "Pennywise the Dancing Clown." Bob Tarte's mention of "turtle coincidences" is interesting, because the gang of outcast children in IT learn of another cosmic being: "Before the universe there had been only two things. One was Itself and the other was the Turtle. The Turtle was a stupid old thing that never came out of its shell." [King, p. 965] In an afterword, King states that IT was "begun in Bangor, Maine, on September 9th, 1981, and completed in Bangor, Maine, on December 28th, 1985." [King, p. 1090] The Fortean Times articles were published within this period.

Since the time of Tarte and Holm's clown coincidences, a wave of coulrophobia has swept the world. Nowadays almost everyone claims they were frightened of clowns as children. Stephen King's IT, the movie Killer Klowns from Outer Space, and other films and stories have given us evil, grease-painted mountebanks by the clown-car-full.

Loren Coleman's Mysterious America, mentioned above, documents the clown "invasion" that started in Boston, Massachusetts, in the spring of 1981. Clowns, usually driving vans, were supposedly harassing schoolchildren, chasing them, or trying to lure them into their vehicles with candy. After a fruitless investigation, the police disregarded the reports, but sightings spread into surrounding cities and south to Providence, Rhode Island. Then clowns popped up in Kansas City – of both Kansas and Missouri. Next, they showed up in Pittsburgh and other Pennsylvania cities, then sporadically throughout the nation. In those pre-Internet times, says Coleman, the newspapers and police of the individual cities seemed unaware that clowns were appearing elsewhere. "Something quite unusual was happening in America in the Spring of 1981." [Coleman, p. 269]

In May 1992, police in Minneapolis, Minnesota, received reports of "suspicious activity" by a clown with a white face, red hair, and a green-and-white polka-dotted costume. The clown was seen lurking in the woods near Vadnais Heights Elementary School. Residents of the Vadnais Heights neighborhood found him or her standing on their property at night.

In June 1994, around Alexandria, Virginia, and Washington, D.C., there were nearly a hundred reports of clowns driving white vans trying to lure children into their vehicles. Authorities dismissed the sightings as rumors. A police spokesman said, "The children may just be seeing the bogeyman. Any time people see a white van, they see a clown too."

A clown in Billericay, Essex, UK, got up close and personal. On October 4, 1995, he entered St. Andrew's Hospital and told the nurses he was delivering flowers and a telegram to a patient. Upon reaching the patient's room, the clown pulled a sawed-off shotgun out of his bouquet and shot him.

Finally, on November 2, 1995, sixty professional clowns in Tegucigalpa, Honduras, burned their costumes to distance themselves symbolically from evil harlequins. Over the previous two years, about 300 children had been reported missing, many supposedly dragged into vans by men dressed as clowns. The Honduran police suggested that "the children are either being sold for adoption, turned into drug smugglers, or butchered for the spare-parts trade." ["Fears of a Clown," p. 17]

The last word on clowns, however, must go to one Brian Chapman of Victoria, British Columbia, in a letter to the Fortean Times. Mentioning the fact that apelike Bigfeet, mysterious black panthers, and other unexplained beasts or monsters are often blamed on animals escaping from derailed circus trains, he writes, "Your round-up of reports of malevolent clowns [FT85:17] brings up the question: why has no-one ever suggested that such a clown probably escaped from a circus train wreck?"

Chapman, Brian, "Runaway Clowns," Fortean Times no. 91 (Nov.

1996), p. 53.

Coleman, Loren. Mysterious America: the Revised Edition (New York: Paraview Press, 2001).

"Fears of a Clown," Fortean Times no. 85 (Feb/March 1996), p. 17.

Jobe, Gertrude. Dictionary of Mythology, Folklore and Symbols Vol. 2 (New York: Scarecrow Press, 1962).

King, Stephen. IT (New York: Signet Books, 1986).

Rickard, Bob, "Reflections: Circle of Clowns," in Fortean Times no. 39 (Spring 1983), p. 27.

Tarte, Bob, and Bill Holm, "A Circle of Clowns," in Fortean Times no. 38 (Autumn 1982), pp. 46-48.

Bob Tarte re-wrote his article on Bobo and 22 for Yellow Silk Magazine in 1991: see Bob Tarte's "Technobeat" Archives: http://www.technobeat.com/COLUMNS/BOBO.html

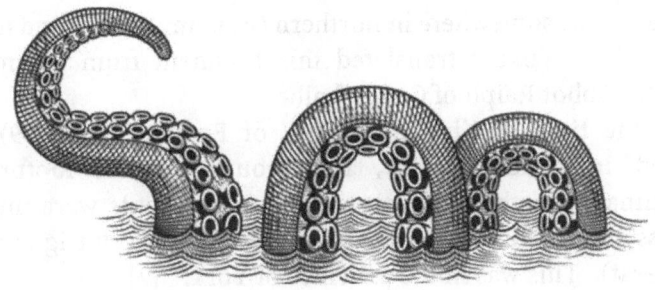

- Burning Man
- Fiery humanoid
- Germany: "Human torch"
- "Human Torch" specter

The Burning Man

A truly frightening creature is described in the old Deutsche Sagen of the Brothers Grimm: "'In this year (1125) we saw a fiery man walking between the two castles called Gleichen. It was right at midnight. The man walked from one castle to the other, and he burned like a bright flame.' The sentries who tell this story report that he did this for three nights and no more."

Shades of the Human Torch! The Grimms continue: "George Miltenberger, who lived in the so-called Hoppelrain near Kailbach in the region of Freienstein, tells the following story. 'It was on the first Sunday of Advent between eleven and twelve o'clock when I saw, not far from my house, a man who was completely enveloped in fire. One could count all the ribs in his body. He remained on the road from one milestone to the next until right after midnight, when he vanished.'" [1]

The creature was able to spew fire from its nose and mouth, terrifying anyone who encountered it. Folklore professor Donald Ward, in his translation of The German Legends of the Brothers Grimm, reports that the Brothers combined two stories into one. The first takes place somewhere in northern Germany, the second in Hesse.

Harold T. Wilkins translated this fragment from the medieval chronicler Abbot Ralph of Coggeshall:

"'In the time of King Richard I, of England' (1189-99), 'there appeared in certain grassy, flat ground human footprints of extraordinary length; and everywhere the footprints were impressed the grass remained as if scorched by fire (herba velut igne ustulata remanserat). This was in the province of York.'" [2]

Philip MacLeod writes of a German bogey called the Puhu, or Fiery Man, in a 1915 article from Occult Review:

"There is a curious legend of a girl who was induced to call from a window, 'Come and kiss me, Fiery Man!' Presently the terrified company heard a swift foot upon the stair and a panting breath at the door, which they dared not open. Suddenly two hands were struck on the wood, and the steps retreated again, but on the door there remained the deep charred marks of two fiery hands."

It sounds as if this young woman came perilously close to a terminal case of chapped lips! A Pastor Schneider of Feldberg saw the Burning Man more than once, as he describes in a letter published in 1850:

"Last year I saw a puhu again. It was in the autumn; I was returning with my children from a walk to M_____. As we came into our little vale, a puhu was hurrying to and fro on the top of the hill between this place [Felding?] and O.E. We followed the burning apparition with our eyes for a long time. When we got home, I took the telescope and very attentively observed the apparition with that instrument. It was just like the other appearance described above: round, and blazing with many pale flames, and of the size of a basket. For a long time it ran to and fro upon the hill opposite the parsonage, till at length it went down into the valley and disappeared among the houses." [3]

This was a nasty little story to come across at age 11. Since most monsters of legend and film hated fire, I felt I would be safe in any horror movie-type environment if I stayed near a campfire or torch. But the Burning Man would just love that!

1. Grimm, Jacob and Wilhelm. German Legends of the Brothers Grimm (1812-1814). New edition edited and translated by Donald Ward (London: ISHI, 1981), Vol. I, p. 231.
2. Wilkins, Harold T. Strange Mysteries of Time and Space (New York: Ace Books, 1958), p. 197.
3. MacLeod, Philip, "The Fiery Man," Occult Review Vol. 21 (1915), pp. 286-288.

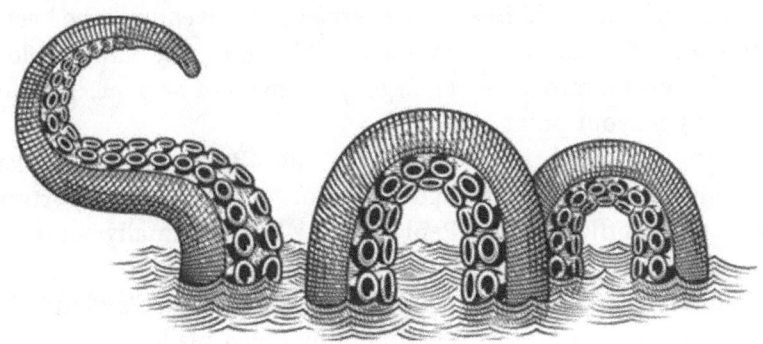

- California: Actor sees men with dog's heads
- Marco, Paul (Ed Wood actor) reports dogmen
- Plan 9 from Outer Space actor reports dogmen
- Wood, Ed, actor sees dogmen

Can Your Heart Stand the Shocking Facts about Hollywood Dogmen?

It was not until her fourth book on unidentified bipedal canines that reporter/author Linda S. Godfrey uncovered any reports of "dogmen" or "manwolves" from southern California, and three of those were actually of a creature that "looked like a lynx but was the size of a Doberman." [1] (See also "Legend Trips" elsewhere in this volume.) There seem to be few sightings in general of such cryptids in the western United States. Perhaps, however, we have overlooked an early witness to the dogman phenomenon.

Born and raised in the Los Angeles/Hollywood area, Paul Marco (1927 - 2006), birth name Angelo Inzalaco, went into show business "because I liked acting and being funny, and, well, I didn't know what I was doing," as he said in a 2005 interview. [2] Eventually he became friends with the infamous filmmaker Ed Wood, Jr., who employed Marco in several movies -- which may or may not be a success story, depending on your point of view.

Marco appeared in Wood's 1955 film Bride of the Monster, alongside horror stars Bela Lugosi and Tor Johnson. Marco portrayed a timid police officer named Paul Kelton, which eventually became his signature role.

Filmed in 1956 (but not released until 1959), Wood's Plan 9 from Outer Space, often dubbed "the worst movie ever made," brought back Marco as Officer Kelton, who bemoans the fact that he gets all the weird assignments. The patrolman knew of which he spoke, because he appeared again in Wood's Night of the Ghouls, a sequel to Bride of the

Monster.

Unfortunately, after a few more movie and TV credits, Marco faded from the scene for nearly a quarter century. Then, in the cinema magazine Cult Movies (#16, 1995), publisher Buddy Barnett reported: "Ed Wood actor Paul Marco (Kelton the cop) has been admitted to the county psychiatric hospital for evaluation. Allegedly, Marco was seeing men with dog heads invading his property."

Marco summoned the police, and the responding officers, predictably, found nothing. "Marco was taken into custody after a brief altercation with the officers." [3]

I'm surprised more witnesses of dog- or wolf-headed humanoids don't get taken in for evaluation -- or get into "brief altercations" if they don't wish to go. Perhaps after so long out of the spotlight, Marco's life was taking a final, sad turn.

Or was it a sad turn? Sometime in that year of 1995, Marco (as Kelton) cut a record with Dionysus Records, "Home on the Strange." In 2005 he played Kelton in a movie called The Naked Monster, a spoof which starred several actors from 1950 sci-fi films. [4] In 2006, "Kelton's Dark Corner" was slated to be an independent TV series, directed by Russian rock-and-roll star Vasily Shumov and starring Marco as the bumbling cop, encountering strange beings and situations a la the 'seventies show Kolchak: The Night Stalker. Unfortunately, Marco died during production, and the existing footage was edited and padded to make one feature-length film, Kelton's Dark Corner, Trilogy One. [5] (Marco shared the cinematic fate of his former co-star Bela Lugosi, who died during the production of Plan 9, and whose existing scenes had to be padded out by a body double, Ed Wood's chiropractor.)

Perhaps seeing dog-headed men was a prophecy of better times to come. Or perhaps it was just the sort of thing that happened to Officer Kelton.

1. Godfrey, Linda S., Real Wolfmen: True Encounters in Modern America (New York: Tarcher/Penguin, 2012), p. 95.

2. Sloan, Will. "Can Your Heart Stand the Shocking Facts About

Kelton the Cop, aka Paul Marco?" Filmfax No. 106 (April-June 2005), p. 88-89.

3. Barnett, Buddy. "Cult Movie Stuff," Cult Movies No. 16 (1995), p.20.

4. http://en.wikipedia.org/wiki/Paul_Marco

5. http://www.keltonsdarkcorner.com/

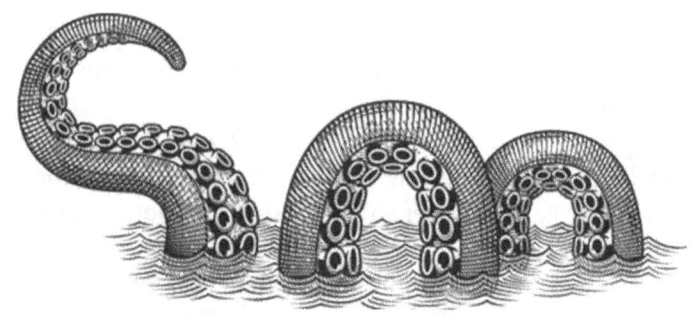

- Bicyclist's pants catch fire
- Poland: Speedy cyclist's pants catch fire

Chariots of Fire

For the Fortean Times no. 308 (Jan. 2014), to celebrate forty years of strange stories, readers and contributors were asked to choose the top forty best articles from the magazine printed since 1973. After that two-score collection of strange tales had been tallied, there were a residue of items that people recalled but the whole magazine staff could not locate (see "Toxic Waste Creatures" for another example).

One mystery story was described by Mikita Brottman: "It might have been in 'Strange Deaths.' It was an item about a man – I think it was in China, for some reason – who rode his bicycle so fast that his trousers caught fire." [1]

The writer seems to be referring to an item in FT no. 237: "A Polish cyclist received second-degree burns after apparently pedaling so hard his trousers caught fire." The unfortunate bicyclist, Mieczyslaw Jasinski, in good shape for age 55, smelled smoke as he rocketed through the town of Koroszczyn. "'Witnesses said he was like a human torch cycling along,' said police." Fortunately, Mr. Jasinski stopped, dropped, and rolled. [2]

While not really spooky or paranormal, the flaming cyclist story demonstrates how a casual reader can recall the general outlines of an event but forget the specifics, filling them in with false details. This is a normal response, because the story – even as an outline or query – sounds too fragmented otherwise to the human mind. Somehow, over the space of six years, Mikita shifted our racing hero from Poland to China and even had him die at the end.

No, not paranormal, but as Brottman concludes, "It was the essence of forteana – concise, highly improbable but not actually implausible, and makes the universe suddenly seem full of all kinds of previously unimagined accidents."

1. Emerson, Hunt, "Fortean Top 40," Fortean Times no. 308 (Jan. 2014), p. 31.
2. "Trouser Kindling," Fortean Times no. 237 (special issue 2008), p. 8.

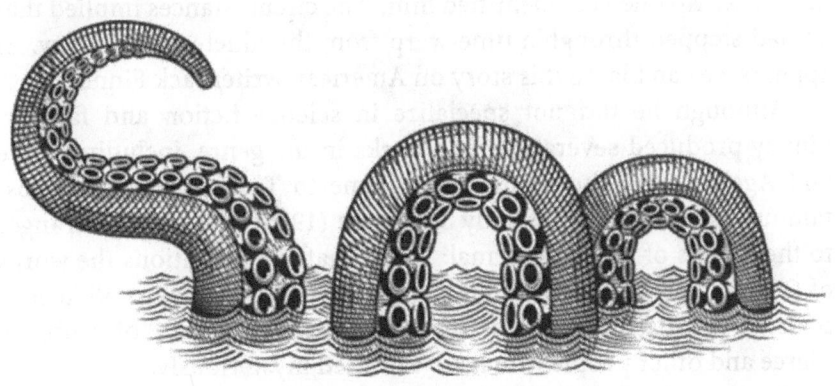

- Man from the 1870s appears in Time Square
- Nineteenth century man appears in New York City
- Time traveler hit by car

The Chronokinesis of Rudolph Fentz

"Do you remember the account that appeared in Collier's magazine some years ago?" anomalist and paranormal author John Keel once asked Brad Steiger. [1] "A man dressed in period clothing had simply blundered into the traffic in Times Square in 1950, got hit by a cab, and was killed. It turned out that this man had disappeared around 1879 – he had gone out for a walk and had never come back."

A tale or rumor I often "heard about" concerned a man dressed in old-fashioned clothing who simply appeared in the middle of a modern city, in the middle of a street full of traffic, and rather conveniently managed to get run over before he could tell anyone who he was. The police went through his pockets and found only coins and papers dated the 1870s. No one ever identified him. The circumstances implied that he had stepped through a time-warp from the nineteenth century. It appears we can blame this story on American writer Jack Finney.

Although he did not specialize in science fiction and fantasy, Finney produced several famous works in the genre, including Time and Again (1970), its sequel From Time to Time (1995), and most famously Invasion of the Body Snatchers (1955). He was no stranger to the realms of the paranormal: Body Snatchers mentions the works of Charles Fort in regard to falling objects (in this case the alien seed pods). "Of Missing Persons" reveals to us the final fate of Ambrose Bierce and other people who have vanished mysteriously.

In Finney's short story "I'm Scared," an old, retired gentleman, settling back with a mystery novel, hears a radio program that went out over the air five years earlier. Mentioning the odd event to others seems to prompt every friend and acquaintance to tell him of similar strange occurrences:

"A man on Long Island received a telephone call from his sister in

New York one Friday evening. She insists that she did not make this call until the following Monday, three days later. At the Forty-fifth Street branch of the Chase National Bank, I was shown a check deposited the day before it was written. A letter was delivered on East Sixty-eighth Street in New York City, just seventeen minutes after it was dropped into a mailbox on the main street of Green River, Wyoming." [2]

The mixed-up time events grow stranger and more disturbing, and the final story he collects is the most bizarre, given to him by the police captain who handled the case: "Eleven-fifteen at night in Times Square – the theaters letting out, busiest time and place in the world – and this guy shows up in the middle of the street gawking and looking around at the cars and up at the signs like he'd never seen them before ... A cab got him and he was dead when he hit." [3]

Coins, bank notes, and letters on the dead man's person are dated 1876 or earlier, and in his wallet are the business cards of a Rudolph Fentz. The police captain digs through old records, and yes, a man named Rudolph Fentz went out for an evening stroll in 1876 and never returned.

It is not all that strange Finney's story was taken for fact: the unnamed narrator meticulously gives us precise dates, names, and addresses. There is also no proper ending to the story, as with real-life accounts of the paranormal, only the narrator's growing concern that such events are happening more and more frequently, perhaps to end someday with the space-time continuum ripping apart. We ought to be happy, then, that this recurring rumor turns out to be fiction – however gripping.

1. Steiger, Brad. Mysteries of Time and Space (New York: Dell Books, 1974), p. 220.
2. Finney, Jack, "I'm Scared" (1951), in Heinlein, Robert (editor). Tomorrow, the Stars (New York: Berkley Books, 1983 [1952]), p. 4
3. Ibid., p. 12.

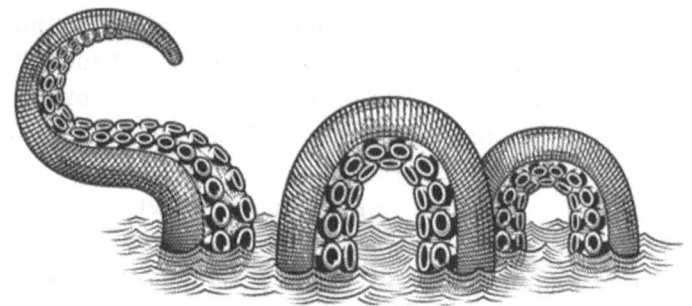

- France: Stones fall from sky
- Girls pulled upward as stones fall down
- Sky falls: Stones
- Stones fall from the sky; girls pulled upward

Clavaux Stone Falls

In Chapter Four of Charles Fort's LO!, the pioneer anomalist lists numerous accounts of objects or substances falling from the sky or flying up from the earth. He writes of an incident near Clavaux [also spelled Glaveaux], France, in which two young girls, clearing the ground of leaves, suddenly noticed stones dropping around them, not so much falling as drifting down, as if they partly defied gravity. The girls fled the area and returned with their skeptical parents.

The stones continued falling. "There was another phenomenon, an upward current, into which the children were dragged, as if into a vortex. We might have had data of mysterious disappearances of children, but the parents, who were unaffected by the current, pulled them back." [1]

Fort's source was the London Times, January 13, 1843, which in turn took the story from a French newspaper, Courrier de l'Isere. The Times account does not quite agree with Fort's: "The parents, taking the hands of the children to take them away, found themselves, to their great surprise, drawn within the sphere of attraction, and perceived the stones just above their heads, which, the moment after, fell on them, and rolled on the ground."

The Times account goes on to say that several other people, including members of the clergy and a respected doctor, saw the rocks fall, and that even if the missiles struck anyone, the victim received no injury, except for one person with a "hand slightly swelled."

"About 60 of them [the stones] have been picked up, but they present nothing particular in appearance."

That might have been the last of the matter were it not for the indefatigable Theo Paijmans, a researcher who specializes in ferreting out strange tales from earlier centuries. Paijmans, always fascinated by this anecdote, dug up a 1936 issue of a scholarly French publication that expanded on the Clavaux fall. [2] The author of the article, one M. Michea-Bonnardon, was himself quite the researcher; among other things, he reprinted the original French news story.

According to the French account, the two girls had been raking leaves into sacks. When they sat down to rest, stones started dropping around them. They fetched their parents, who did not even see the stones until they took the girls' hands. Soon "the directors of the foundry of Riouperoux" and "the inhabitants of Bourg d'Oisans" came to see the falling stones. After a few days, a physician from Vizille, very skeptical, visited Clavaux, and, "taking the two children by the hand," not only saw the falling stones, but got hit on the cheek by one. The phenomenon stopped after a few days.

Yet there was still more. M. Michea-Bonnardon knew the story because the skeptical physician was his own grandfather, Leonce Bonnardon, who eventually became mayor of Vizille. The elder Bonnardon wrote his own account of the affair, which supplied all details of the strange events connected with "these two 14-year-old girls: Marguerite Pinel and Marie Genevois, of Glaveaux, a hamlet of Livet."

The falling stones were seen by over eighty witnesses, including "Belion, parish priest of Sechilienne; Dumas, director of the foundry of Riouperoux; Paturel, justice of the peace; Viallet, bailiff," and many more. The phenomena lasted from December 12, 1842 until February 17, 1843 – no less than sixty-seven days. Unlike Fort's usual sky falls, the stones were often spotted rising from the earth and sailing in an arc toward the children.

Even more incredibly, the stones sometimes appeared when the girls were inside closed rooms. In the Pinel house, one Antoine Michel saw a stone simply appear behind the girls, bounce off Marie's head, and hit the hand of Marguerite's mother (this might be the case of the "swelled hand," mentioned in the Times, since the stones seemed to regain acceleration after touching something).

On the morning of Wednesday, January 18, 1843, while Marie was asleep in the same bed as Marguerite, no less than three stones hit her on the head; none of these rock missiles could be found – perhaps here was a small example of a disappearance with the appearances.

Michea-Bonnardon concluded with – no conclusions. "The field remains open for researchers." [3]

"If I could appeal to what used to be supposed to be known as common sense, I'd ask whether something that mysteriously appears somewhere had not mysteriously disappeared somewhere else." [4]

The Clavaux story looms large in Fort's compendium because it supplied an almost-disappearance to balance the stones' appearance. The cover of the ACE edition of LO! (1974) depicts two children being drawn into a tornado full of human bodies while their parents, feet planted firmly on the ground, pull them back – an illustration obviously based on the French incident.

Fort nearly went blind reading through thousands of journals and newspapers, and his surviving notes show that he scribbled sources and synopses frantically in a code of his own creation. He can be forgiven for conflating the parents' attempting to pull the children away with being "drawn within the sphere of attraction." One should not dismiss the Clavaux events, however: they were witnessed by dozens of people, and they continued off and on for several weeks. While poltergeists are infamous for haunting teenage girls, the Clavaux phenomena remained mostly an outdoor activity, never expanding into vocalizations, knockings on walls, or spontaneous fires. It seems to linger halfway between a poltergeist outbreak and Fort's quasi-meteorological sky falls – an event difficult to classify in a field where categories and distinctions are already frequently inclined to change.

1. Fort, Charles. Complete Books (New York: Dover Books, 1974 [1941]), p. 559.
2. Paijmans, Theo, "Mysterious Falling Stones at Glaveaux," Fortean Times no. 317 (Sept. 2014), pp. 28-29.
3. Michea-Bonnardon, M., "Un phenomene ou pretendu tel survenu a Livet en 1842," Bulletin Mensuel de l'Academie Delphinale, no. 7, 1936.
4. Fort, p. 568.

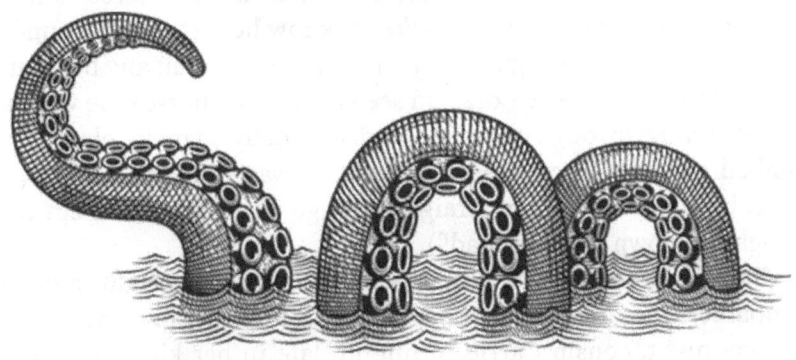

- Spontaneous Life?
- Virginia: Tiny humanoid

Coffee Pot Creature

Paranormal and Fortean researchers come across an amazing variety of bewildering monster reports – just see "Dart Creature," "The Flying Clam," and "Giant Shrimp in the Laundry Room" elsewhere in this volume. But I personally would give the Strangest Creature Ever Reported Award to the following short and poorly-detailed anecdote.

Georgia native Chuck Perdue (d. 2010) had a degree in geology and a Ph.D. in folklore. In 1964 or -65 he met and befriended a black couple, John and Cora Jackson, of Rappahannock County, Virginia. While gathering folk stories, jokes, and anecdotes for a folklore article, Perdue decided he should interview John, who was a noted musician and storyteller.

John Jackson (b. 1924) and his wife Cora (b. 1926) had dwelt in Rappahannock County all their lives. For years they worked on a set of small farms surrounding a huge, pre-Civil War mansion, an estate that looked no different in the 1960s than it did in the days of slavery. Eventually John became a chauffer and handyman, and at the time of the interview (1969), he was a gravedigger and "odd-job man" in Fairfax, VA.

During his life in Virginia, John Jackson had run across strange animals, such as a giant black snake ("I know he was as big around as a gallon bucket"), and a giant hog ("He was bigger than any beef cattle you ever saw"). His wife Cora had seen a phantom horse ("he was just, just wobbling through the air") and a ghostly man in black ("We climbed over the fence and we thought he was gonna climb over the fence, but he walked right straight through that fence and kept right straight on down that old road").

But the Jacksons' strangest experiences were downright mundane compared to something that happened to John's cousin Carrie.

One night, cousin Carrie, sitting up late in her kitchen drinking coffee, heard a noise. Her coffee pot had fallen off the stove. According to John Jackson, "she jumped up cause she know it was hot coffee and she looked and this thing was coming out of the pot. And said just commenced – said she never seen such a terrible looking thing in all the days of her life. It was a little terrible looking man – said she never seen such a terrible looking thing."

Chuck Perdue asked for more details, but Jackson could not deliver. "[S]he never said exactly how it looked. She said it was the horriblest looking thing she ever seen." We are not told what Carrie did next or what happened to the little monster. One thing Mr. Jackson could say – Carrie never made or drank coffee again.

A spontaneous Homunculus? Maybe it was time for cousin Carrie to cut back on the caffeine.

Perdue, Chuck, "I Swear to God it's the Truth if I Ever Told it!", Keystone Folklore Quarterly Vol. XIV, no. 1 (Spring 1969), pp. 1-56.

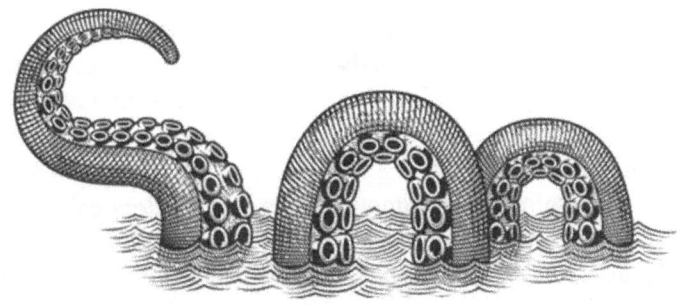

- Arizona: Dinosaur reports
- Colorado: Dinosaur reports
- Living dinosaurs?
- Texas: Dinosaur reports

Colorado Raptors

It all started innocently enough when Ms. Myrtle Snow of Pagosa Springs, Colorado, sent a letter to the Denver Post's Sunday supplement, Rocky Mountain Empire Magazine. The letter was published in its August 22, 1982 edition. Ms. Snow had lived in the Pagosa Springs area all her life, and she had encountered some very intriguing creatures.

In May of 1935, when she was three years old, Myrtle claimed she and a friend discovered five "baby dinosaurs" in a "nest" in an outhouse. The friend's mother couldn't identify them; the unnamed friend decided they were "snakes with legs." The girls finally threw them out into a field.

Several months later a farmer named John Martinez began losing sheep to an unknown predator in a canyon about five miles from his ranch. Eventually he shot the culprit, and what a culprit it was!

An Apache youth dragged the carcass back to the ranch with a team of mules. Martinez put the corpse in a barn, and the local farmers came to gawk at it. "My grandfather took us to see it the next morning," writes Ms. Snow. "It was about seven feet tall, was grey, had a head like a snake, short front legs with claws that resembled chicken feet, large stout back legs and a long tail." [Rickard, p. 8] Years after writing her letter, in an interview with Nick Sucik, she added that "its body was covered in fine gray hairs." [Sucik, p. 144] (Could the "hairs" have been downy feathers? Velociraptors and similar dinosaurs are now thought to have been partly covered with feathers.) No one could figure out what it was, but the Apache boy thought it was something his tribal elders called a "Moon Cow" – always rare and hardly ever seen in the modern era.

Two years later, according to Ms. Snow, she visited a friend well out in the country and went exploring in the woods by herself. She found a shallow cave, and while examining it she heard a loud snakelike hissing. She froze, then she realized the hissing came from a tree some distance away. There was a dinosaur-ish creature by the tree, like the one she'd seen in the Martinez barn. It stood erect, possibly because it was after something in the tree, and it was green from the waist up and brown from the waist down. The brown areas seemed to be hair-covered. A line of "humps" ran down its back.

The beast snatched something out of the branches and held it for a moment in its foreclaws as if examining it. Then it shoved its catch into its mouth. Myrtle was able to sneak away unseen, or perhaps the creature just ignored her.

One can dismiss recollections from early childhood, when the boundaries between reality and imagination are somewhat plastic, but in her letter Ms. Snow mentioned one more encounter as an adult: "On Oct. 23, 1978, as I was returning from Chama, NM, about 7:30 pm, in a driving rain, I saw another one going through the field towards the place where I had seen the one in 1937." (Chama is about thirty miles southeast of Pagosa Springs, just across the New Mexico border).

When Nick Sucik interviewed Myrtle Snow (ca. 2000), she told him that she had seen another bipedal saurian on the same stretch of highway a few years after writing her letter. A passenger this time, the driver also saw the creature.

Sucik took it upon himself to locate witnesses to bipedal "dinosaurs" in the Colorado area. Finding witnesses turned out to be nearly as hard as finding dinosaurs. Myrtle Snow knew of several, but they were all either dead or had moved away, she didn't know where.

A buddy from Sucik's Marine days recalled an episode of Sightings or Unsolved Mysteries in which a couple of ranchers on horseback come upon a "dead dinosaur" near Cortez, Colorado. Other people remembered the show, but neither TV series listed such an episode.

Sucik put an ad in the Cortez Journal requesting stories or sightings of little "dinosaurs". He expected a stream of hoaxes and jokes, but he received only one response: A man had seen something like that in California in the 1950s.

An abortive house-to-house survey brought forth no dinosaur witnesses, only a few angry dogs.

Finally, he scraped together a few sightings, mostly of two-legged creatures dashing across roads in front of cars. Some sounded like collared lizards. Some sightings were due to an escaped emu. One drawing of a creature was obviously a coatimundi, a relative of the raccoon.

He heard a story about "baby dinosaurs" sent to the Cortez Museum in 1963. It turned out to be a box of baby dinosaur fossils – which in turn proved to be bones of various mammals mixed together.

Yet there were enough stories to keep Sucik interested. When he worked for the Navajo Nation, there were many rumors of giant reptiles being seen, but the subject was taboo among that First Nations people, so he could dig up no specifics.

On February 17, 1993, two truck drivers in a convoy saw a creature cross the road in front of them somewhere between Snowflake and Heber, Arizona. It stood ten to twelve feet tall and had small arms like a Tyrannosaurus rex.

A man told Sucik about his two aunts – sisters – who traveled with their parents during the Depression to work on farms. A bizarre little creature started eating scraps at their campsite. The sisters caught it and put it in a birdcage. It looked exactly like a T. rex, but it was only the size of a kitten. Eventually their father made them to let it go.

As if to bring things full circle, Sucik started receiving reports of a quadrupedal "dragon" – not a two-legged quasi-Velociraptor – being seen near Pagosa Springs. Former police chief Leonard Gallegos claimed to have seen it back in the 1950s, when he was a schoolboy. It resembled a Komodo Dragon, greenish-gray and "at least the size of an alligator."

"Sightings continue to this day," writes Sucik.

Meanwhile . . . In 1993 Texas UFO researcher Jimmy Ward published an article called "The Mountain Boomer," a collection of folktales from the Big Bend National Park area of Texas (almost as far west as Pagosa Springs but much further south). A "Mountain Boomer" was supposedly a "giant lizard that walked on its hind legs and whose voice sounded like the roll of distant thunder." The creatures were usually greenish or brownish, standing five or six feet tall, their short forelegs held like arms. While hunting down stories, Ward met up with a Connecticut family who spotted such a creature while en route to California. They agreed that it was the very image of the nasty Dromaeosaurs of Jurassic Park fame. (One should point out that the eastern collared lizard is sometimes called a mountain boomer, and that it can run on its hind legs when threatened.)

Cryptozoologist Chad Arment suggests that some "baby dinosaur" stories might be caused by people seeing species of lizards that can run (momentarily) on their hind legs, like the real mountain boomer or the South American basilisk (presumably escaped pets). How to explain reptiles standing six or even ten feet tall, though?

Although skeptical of the Texas and Colorado stories, Arment mentions that: "Some friends of mine in the reptile trade had done business a few years ago with an individual who had collected some Colorado species and had offered to catch some 'river dinos' for them." [Arment, p. 39] Arment's friends didn't have the money, but yes, the description given of a Colorado "river dino" was of a bipedal, theropod-dinosaur-ish reptile. The hunt continues.

When I was a dinosaur-crazed kid, I hoped that remnants of the great reptiles survived somewhere, hidden from men, maybe in Asia, Africa, or South America. Perhaps I don't have to travel so far, after all, to find a "lost world." But I might regret finding it, if I did.

Arment, Chad, "Dinos in the U.S.A.: A Summary of North American Bipedal 'Lizard' Reports." North American BioFortean Review Vol. II, No. 2, (2000), pp. 32-39.

Gerhard, Ken, and Nick Redfern. Monsters of Texas (Bideford,

North Devon: CFZ Press, 2010).

Rickard, Bob, "A Reprise for 'Living Wonders.'" Fortean Times no. 40 (Summer 1983), pp. 4-15.

Sucik, Nick, "'Dinosaur' Sightings in the United States." Cryptozoology and the Investigation of Lesser-Known Mystery Animals (Landisville, PA: Coachwhip Publications, 2006), pp. 137-168.

Ward, Jimmy, "Mountain Boomer." Far Out Vol. 1, no. 4 (Summer 1993), pp. 45-46.

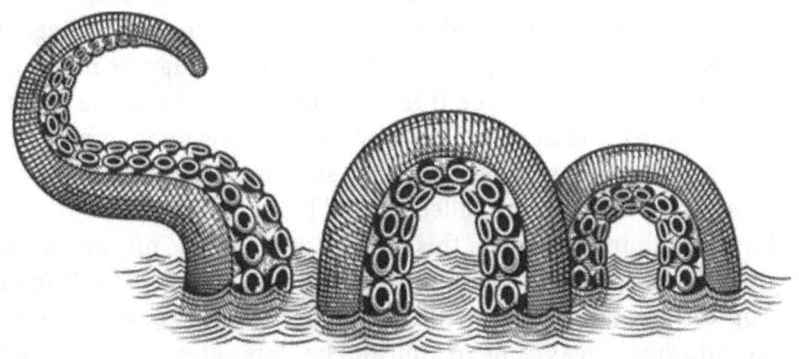

- Bradbury, Ray – witnesses strange occurrence
- Parahumans/ultraterrestrials/spirits mingle with people?
- Strange people seen at accidents

The Crowd

> ". . . that numerous piece of monstrosity, which, taken asunder, seem men, and the reasonable creatures of God, but, confused together, make but one great beast, and a monstrosity more prodigious than Hydra."

-- Sir Thomas Browne, Religio Medici

Before becoming known for such SF classics as The Martian Chronicles, Ray Bradbury wrote a number of bizarre horror and fantasy tales. (The best of these can be found in his collection, The October Country.) His most effective horror story, in this writer's opinion, was "The Crowd" (1943).

"The Crowd" is the story of Mr. Spallner, who is involved in an auto accident and is amazed at how quickly a morbid crowd assembles to stare. Studying pictures of and newspaper clippings about car accidents, he notices that the same people are standing in the background -- part of the crowd that always gathers to stare at tragedy. No matter where in the city, or at what time of the day or night, the same ghoulish people emerge from the shadows to form the Crowd. "They have one thing in common, they always show up together. At a fire or at an explosion or on the sidelines of a war, at any demonstration of this thing called death." [1]

Ray Bradbury claimed this story was based on an actual occurrence. In an article called "Run Fast, Stand Still, or, The Thing at the Top of the Stairs, or, New Ghosts from Old Minds," he discusses how certain story ideas came to him, and he elaborates on "The Crowd" in particular.

It was Bradbury's manner of writing to scribble down lists of possible titles, mostly simple nouns, which often suggested stories to him. Once he wrote the words THE CROWD, and he recalled something that happened when he was fifteen. While at a friend's house, he heard a terrible crash and ran outside to find that a car full of people had hit a telephone pole head-on. Four passengers died immediately, and the fifth died the next day. It took the young Bradbury months to recover emotionally from the scene.

"The accident had occurred at an intersection surrounded on one side by empty factories and a deserted schoolyard, and on the opposite side, by a graveyard," writes Bradbury. "I had come running from the nearest house, a hundred yards away. Yet, within moments, it seemed, a crowd had gathered. Where had they all come from? Later on in time, I could only imagine that some came, in some strange fashion, out of the empty factories, or even more strangely, out of the graveyard." [2]

The eminent scholar and ghost story writer Montague Rhodes James made a similar observation in "After Dark in the Playing Fields," published originally in the periodical College Days (June 28, 1924). The story is an oddity for James, concerning not his usual unspeakable horrors but the narrator's comical conversation with a barn owl. Near the end there is an even stranger aside:

"I do not like a crowd after dark – for example at the Fourth of June fireworks. You see – no, you do not, but I see – such curious faces: and the people to whom they belong flit about so oddly, often at your elbow when you least expect it, and looking close into your face, as if they were searching for someone – who may be thankful, I think, if they do not find him. 'Where do they come from?' Why, some, I think, out of the water, and some out of the ground." [3]

Reporter Connie Fletcher has written a number of books about real police on the beat, beginning with What Cops Know (1990). The stories are given by the officers themselves, in their own words (but anonymously for their protection). An arson squad detective from Chicago PD told Ms. Fletcher: "We see the same people all the time, every fire scene. They all look like suspects. They look catatonic . . . You could arrest a lot of these people just on looks alone." [4]

As John Keel might have asked, "Who are these 'people'?" Perhaps the present readers will watch for them, if they ever find themselves at the site of a disaster or wreck. But be careful on the way home . . .

1. Bradbury, Ray. The October Country (New York: Ballantine Books, 1972 [1955]), p. 153.
2. Ibid. "Run Fast, Stand Still, or, The Thing at the Top of the Stairs, or, New Ghosts from Old Minds." In How to Write Tales of Horror, Fantasy, and Science Fiction, ed. by J. N. Williamson (Cincinnati, OH: Writer's Digest Books, 1987), pp. 16-17.
3. James, Montague Rhodes. Collected Ghost Stories (Ware, Hertford, UK: Wordsworth Press, 1992), p. 624.
4. Fletcher, Connie. Pure Cop (New York, NY: St. Martin's Press, 1991), p. 48.

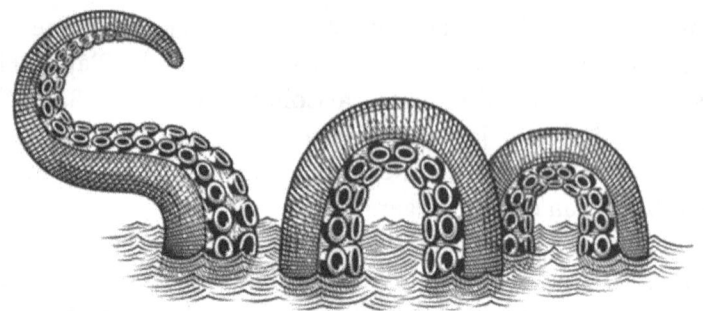

- Bierce, Ambrose: "The Damned Thing"
- Invisible Monster
- New Hampshire: Invisible monster
- Texas: Invisible monster

Damned Things

Ambrose Bierce's most famous short story, "The Damned Thing," concerns an invisible monster on the loose in the Old West, evidenced only by its effect on plants, animals -- and people:

"I was about to speak further, when I observed the wild oats near the place of the disturbance moving in the most inexplicable way. I can hardly describe it. It seemed as if stirred by a streak of wind, which not only bent it, but pressed it down -- crushed it so that it did not rise; and this movement was slowly prolonging itself directly toward us."

According to Paul Fatout's biography Ambrose Bierce: the Devil's Lexicographer, "The Damned Thing" was based on an actual occurrence:

"Another story pertinent to character was 'The Damned Thing,' published in the 1893 Christmas number of the New York Town Topics. Similar to Maupassant's "Le Horla," the tale is of a spectral presence, sensed but unseen: an emptiness that moves and terrifies. It was suggested, the author said, 'by a rather disquieting personal experience while gunning': 'I am convinced that in daylight and on an open road I stood in the immediate presence of a wild beast invisible to me but sufficiently conspicuous to my dog, and sufficiently formidable to frighten it exceedingly.'" [1]

Texas hosts a similar invisible monster, according to Lone Star historian William Edward Syers. The Ottine Swamp flanks the San Marcos River southeast of Austin and encompasses Palmetto State Park. About 1980, Syers interviewed Berthold Jackson, an A&M graduate and woodsman, one of many hunters and fishermen who have encountered the "thing" in the swamp. "He had never read Ambrose Bierce's masterpiece, 'The Damned Thing' . . . Yet that is precisely what he described to me over early coffee on a fine spring morning."

One night, Jackson was hunting with a friend, Johnny Boehm of Gonzales, Texas:

"'Johnny was behind me, maybe fifty yards. I could see his light, and he could see mine. The damned thing got right between us. We could see the brush move.' He gestured the rippling movement of passage. 'We could hear brush snap underfoot. But we couldn't see a thing except that brush moving. Not the thing itself. And that close, an animal's eyes would show like headlights.'"

Jackson and other locals had put big lights on "it" multiple times; nothing -- except the movement of undergrowth -- was ever seen.

Jackson named several others who had encountered the thing, from Luling and Gonzales, TX. Two men, Billy Webb and Ab Ussery, running a trotline one night, saw an expanse of bloodweeds along the riverbank move as if something large were passing through it, following them. They shone a large light at the disturbance from only 20 feet (six meters) away but still saw nothing.

The "Thing" seems to be attracted to vehicles parked on Lookout Hill, which lies near the entrance of Palmetto State Park. Two young men, Brewster Short and Wayne Hodges, loading up to go home from a hunting trip, claimed that something unseen reared up on the back of their car. They fled hastily, leaving their dogs behind. This experience so disturbed Wayne that he moved into his parents' bedroom. Lamar Ryan, Jackson's cousin, was parked one night on the hill with his fiancée when something started shoving his pickup towards the edge of a steep drop-off. Lamar jumped out, but he could see nothing, despite the moonlight. He and his wife-to-be left hastily.

Jackson's son spoke to a couple who lived in a trailer house near the swamp. He was informed that something had once or twice shook the trailer "like a box," and that the couple had come home one day to find the wife's best dress, which had been on a clothesline, "torn in half, and each half rolled in a ball and stuck under each bed." [2]

The unseen being of Palmetto State Park still roams about, at least according to the author of an anonymous letter sent to Wesley Treat, Heather Shade, and Rob Riggs, authors of Weird Texas. "Many years back," after receiving a camera from his wife for Christmas, the author drove out to the park to take pictures. He began to feel that someone was following him. He headed for his vehicle, but the feeling grew so intense that he started running. He tripped and fell, looking back as he rolled over to get up.

"I saw the tall grass off to the side of the trail getting flattened and parting, as if someone was pushing their way through it. But there was no one there. I jumped up and broke out into a full sprint until I was inside my car. I quickly took off, without even catching my breath, and felt something hit the car from behind." [p. 105]

The author wondered if he was going crazy, but eventually he heard the stories about an "invisible man" in the park. [3]

Jody Noller of Connecticut provided a similar "invisible thing" report for Joanne Austin's Weird Hauntings. The year is unspecified, but the event occurred at a YMCA camp near Washington, New Hampshire, when the witness was fourteen. One night at about 2:00 am Noller woke to "heavy footsteps" in the leaves. "I heard brush being swept aside and a kind of low-pitched wailing I couldn't identify," he reports. He claims to have been familiar with most animal noises (and teenage camper noises, for that matter). Noller woke his tentmate Bruce, and both looked out with large flashlights. "The leaves and branches were being pulled off trees and thrown around, as if something very large and invisible was deliberately destroying the trees."

The boys naturally yelled for help, but the camp counselors who responded were equally mystified. One counselor, Jim, left and returned with a shotgun. As the other counselor held a light, he fired into "it" twice from 20 feet (six meters) away. "It" did not seem to be harmed, but now "small- to medium-sized rocks" came flying out of the trees. One hit Noller painfully in the head. The thing moved noisily into the deep woods, wailing again.

By now, all the young campers were awake and screaming. The counselors called the state police, who found nothing but torn saplings and underbrush. From then on, several counselors sat up at night with shotguns, but the "Camp Morgan Thing" never returned. [3]

There is a running thread in these stories of something massive and powerful close by yet as clear as air, a solid and destructive "emptiness" -- an incongruity Charles Fort would have liked.

    1. Paul Fatout. Ambrose Bierce, the Devil's Lexicographer (Norman, OK: University of Oklahoma Press, 1951), pp. 202-203. The quote within the quote comes from the San Francisco Examiner, May 27, 1894.

    2. Ed Syers. Ghost Stories of Texas (Waco, Texas: Texian Press, 1981), pp. 22-25.

    3. Treat, Wesley, et al., Weird Texas (New York: Sterling Publishing, 2005), p. 105.

    4. Joanne Austin. Weird Hauntings: True Tales of Ghostly Places (New York: Sterling Publishing, 2006), pp. 141-142.

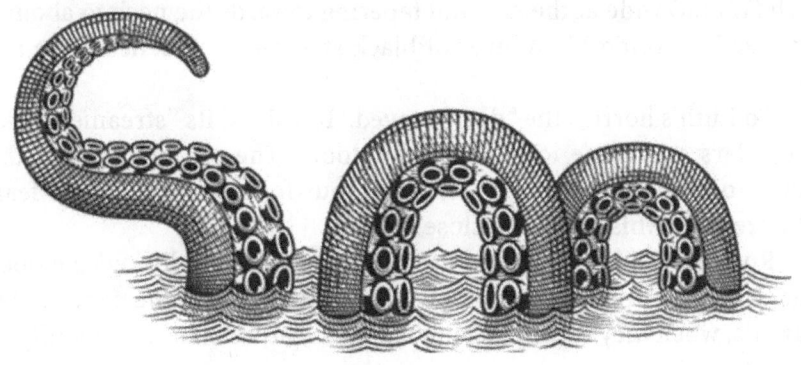

- Derbyshire, UK: Flying dart creature
- Flying arrow/dart creature
- Living arrow/dart
- Northumberland, UK: Flying dart creature

Dart Creature

One candidate for "weirdest creature ever" must be the living, flying killer dart:

When Ruth Summersides was 11 or 12 (in 1960-61), her family lived near Acomb, Northumberland. One warm July day, while her parents were out, she set up an easel in the yard and started painting.

She heard a whistling and whooshing sound and glimpsed something shooting through the air at her. She dropped flat, and the missile hurtled onward to "thunk" into the front door of her house like an arrow.

The girl rose and investigated the object. It drooped down to hang beside the doorknocker, as if it weren't wedged in very tightly.

"The thing had a black pointed head, with a frilly ruff around the short neck part," she recalled decades later. "The body was black and very shiny, about as thick as my index finger. Hanging from the neck were about six very shiny red, ribbon-like 'streamers', about half an inch (12mm) wide at the end and tapering towards the neck to about a quarter-inch (6mm)." A layer of black streamers lay beneath the red ones.

To Ruth's horror, the "dart" moved. It whirled its "streamers" like propellers and came loose from the door. The girl ran around the house to the back yard, easily leaping a four-foot stone wall in her fear. The creature whistled along close behind.

Ruth reached the back door and jumped in. She locked the door and dragged a dresser over to block it. Then she hid in the pantry. Her parents, when they returned, laughed the creature off as a dragonfly or hornet.

Ruth told an old man in the nearby village about the "dart", and the oldster responded, "I haven't seen one of those things for over 50 years. They're called flying arrows."

Although Ruth checked through many books about insects as she grew older, she never found anything remotely resembling the "flying arrow."

It may be that another young girl did, though! Around 1998, when Brenda Ray of Allestree, Derbyshire, was 6 or 7, she returned from school to find herself locked out of the house. Her mother had left (for reasons not given), and Ruth had no key.

The young girl wondered what to do. The house was surrounded by waste ground and trees, so there was no one near to ask for help. She remembered that sometimes a spare key was kept in the coal shed, a brick structure attached to the house, so she started for that.

Suddenly something zipped by her head ("I can still sense the draught it made!") and crashed into the brickwork of the shed or the front porch. At six inches long, the flying thing seemed too big to be an insect, but it certainly was not a bird. "Whatever it was had black whirring strands attached to it and made a noise not unlike one of those rotating bird-scarer rattles kids used to swing round at football matches," Brenda writes. "Whatever it was gave the impression it was trying to get in the house."

To the young girl's mind, the creature most resembled a black shuttlecock or a squid. She felt it to be malevolent, but she can't recall what she did next. "I must have put it out of my mind." Eventually someone came home and let her in.

Many years later Brenda bought a Spanish-style comb at a flea market. It struck her that the comb, with its semicircle of "rays" and spike-like teeth, resembled the flying entity. Could it have been an artificial construct, like a toy ornithopter? "It certainly gave the impression of being alive."

To the present writer, the "flying arrow" sounds almost like a weapon. Bio-technology, anyone?

Ray, Brenda, "Frightening Insect," Fortean Times no. 344 (Oct. 2016), p. 73.
Summersides, Ruth, "Flying Arrow," Fortean Times no. 237

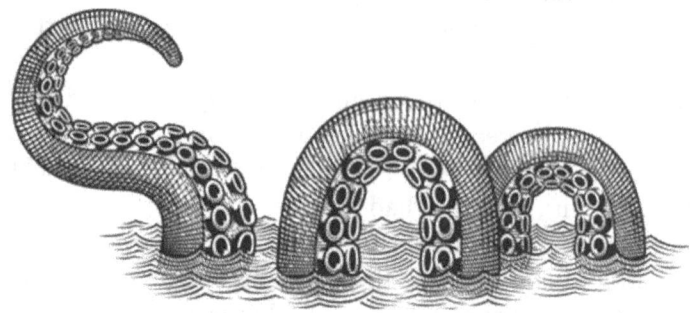

- Illinois: Space-time displacement
- Space-time anomaly, Illinois
- Train station, supernatural

The Depot

In 1934, young Miriam Golding and her husband-to-be, Stan, lived in Chicago. They were both music students, quite dedicated ones apparently, as one autumn afternoon they marched straight from a concert to a music store. They lost themselves among musical instruments, scores, and magazines until Stan pointed out that they were expected at his parents' house for dinner.

The couple headed for the elevators but became separated in a rush of people. Miriam tried to get off on the first floor, but more people pressed her in. She decided to ride all the way down and back up.

Unfortunately, when the car thumped to a halt below street level, the operator insisted that everyone disembark. Miriam obeyed, but to her surprise she found herself in a huge basement area, far too big for the modest music store: "There were boxes and crates stacked everywhere," she wrote years later. "Grainy, perspiring men pushed carts or rode little trucks loaded with trunks and baggage."

She found a staircase and climbed to street level. Her surprise became shock as she found herself in the middle of a huge railroad station. There were no signs of the music store or of the streets and buildings surrounding it.

Miriam grew ever more frustrated as she tried to understand the situation. Many people bustled around, but when she apologized to one woman she literally ran into, the woman ignored her. There were signs reading "To Trains," "Waiting Room," "Tickets", and the like, but no timetables of arrivals and departures. A voice on the loudspeakers rattled off destinations, but Miriam couldn't make out one word. She stood in line for a long time at an information booth, but, upon reaching the front, it seemed as if the woman in the booth could neither see nor hear her.

Miriam followed a sign reading "To Seventh Street" and found herself on an ordinary street, lined by large trees, under a blue sky. Across from the station a red brick building, possibly a church, was being built. The leaves were turning color, so it was autumn here – wherever "here" was. The people on the street seemed happy and contented, but none of them noticed her, and she could not understand a word they said. The community seemed perfectly ordinary, but Miriam grew ever more confused as she ambled along the sidewalk.

She stepped around a blond teenage youth on the sidewalk. He, however, touched her arm. The woman paused.

"I guess they let you off at the wrong stop, too," said the young man. He and Miriam talked and realized that they had undergone similar astonishing experiences.

"I was playing tennis back home and went to the locker room to change my shoes. When I came out I was in that depot," the young man said.

"Home" for the young man, however was Lincoln, Nebraska, not Chicago. The puzzled pair walked on, trying to dredge up anything they'd ever heard or read about time travel, teleportation, dimensions, and the like.

The street sloped downhill, and the town fell behind. They wandered through open country and ended up on the sandy beach of a lake or ocean. The sun dipped toward the watery horizon, which indicated they had been hiking west – but could they even take that for granted?

Miriam heard someone calling her name from a sandbar some distance offshore. To her ever-increasing amazement, it was Stan's sister. She and several other young women waved and shouted to her.

The tennis player stripped down to his shorts. "I'm going out there! They see us! They know you!" he cried. Perhaps, he suggested, they were a "link" that could draw the lost pair back to the real world.

The youth plunged into the water and swam toward the sandbar. The people on the sandbar still called, but the islet itself seemed to pull away from the beach. The swimmer finally gave up and returned to shore, exhausted and discouraged. According to Miriam the sandbar simply vanished.

Before the lost duo could discuss further options a blanket of darkness enveloped them. Miriam felt as if she "floated in space," then she came to, sitting on a stool back in the music store. "A clock was striking, and the clerks were tidying up the counters, preparing to close." Miriam left – careful to use the stairs – and walked to Stan's house.

According to her fiancé, he lost her at the elevators. He stepped out on the ground floor and waited, but Miriam never appeared. He assumed she had left via some other exit, so eventually he went home. Miriam showed up just as dinner was being served.

One more surprised awaited Miriam: Stan's sister and her friends were among the dinner guests. The sister remarked, "We saw you in town, but you were so engrossed in each other you didn't even hear us!"

Miriam eventually married Stan, despite being late for dinner with the 'rents. Apparently, nothing like this ever happened to her again, which was just as well, because according to her the mere memory of the Depot "still fills me with chills of apprehension."

Being one of the most elaborate space-time anomalies ever reported, the tale of "The Depot" can't help but seem strange. Although Stan in "reality" apparently waited some time at the music store and at home for Miriam to show up, Miriam's adventure sounds like it took longer – in the same period of time – with her misadventures in the train station and her walk out into the country to the sea.

"The [Golding] experience is unique insofar as she apparently met another individual who was as lost as she was in an unknown dimension," remarks one investigator of time anomalies. [Heffern, p. 45] Miriam from Chicago could interact with the young man from Lincoln but not with the people of "the Depot" and its surrounding town. Stan's sister and her friends apparently saw her in some normal setting, while she saw them standing on a sandbar (presumably they were on a sidewalk in Chicago).

Other people have reported strange events in train stations, but this depot sounds like something out of Harry Potter. Did Miriam's brain interpret something beyond her comprehension in terms she could understand? A weird, four-dimensional construct that sends people across space and time – in function it might seem like a train depot, with travelers heading for various destinations.

Could the event have been a hallucination on Miriam's part? Did she fall asleep while thumbing through a magazine and dream the event? Yet she apparently accompanied Stan to the elevators at least, and Stan's sister spotted her – somewhere. One wonders what would have happened if the sister had decided to walk over and join Miriam. As a matter of fact, the sister and her friends apparently saw the time-lost tennis player as well, mistaking him for Stan ("you were so engrossed in each other").

One wonders if Miriam ever tried to locate the young man from Nebraska, though admittedly that would have been a daunting task for a college student in another state in 1934.

. . . So, people encountered during a time-space displacement neither see nor hear the victim. I always wondered what would happen if the victims got more aggressive – punching out passersby or causing property damage. Would they notice that?

Miriam and her companion hailed from known cities of this earth. Where were the train station, the unknown town and its environs? If the sun was sinking into the sea, that would put it on the West Coast (or a west coast, somewhere). The comments that the people all looked "healthy, pleasant, and contented" reminds one of visions of Heaven, but perhaps it was just a nice fall afternoon in – wherever.

Another detail common in paranormal reports is the claim that people (or ghosts, or mysterious voices) are audible and apparently speaking English, but the English-speaking percipient can't understand what is being said. People who have been unconscious or badly injured sometimes make similar statements about the doctors and visitors around them.

A friend of mine who has traveled the world made an off-hand remark that I find interesting: Of all the languages he has ever heard, Danish is the only one similar to English in tone, cadence, pronunciation, and accent. One knows when one is hearing German or French, even if one doesn't understand the language. When my friend traveled through Denmark, however, it "felt" like the conversations and intercom announcements were in English – until he concentrated on them, whereupon he realized he couldn't understand a word. Except for the fact that "the Depot" signs were in English, I might suggest that it was in Denmark!

Golding, Miriam, "I Was Lost in the Fourth Dimension," in Kenner, Corrine and Craig Miller, Eds., Strange But True: A Collection of True Stories from the Files of FATE Magazine (Woodbury, MN: Llewellyn Publications, 1997), pp. 18-21.

-- reprinted from Fate Magazine no. 9 (Sept. 1956), pp. 61-64.

Heffern, Richard. Time Travel: Myth or Reality? (New York: Pyramid Books, 1977).

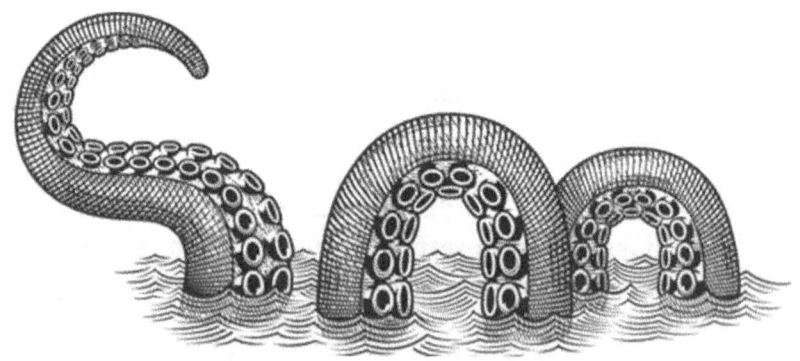

- Carnivorous plants
- Mexico: Carnivorous plants
- Nicaragua: Carnivorous plants
- Tree, carnivorous
- Vampire plants
- Vines, moving/blood drinking

The Devouring Vine and the Snake-Tree

Throughout the 1880s and 1890s, Dr. Andrew Wilson's column "Science Jottings" could be found in most issues of the Illustrated London Times. His column for August 27, 1892, concerning a "very singular plant," brought his readers to the very limits of conventional biology:

"It appears that a naturalist, a Mr. Dunstan by name, was botanising in one of the swamps surrounding the Nicaragua Lake. The account goes on to relate that 'while hunting for specimens he heard his dog cry out, as if in agony, from a distance. Running to the spot whence the animal's cries came, Mr. Dunstan found him enveloped in a perfect network of what seemed to be a fine, rope-like tissue of roots and fibres. The plant or vine seemed composed entirely of bare, interlacing stems, resembling more than anything else the branches of a weeping willow denuded of its foliage, but of a dark, nearly black hue, and covered with a thick, viscid gum that exuded from the pores.'"

Mr. Dunstan was barely able to free his dog with his hunting knife, and "the twigs curled like living, sinuous fingers about Mr. Dunstan's hand." The dog survived, but it was covered in blood, its skin "sucked" and "puckered". The local natives were supposedly well acquainted with this vampiric plant, explaining that "in five minutes it will suck the nourishment from a large lump of meat, rejecting the carcass as a spider does that of a used-up fly."

In the September 24, 1892, issue of the Illustrated London Times, Dr. Wilson reports further:

"The 'snake-tree' is described in a newspaper paragraph as found on an outlying spur of the Sierra Madre, in Mexico. It has movable branches (by which I suppose, is meant sensitive branches), of a 'slimy, snaky appearance,' which seized a bird that incautiously alighted on them, the bird being drawn down till the traveller lost sight of it."

The unnamed witness to this botanical monster claimed that feathers and bones littered the earth surrounding it. Eventually the avian victim dropped from the tree, "flattened out." Like Mr. Dunstan, our "traveller" simply had to touch a branch. "It closed upon his hand with such force as to tear the skin when he wrenched it away." The branches had suckers resembling those of an octopus.

Dr. Wilson ends: "I give the story simply for what it is worth. A lady correspondent, however, reminds me that in Charles Kingsley's West Indian papers he describes a similar tree to the Nicaraguan plant of Mr. Dunstan."

Perhaps identical to the Snake-Tree is the hideous "Rattle-snake Bush" of Mexico, mentioned by folklorist Charles M. Skinner, which was "a tree of serpents that wound its arms about men and animals that tried to pass, and stung and strangled them to death."

Skinner, Charles M. Myths and Legends of Flowers, Trees, Fruits, and Plants (Philadelphia: J. B. Lippincott, 1911).

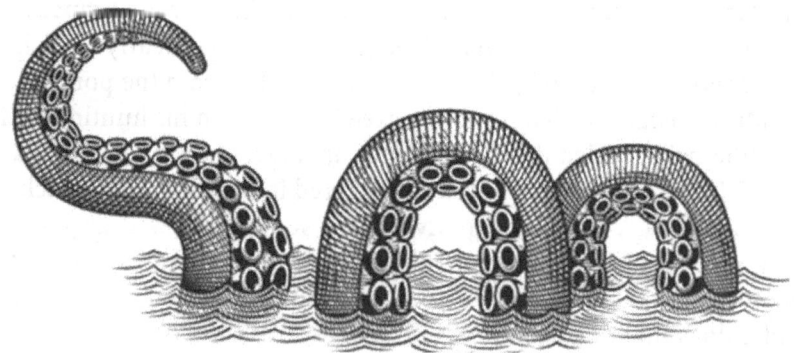

- Alabama: Farmer disappears near Selma
- Bierce, Ambrose – "Mysterious Disappearances"
- Disappearance – farmer crossing a field
- Tennessee: David Lang hoax

The Difficulty of Crossing a Field – and of Crossing off an Old Story

David Lang

When I was a boy, being taken to a new library was almost as exciting as going to Disneyland. One day I was dropped off at a very small library on 21st Street in Tulsa, Oklahoma, in a building which is now a dentist's office. I ran into the first bookshelves the moment I stepped in, space being at a premium, and, as the library used the Dewey Decimal System, the first section I faced was 001.9, "Wonders and Miscellanea." The first book on that first shelf was Stranger than Science by Frank Edwards, and upon cracking open this ominous-sounding tome, the first story I found was "The Disappearance of David Lang."

The first story in the first book on the first shelf of the library was pretty startling. On the afternoon of September 23, 1880, David Lang, a farmer living near Gallatin, Tennessee, started out across the field facing his house to check on some horses. His wife sat on the porch and his two children played in the yard. Judge August Peck and his brother-in-law happened at that time to be riding up to the Lang property in a horse-and-buggy. Lang waved to them from the field. Peck drew in a breath to call hello, when suddenly, in full view of his family, the judge, and the brother-in-law, David Lang abruptly vanished.

The grass in the field had been closely cropped by horses. There were no boulders or trees to obscure the view. Mrs. Lang and the visiting men ran out into the field and studied every inch of ground.

Over the next week hundreds of other people did the same. There were no holes, cracks, cave openings, old wells, or mineshafts into which Lang might have fallen. A county surveyor reported that bedrock began only a few feet under the topsoil; there simply couldn't be any caves below. At any rate, David Lang was never seen again – but that was not the end of the story.

The following April, the Lang children, George, age 8, and Sarah, age 11, noticed that at the point where their father vanished, a circle of grass about fifteen feet in diameter looked stunted and yellow. They ventured out into the field and, on impulse, Sarah called to her father. To their shock, the children heard a faint voice calling for help. Mrs. Lang and others heard the voice too, but over the next few days it grew fainter and fainter, and finally it faded away altogether.

Such was the story of David Lang, as described by Frank Edwards, Dr. Nandor Fodor, Harold T. Wilkins, and various other purveyors of the mysterious and paranormal. They all drew upon an article called "How Lost Was My Father" by Stuart Palmer, from Fate Magazine (July 1953). In this article, Palmer claimed to have interviewed Sarah Emma Lang, David Lang's daughter, in 1931. According to Sarah, one of the "curious" who harassed the family after her father's disappearance was a writer and journalist named Ambrose Bierce (bear that in mind). Mrs. Lang pined away and died, and the Lang children were raised by their grandparents in Virginia.

When Sarah reached adulthood, she consulted several mediums, hoping to contact her father and learn the secret of his disappearance. Strangely, she received only a message from her mother, suggesting that Sarah herself might become a medium. She developed the ability of automatic writing – allowing an external intelligence to write messages with one's hand – and received more communications from her mother. Finally, one day, she received the following message: "Together now and forever after many years God bless you."

Sarah dug through old keepsakes and discovered a sample of her father's handwriting. It matched that of this final communication.

Stuart Palmer passed on samples of Sarah Lang's automatic writing, David Lang's handwriting, and an affidavit from Palmer and Ms. Lang attesting to the truth of the matter, all of which were reprinted in Fate. The evidence was impressive . . . but some researchers just can't leave well enough alone.

In 1976, Bob Rickard and Robert Forrest of Britain's Fortean Times decided to investigate the David Lang story. They discovered that they were not the only ones interested in the matter. Herschel G. Payne of the Nashville and Davidson County Public Library had investigated it himself.

Payne writes: "The story is supposedly only a fabrication which was told by one Joe Mulhatten, a travelling salesman who was in these parts during the 1880s. There were, at that time, lying contests in which men vied for the title of 'biggest liar' and Joe Mulhatten was a champion." [Rickard and Forrest, p. 7]

Payne consulted librarians, historians, and other knowledgeable people in the Gallatin area. He reviewed old newspapers, genealogies, and the census reports for 1830, 1850, and 1880, but there was absolutely no record of a David Lang or Judge Peck ever living in the area.

But what of Sarah Lang's account? Since Stuart Palmer had provided copies of Sarah's handwriting, an affidavit of truthfulness, and other evidence to Fate, the staff of that magazine decided to put the "proof" to the test. Writer Robert Schadewald and Fate editor Jerome Clarke brought in Ann B. Hooten, an expert in handwriting analysis ("Examiner of Questioned Documents and a member of the prestigious American Society of Document Examiners," as Schadewald put it). Hooten's five-page report concluded that the signatures of Stuart Palmer, Sarah Lang, David Lang (pre-disappearance), Mr. and Mrs. Lang (via automatic writing), and even the notary from the affidavit were all written by the same person. [Schadewald, p. 59.] Mr. Palmer, whoever he was, put out an awful lot of effort to get one little article into one little magazine, but stranger things have happened.

Orion Williamson

. . . But wait! What about this Ambrose Bierce fellow "Sarah" mentioned? Bierce, of course, was the nineteenth-century journalist and writer famous for Civil War stories, cynical humor like The Devil's Dictionary, and horror tales. With his tales of terror, Bierce carved a solid niche for himself in the genre between Poe and Lovecraft.

One of Bierce's most famous and eerie stories was a mini-anthology of vignettes called "Mysterious Disappearances." The first sub-tale, "The Difficulty of Crossing a Field," is concerned with a farmer from Selma, Alabama, named Williamson. One morning in July, 1854, while his wife and son watched from the front porch of their house, and while a neighbor, Armour Wren, was approaching in a carriage with his son James, Williamson hiked out into a nearby field and disappeared.

Sound familiar? Rodney Davies, author of Supernatural Vanishings, investigated the vignettes of "Mysterious Disappearances." "They are fascinating stories," he admits, "but unfortunately I have likewise found nothing definite to substantiate them." In fact, knowing of Bierce's wry sense of humor, Davies suggests that Bierce borrowed from Joe Mulhatten's tall tale: "Bierce's 'Armour Wren' is immediately recognizable as Palmer's 'August Peck,' whose surname surely derives from the tongue-and-cheek association of 'a wren is a bird, and birds peck!'" [Davies, p. 136]

One would expect the trail to end there, but Mr. Williamson, instead of fading into fiction as he faded into an Alabama field, has taken on a life of his own. In Jay Robert Nash's book Among the Missing, the story of David Lang is dismissed as a "gross fabrication": "No such person as David Lang ever existed in Gallatin, nor did any family named Lang during this period." Bierce's Williamson, however, was a "real, live resident of Selma, Alabama." Nash even gives us Williamson's first name, Orion. This all comes from "a thorough investigation on the part of the author and his staff." [Nash, p. 330]

Nash is a prolific writer of true crime and a recipient of the Edgar Award, and Among the Missing provides an impressive list of reporters, archivists, court officials, and staff members consulted, but book reviewers like Sally G. Waters of the Library Journal and Richard Maxwell Brown in the Journal of American History have reported numerous errors in Nash's books.

Searchers may be digging through that grassy field looking for

Orion Williamson for another century or two.

Isaac Martin

"In the New York Sun, April 25, 1885, it is said that Isaac Martin, a young farmer, living near Salem, Va., had gone into a field, to work, and that he had disappeared. It is said that in this region there had been other mysterious disappearances."

Charles Fort, LO!, chapter 17

Another farmer in another field – we should make short work of this, right? Theo Paijmans, a specialist in nineteenth-century oddities, decided to track down this tidbit from Charles Fort (who, strangely, passed over the Lang and Williamson stories). The newspaper Fort refers to was actually The Sun – a Baltimore, Maryland, periodical. "This is the second case of mysterious disappearance in that immediate neighborhood in the last two weeks," proclaimed the April 25 issue.

Paijmans reviewed other old newspapers. There did seem to be a plague of missing persons. "The list of such disappearances in the western portion of Virginia in the past few months is remarkable . . . and no clue has ever been discovered in any of them," says the Statesville, NC Landmark for May 1, 1885.

Isaac Martin, however, didn't stay missing. He was discovered in late May, hanging by the neck from "a tree not far from his home" and only two-and-a-half miles from Salem, according to various newspapers. He had been dead about five weeks.

This brings in a new mystery. It was assumed that Martin committed suicide. But people surely searched for him. How did searchers miss him for five weeks if he was hanging from a tree near both his home and a sizable town? Readers of David Paulides' Missing 411 series will recognize this detail: a person missing for days or weeks, suddenly turning up (usually dead) in a spot where search parties could not have possibly missed him or her.

Paijmans kept up the microfilm-diving, hoping to find out more about the other Virginia disappearances. He didn't find anything about the Virginia cases, but:

"I did find an abundance of reports on mysterious disappearances. It appears that Bierce and Fort tapped into a tradition of events where men stepped into fields and yards – and then nothing." [Paijmans, p. 30]

While we were all beating the dead horse farmer David Lang, perhaps we missed the real strangeness surrounding us.

Bierce, Ambrose, "Mysterious Disappearances," in Ghost and Horror Stories of Ambrose Bierce (New York: Dover Books, 1964), pp. 86-91.

Davies, Rodney. Supernatural Vanishings (New York: Sterling Publishing Co., 1995).

Nash, Jay Robert. Among the Missing: An Anecdotal History of Missing Persons from 1800 to the Present (New York: Simon and Schuster, 1978).

Paijmans, Theo, "Mysterious Vanishings," Fortean Times no. 262 (June 2010), p. 30.

Palmer, Stuart, "How Lost Was My Father," Fate Magazine (July 1953).

Rickard, Bob, and Robert Forrest, "Disappearance of David Lang," Fortean Times no. 18 (October 1976), pp. 6-7.

Schadewald, Robert, "David Lang Vanishes . . . Forever," Fate Magazine Vol. 30, no. 12 (Dec. 1977), pp. 54-60.

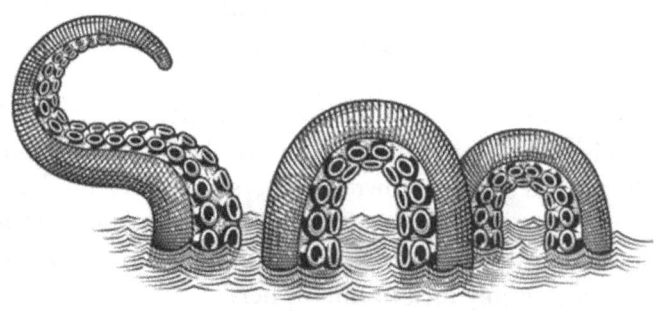

- Dreams that come true
- Precognition/foretellings
- Psychic powers

Diving Boards

I decided on this term after reading parts of the Society of Psychical Research's huge compendium Phantasms of the Living with growing frustration and puzzlement.

Beginning on page 64 of the University Books edition we are told of the psychic adventures of Mrs. Medora C. Adams. One evening, while entertaining visitors at an "at home", she tried to receive impressions from a young man she had never before met. She suggested that he had just sold a parcel of land to a man named O'Brien. This was completely incorrect, but the woman accompanying the man -- also unknown to Mrs. Adams -- said "That is very strange, for I sold a piece of land to-day to a man named O'Brien." On another occasion, as Mrs. Adams and her nephew were watching troops depart (during the Spanish-American war), Mrs. Adams' gaze fell upon "a little woman with a faded shawl over her shoulders." She was suddenly sure the woman was named Smith, and that she had been born in Dumfries, Scotland. Mrs. Adams' nephew accosted the woman and verified the information as true.

We are given other accounts of minor telepathic events in letters from Mrs. Adams and various witnesses. Then, in her own account, just before signing off, Mrs. Adams adds:

"When a girl I was often followed on the street by both men and women who later told me that they could not help it. And once at the theatre I was admiring a lady's gown through my opera glasses. A few moments later the lady in question came to where I was seated and said that she was dominated by an impulse that she could not explain."

And so ends Mrs. Adam's letter. This bizarre aside left me hanging. Did she possess some Pied-Piperish ability to control people? If she concentrated, could she have forced them to perform more complicated tasks against their will? In a comic book story, she might have gone on to conquer the world!

(Can you imagine what would happen today if a man followed a little girl all over town for no apparent reason? "Honest, Officer, some strange force is dragging me after that little girl." "Up against the wall, you perv!")

It just seemed like this statement could have led to a whole new line of inquiry for the SPR. Instead they move on to some story about a housekeeper losing a latchkey. Mrs. Adams' claim just hangs there like a diving board over a pool.

Several pages along in Phantasms we come to a case listed as "transferred emotion" (what is nowadays called empathy rather than telepathy). One Donald Hutchinson of Lowestoft wrote in, stating that he had been invited to see the Observatory at Cambridge on Saturday, October 14, 1911. On that Friday Mr. Hutchinson had the sudden intense feeling that some disaster would take place, and he took out insurance on himself. This feeling appeared late in the day, and he had some trouble getting the matter taken care of, but he was insistent. This was despite the fact that he had motored all over England and Scotland for ten years without ever having an accident, and that he had never felt any need for insurance before.

To prepare for his long journey, Mr. Hutchinson rose at 4:15 am to dress. Soon he heard his six-year-old son crying for him upstairs ("it was a most unusual thing for the boy to wake up at that hour of the morning"). Hutchinson climbed to the boy's room, and the boy threw his arms around his neck, begging him not to undertake the journey. Hutchinson writes that he carefully kept his anxiety over the trip to himself, and that his son had not been told "anything very much about" the affair.

Hutchinson could not comfort the boy, so he took him down to his wife as he finished dressing. The boy fell asleep again after Hutchinson left.

And that's it. Once again, we are left hanging, as if at the edge of a diving board, waiting to hear of a horrible accident. Phantasms notes that the story is presented for the boy's empathy, but that it reads like many of their premonition tales -- except nothing happened.

Three or four pages after this, letters from a woman called "E.M." are printed. On February 3, 1889, E.M. woke with the conviction that a man she knew in America was mailing her a marriage proposal. She was thoroughly convinced of this despite the fact that she believed him to be engaged at the time. Indeed, on Feb. 13 she received a letter from him stating that he had decided to marry an American woman.

On the 15th, as E.M. expected, a letter arrived asking for her hand in marriage. Her correspondent could not bring himself to propose to the other woman. The letter had been written about the time E.M. woke with her impression on the 3rd.

A minor account of an apparent psychic influence, all well and good. E.M. goes on to say that she has, in fact, never had a dream that did not come true -- except one that recurred about once a year:

"I wake up dreaming that a man with red hair and a red beard is leaning over my bed with a knife in his hand. Sometimes he has hold of my shoulder. For some minutes after I am awake I still seem to see and feel him, his hot breath coming on my face... It is always the same face, and I cannot -- since I first had the dream about six years ago -- conquer my horror of red-headed men... I have tried moving my bed to another part of the room, but the dream still comes."

And that's all. Would you have been surprised if a postscript stated that E.M. had been murdered recently by a man with a red beard? Well -- we never find out. Hopefully not, but again I felt like I'd come abruptly to the edge of a diving board.

Sidgwick, Eleanor Mildred, et. al. Phantasms of the Living (New Hyde Park, NY: University Books, 1962 [1886]).

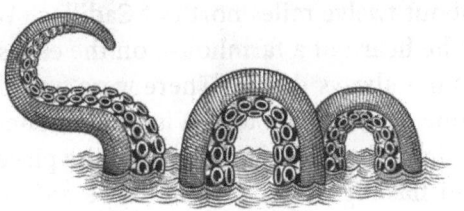

- Bury St. Edmonds, Suffolk, UK: Vanishing houses
- Dartmoor, UK: Vanishing house
- Illinois: Disappearing, moving house
- Michigan: Vanishing farmhouse
- Missouri: Phantom cabin
- Vanishing houses

Dream Houses

Vance Randolph, in Ozark Magic and Folklore, mentions that "Mrs. C. P. Mahnkey once saw clearly a little cabin on a ridge in the old McCann game park, near her home at Mincy, Missouri." She got a pair of binoculars and studied it, noting that smoke was rising from the chimney. By the next day, the cabin had vanished again. Her neighbors informed her that no cabin ever stood there to their knowledge. [1]

Richard T. Crowe, an expert in ghostly phenomena (particularly as it pertains to Chicago, Illinois) tells of a similar "Dream House" located near the infamous Bachelor's Grove Cemetery:

"'As if the thing were not mystery enough,' Crowe went on, 'old records show that there never has been a house there. But the ghost house appears on either side of the road, at different places. Witnesses always describe it in the same way: wooden columns, a porch swing, and a dim light glowing within.'" [2]

Crowe says that no one has ever reported entering the house, but that maybe those who do don't come out again! If so, Don Frosty of Michigan and his girlfriend may have had more than one lucky escape.

Manton is a small town in northwestern Michigan just west of Highway 131, about twelve miles north of Cadillac. When Don Frosty was a teenager, he heard of a farmhouse on the east side of town that supposedly was not always there. "There were two old mining roads, and it was off one of them," he told Wisconsin writer Linda Godfrey. Frosty and his high school girlfriend visited the place multiple times, armed only with flashlights. It seemed to be an ordinary two-story farmhouse.

"I don't recall any furniture in it," he explained to Godfrey. "It was empty like an abandoned house with a wooden floor and no drapes on the windows. The windows were intact. But when we would go back there the next day, there was nothing. Just a field." The house has not been reported, apparently, in recent years. [3]

A number of Dream Houses seem to haunt the small English town of Bradfield St. George, near Bury St. Edmonds in Suffolk. After hosting a radio program about ghosts in March 1934, Sir Ernest Bennett received a letter from a Miss Ruth Wynne, a teacher, who lived in the area in 1926. Miss Wynne and her fourteen year old pupil Miss Allington, taking a walk on a "dull, damp afternoon, I think in October '26," came upon a mildly interesting sight:

"Exactly opposite us on the further side of the road and flanking it, we saw a high wall of greenish-yellow bricks. The road ran past us for a few yards, then curved away from us to the left. We walked along the road, following the brick wall round the bend, where we came upon tall, wrought-iron gates . . . Behind the wall and towering above it was a cluster of tall trees. From the gates, a drive led away among these trees to what was evidently a large house."

The only thing that struck Miss Wynne as odd at the time was that she had not heard of this large residence in the small hamlet. The following February or March, the teacher and her pupil took a walk along the same road and were astonished to find that both the wall (approximately three hundred yards long) and the mansion had vanished. They thought perhaps the house had been torn down, but as they came nearer they noticed a number of small ponds lying where the house had been. "It was obvious that they had been there a long time."

Miss Allington wrote to Sir Ernest in February of 1937, confirming the incident. Andrew MacKenzie made inquiries in the area and scoured the Suffolk Record Office for evidence that such a house ever existed. There was none. [4]

Wynne and Allington's experience was not unique. Around the year 1860, a man named Robert Palfrey was thatching a haystack near Kingshall Street when he happened to look across the road. There stood a house and garden that hadn't been there before. "The house had solid red bricks and the flower-beds were edged with the same red bricks planted slantwise and half buried." The warm June air turned unaccountably cold. Palfrey went home and returned with his relatives, but the house and garden had vanished. [5]

This story was provided to MacKenzie by the great-grandson of Palfrey, "James Cobbold" (pseudonym). Cobbold himself used to make Saturday deliveries with a butcher named George Waylett. One day when Cobbold was twelve years old, they had just left Kingshall for Bradfield St. George:

"[T]here was a loud swishing 'whoosh' as of air displacement, the air became very cold, the pony reared and bolted, and Mr. Waylett was thrown from the cart. In those fleeting moments Mr. Cobbold most distinctly saw a double-fronted, red-brick house roofed with pantiles, three-storeyed, of pronounced Georgian appearance. In front were flower-beds in full bloom. Mr. Cobbold managed to stop the pony and turned it round, since he feared for Mr. Waylett. Even as he did so, 'a kind of mist seemed to envelope the house, which I could still see, and the whole thing simply disappeared, it just went.'"

Despite warnings from Waylett, young Cobbold ran into the field where the house had appeared. There was no sign of anything untoward amid the young wheat. The butcher admitted that this was his third sighting of the appearing-vanishing house. MacKenzie estimates that the year of this occurrence was 1908.

After writing of his and his ancestor's experiences in Amateur Gardening (December 20, 1975), "a young man from the village told Mr. Cobbold that his father had seen the same happening at least twice during the past ten years (1965-1975)." [6]

Folklorist Ruth E. St. Leger-Gordon writes of a phantom cottage that appears occasionally on a small estate near Haytor, in eastern Dartmoor. Sometime in the early 'sixties a woman visiting the area walked past a thatch of forest on the grounds. She remarked on a "charming cottage" to the owner of the estate. He assured her that no cottage existed there. The next evening, she retraced her path and found no evidence of the cottage.

A new house was built a few months later in a nearby clearing. A young woman living in the bungalow asked the owner of the land if he also owned the cottage in the woods, as she couldn't find a way down to it. The landowner, now puzzled, sought any record of a cottage in that area, to no avail. "Nor, after careful search, can he find any traces suggestive of old foundations." [7]

St. Leger-Gordon's book Witchcraft and Folklore of Dartmoor was first published in 1965. In the 1972 reprint, she has more to say on the phantom cottage. An Ordnance Surveyor assigned to the area happened upon her book and sought her out the very next day. "He told me that he had just been sent to survey in detail a small area in the Haytor district. Looking down on this terrain from a high vantage point to check his map, he noticed one cottage that he had apparently missed. Smoke was rising from the chimneys and clothes blowing on a line." As a surveyor, he could pinpoint the exact spot, and he did so. A thorough search of the area revealed no trace of any dwelling, however. He did find a woman walking her dog, and he asked her about the cottage. The woman admitted to having seen it once, and never again. [8]

There are many tales of people seeing/entering/spending the night in houses (or inns) that later proved to have burned down years before. These "Dream Houses" are a little different. Most of them cannot be revenants or "time echoes" of houses now demolished, because no house or cottage ever existed at the sites. Some seem to move around, like the house in Chicago and possibly the house[s] in Bury St. Edmonds. Perhaps if they can lure no one in at one spot, they try "fishing" somewhere else. What would happen if you ventured into a Dream House? Would you end up in some strange parallel world?

All in all, I prefer the Holiday Inn.

1. Randolph, Vance. Ozark Magic and Folklore (New York: Dover Publications, 1964 [1947]), p. 217.

2. Steiger, Brad. Psychic City: Chicago (New York: Doubleday, 1976), p. 88.

3. Godfrey, Linda. Weird Michigan (New York: Sterling Publishing, 2006), p. 72.

4. MacKenzie, Andrew. Adventures in Time: Encounters with the Past (London: The Athlone Press, 1997), pp. 71-75.
5. Ibid., p. 75.
6. Ibid., p. 75-76.
7. St. Leger-Gordon, Ruth E. Witchcraft and Folklore of Dartmoor (New York: Bell Publishing Co., 1972 [1965]), p. 100.
8. Ibid., p. 101.

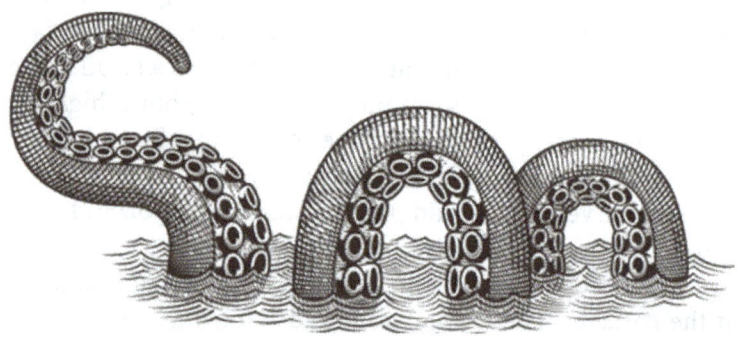

- Haunted house
- Missouri: Haunted house
- Multiple anomaly cluster
- Space/time anomaly, Missouri

The Family That Haunts Together . . .

Starting in the summer of 1982, and off-and-on for the next four years, teacher/coach/writer Jim Longo drove up and down the Mississippi Valley on the Missouri side, interviewing people about ghosts and psychic phenomena. One day, after an unsatisfying interview with an old couple on Altus Place in Kirkwood, MO, Longo was directed to a house only a few doors down.

This house belonged to John and Jean Sears, who, as luck would have it, were hosting a family reunion that very afternoon. Longo was welcomed anyway, and everyone present seemed to have a story about the house.

Mrs. Sears sensed the odd atmosphere of the house as soon as they moved in in 1961. She always had the impression someone was standing beside or behind her. She heard odd sounds, as did nearly everyone in the family, but a particular sound effect singled her out. "Every morning at four AM I'd wake up to the loud sound of an alarm clock," she confided to Longo. However, the Sears owned no alarm clock, and Mrs. Sears was the only one who ever heard it. "But that alarm woke me up every morning for years."

One of the Sears' daughters spoke next. Everyone in the family, she explained, heard the sound of "a man with a cane" wandering throughout the house. When the daughter was a little girl, the footsteps would begin when she stayed home alone, and she would run to her parents' room in terror and lie on their bed. Then, however, a new phenomenon developed: "I'd hear voices that sounded like they were talking quickly, while at the same time, speaking in slow motion." She explained that the voices were deep in tone, like those of men, but gave her the impression of women's voices slowed down. They spoke in an unknown language that sounded vaguely Asian.

A second daughter mentioned the recurrent noise of someone who would enter through the (locked) back door, rummage through the kitchen drawers, then exit the same way. The family then called upon Mr. and Mrs. Sears' son Tom to tell about the "people in the closet." One night circa 1968, as young Tom lay in his bed upstairs, he saw something through the wide-open closet doorway. Although it was a "shadowy, white figure," it was obviously a woman. No mournful specter this: The woman seemed to be washing dishes in a kitchen; at least, in a room much larger than the inside of the closet.

The woman seemed to catch sight of the boy, and the two stared at each other silently for a couple of minutes. The woman stepped out of view but returned momentarily with a man and a small child in tow. "They stared at me as if they'd come to see this remarkable phenomenon." Eventually the "closet people" moved out of sight. "They just seemed to be a regular family with a father, mother and little boy, except they were more like white fog than real people." The phenomenon never repeated.

Eventually, Tom moved to the basement rooms. One of the lights down there could be turned off only by being unscrewed, but when Tom did so at night, the light would pop back on, the bulb having been inexplicably twisted back in. The youth merely slept with the light on. What truly disturbed him was the sense that the house was "alive", with a slow "breath" and "pulse" of its own, which he heard or sensed in the basement.

Stranger still, one night as Tom and a couple of buddies sat chatting in the basement, the three of them "started talking as if we were brothers in the Civil War," as he put it. The gist of the conversation was that one brother, a deserter, had been court-martialed and shot, while the second brother came home to find his fiancée in the arms of the third. The young men snapped out of the spell, and, while driving home, the two visitors swore a man ran into the street and leveled a rifle at them. They roared away without noting more details. "And for several years after that, I had a sore spot in my collar bone, where the Civil War deserter had supposedly been shot," Tom concluded.

The strange events continued right up to the time of Longo's visit. "Just recently," one daughter explained, when she and a girl friend were spending a night alone in the house, they heard footsteps climb onto the porch and enter the front room. The daughter investigated, only to hear the footsteps run out the door onto the porch again. "I looked out, but couldn't see anybody in any direction."

Unexplained noises are common in hauntings, but these seemingly created a special effect for each individual: an alarm clock for one, the "fast-yet-slow" voices for another, the whole house "breathing" for a third. The Sears had purchased the house from a doctor. Mrs. Sears thought perhaps the doctor rose early, and the alarm clock was a "memory" of that time.

Longo hit the supernatural jackpot in the Sears home. The fact that many family members were present that day is one reason, but it truly sounds as if this house in Kirkwood, Missouri, lies in the Twilight Zone as much as Altus Place. The "people in the closet" event is particularly fascinating, as it sounds more like living people in their own home somehow "lapping over" into Tom's closet. I can't help but think that somewhere on earth a woman occasionally tells of the time she glanced toward the kitchen door while washing dishes and saw a bedroom with a boy lying in bed watching her. Naturally she called on the nearest witnesses, her husband and young son, but soon the boy -- no doubt a ghost -- vanished ...

Longo, Jim. Haunted Odyssey: Ghostly Tales of the Mississippi Valley (St. Louis, MO: St. Anne's Press, 1986) pp. 95-101.

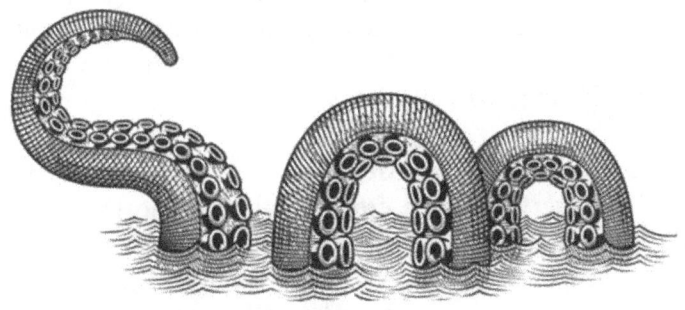

- Chile: Hide/skin creature
- Flat – living rug creature
- Ireland: Rug-like creature
- Living rug creature
- Wellman, Manly Wade – monster of folklore

The Flat

Manly Wade Wellman, the American fantasy writer famous for his tales of John the minstrel, created a pantheon of bizarre creatures for his Appalachian story-cycle, including "the Flat":
"It lay out on the ground like a broad, black, short-furred carpet rug. But it moved, humping and then flattening out, the way a measuring worm moves." [1]

The Wellman book Worse Things Waiting contains an essay called "Up Under the Roof," which he says "is as close to autobiography as I have ever come." [p. xi] If so, it would appear that Wellman's boyhood was haunted by a creature similar to the Flat.

Wellman was the only child in a large, crowded household, and his relatives seemed to resent his youthfulness. He was forced to sleep in a high, dusty, uncomfortable garret. In the summer of his twelfth year he started hearing something between the ceiling and the peak of the roof, a heavy, bulky something that "did not drag or walk, but it moved."

"Years afterward," he writes, "I was to see through a microscope the plodding of an amoeba. The thing up under the roof sounded as an amoeba looks, a mass that stretches out a thin, loose portion of itself, then rolls and flows all of its substance into that portion, and so creeps along."

The humping, flowing noise returned every night, to Wellman's dismay: "I was certain that it crouched there, almost within reach of me, that it gloated and hungered, and that it turned over in its dark sub-personal awareness the problem of when and how to come and take hold of me." [2] The one time he explored the area up under the roof he found nothing, but it appears another young boy had a more blatant run-in with an entity like the Flat, in Ireland, as described in Diarmuid MacManus' book Between Two Worlds.

"Mr. George Hallet, a prominent professional man in the old city of Limerick, had a very queer experience when he was a youngster," during a summer holiday at Mount Temple House, several miles outside that city. Twelve-year-old Hallet slept in a bedroom on the second floor, next to a room full of old furniture and junk. "There were no rugs, a point to be particularly noted."

Hallet had developed a habit of sleepwalking, but he always woke after only a few steps, whereupon he would scramble back into bed. One night he found himself at the opposite end of the narrow room. It was so dark he had to feel his way back.

He did not make it halfway before "one bare foot, put gingerly down as he felt his way, just touched something that was very soft and furry but by the feel of it flat like a rug." The boy froze, foot barely brushing the "rug", greatly disturbed because he knew there was no such item in the room. Then, to his horror, he lost his balance and planted his foot right in the middle of the "rug", which "let out a deafening, reverberating and blood-curdling scream and the fur, though still flat, seemed to come to life under his foot."

Hallet jumped into bed and pulled his blanket over his head. He waited long, agonizing hours until the light of morning [and a maid] came. He was in such a nervous state that a physician was summoned, and the doctor ordered him to stay in bed for two days. There is no mention whether or not it was the same bed in the same room. Adult members of the household searched the room but found nothing. [3]

I wonder if it is significant that both accounts of "Flats" concern boys aged twelve, and that they take place during the summer, in old houses where the layout of the building is important (to show how the boys were isolated near old junk). The stories are even close chronologically: Wellman would have been twelve in 1915, and MacManus' 1977 book claims that Hallet's encounter occurred "fifty-five to sixty years ago," or between 1917 and 1922.

There is, in the folklore of North America, a bizarre critter called the Rumtifusel, an entity that resembles nothing so much as a flat, furry skin with a fine, rich texture like a mink coat. Sometimes an unsuspecting person investigates the Rumtifusel: "With a lightning-fast flick of its blanket-like body the Rumtifusel completely envelops its victim." [4] Off the coast of Chile, according to Jorge Luis Borges, fishermen must beware of "the Hide," which resembles a stretched-out cow hide. "Its edges are furnished with numberless eyes, and . . . whenever persons or animals enter the water, the Hide rises to the surface and engulfs them with an irresistible force, devouring them in a matter of moments." [5] John Michell and Robert Rickard, in Living Wonders (1981), compare the Hide with those hairy bulks from the sea that Ivan Sanderson christened Globsters -- a subject outside the scope of this article.

The Flat strikes this author as a personification of the uncomfortable feeling one sometimes gets in an attic or garage or other musty place full of junk: Could there be something there, something hidden beneath those tables and lamps and boxes, something worse than silverfish or spiders? As for its outdoor equivalents – well, if you ever hike down a forest trail and see an expensive-looking fur coat draped over a stump – you shouldn't take what isn't yours. It just might take you, instead.

   1. Wellman, Manly Wade. Who Fears the Devil? (London: Star Books, 1975 [1963]), p. 98.
   2. Ibid. Worse Things Waiting (Chapel Hill, NC: Carcosa, 1973), pp. 4-8.
   3. MacManus, Diarmuid A. Between Two Worlds (Gerrards Cross, Buckinghamshire: Colin Smythe, 1977), pp. 16-18.
   4. Tryon, Henry H. Fearsome Critters (Cornwall, NY: Idlewild Press, 1939), p. 35.
   5. Borges, Jorge Luis, and Norman Thomas di Giovanni. Book of Imaginary Beings (New York: Avon, 1969 [1967]), p. 100.

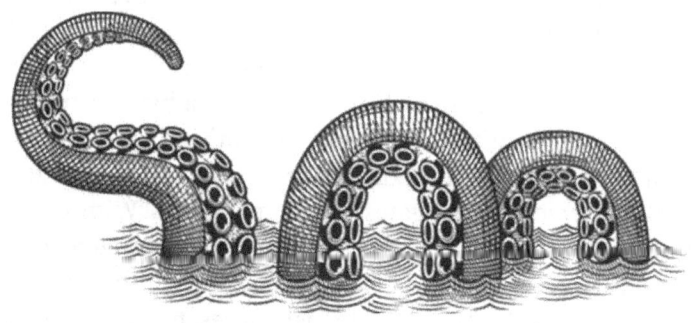

- Coffin, floating/flying
- Floating/flying coffin
- Ghost and spectral coffin
- West Virginia: Flying coffin and ghost

The Floating Coffin

Ruth Ann Musick collected West Virginia ghost stories and folklore for many years. Her books The Telltale Lilac Bush and Coffin

Hollow are considered almost perfect American folk tale collections. Ms. Musick received the following account from one Thomas Leeper of Monongah, West Virginia, in 1949. His relationship to the named witnesses is not known.

"Not long after the end of the Civil War" Mrs. Hess Bender visited the Smith family on her way to her home in Bobtown, near Monongah. She continued traveling after dinner but returned, frightened, half-an-hour later. On a stretch of road passing between Booth's Creek and the woods, "a coffin with a man sitting on it" floated up about head-high from the forest side of the path, quartered across the road, and disappeared over the creek bank.

A local farmer named Isaac Koon later reported an identical apparition. After that several more people reported the flying coffin. It apparently rose from the same point and flew across the road in the same direction, "and was always seen about the same time in the evening." A new road in the area caused the sightings to taper off.

Several years after its initial appearance three young men, Tom Rhea, Barney Whaling, and Will Barnes, after playing in a baseball game at Boothsville, rode homeward along the old road. Barney remarked that this was where the "dead man" was often seen. Tom replied, "I wish I could see him. I would whistle for him to dance."

Immediately the coffin and man appeared, and Tom's horse nearly threw him, indicating the animal's awareness of the entity.

This seems to have been the phantasm's last major appearance. "I have not heard a word about the man and coffin for more than fifty years," said Mr. Leeper in 1949.

William Montell's Ghosts Along the Cumberland (1975) contains some flying coffin stories, and more recently one appears in Steve Stockton's Strange Things in the Woods (2013). Coffins in ghost stories are usually static visions or harbingers of doom. The human apparition using one as a "vehicle" is quite strange. Mr. Leeper mentioned that a man from Pennsylvania had supposedly been murdered along the Booth's Creek road, but had no other explanation for the haunting.

West Virginia seems to have more than its share of off-kilter stories. Tom Rhea spoke disparagingly of the ghost before his encounter, suggesting that his disrespect caused it to appear. This is a common folklore motif. However, the phenomenon seems otherwise to be a vision that mindlessly repeats itself. George Eberhart's Geo-Bibliography of Anomalies lists this tale as a "UFO (CE-1)", which carries totally different connotations.

Musick, Ruth Ann. Telltale Lilac Bush (Lexington, KY: University of Kentucky Press, 1965), pp. 71-72, 173.

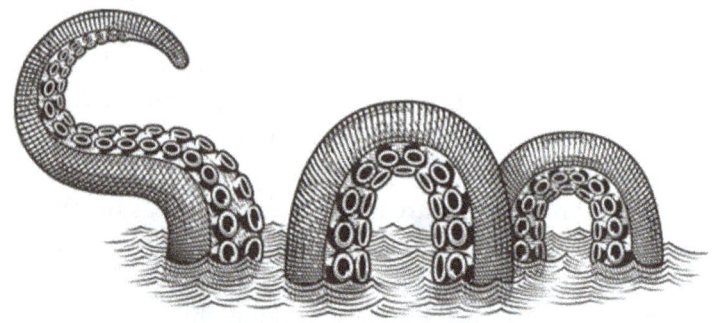

- Constable, Trevor James – theory of living UFOs
- "Critters" – living UFOs
- Flying saucer-shaped creature
- Nevada: Saucer-shaped flying creature
- UFO as living being

The Flying Clam

One day in 1925, pilot Don Wood, Jr., and three other men were flying "Jennies" (Curtiss JN-4 biplanes) over the Nevada desert simply for fun. They knew that the sheer sides of Flat Mesa, near Battle Mountain, Nevada, made it nearly impossible to climb, so they decided to set down on the mesa itself and see what was there. It was about one pm when they landed.

As they hiked around the plateau, they saw something else coming in for a landing. "It was about eight feet across and was round and flat like a saucer," writes Wood. "The undersides were a reddish color. It skidded to a stop about 30 feet away." A classic flying saucer, a good twenty-two years before the term was coined? No: "We walked up to the thing and it was some animal like we never saw before. It was hurt, and as it breathed the top would rise and fall making a half-foot hole all around it like a clam opening and closing."

The creature had no apparent eyes or limbs. Its upper surface glistened with moisture, and its shell possessed a mica-like appearance. A large chunk had been "chewed" out of its otherwise circular rim, and a metallic froth dribbled from this wound. As the astonished fliers approached, the thing breathed faster and tried to lift from the mesa. It rose only a few inches before dropping back down.

The men stood uncertainly, amazed by their find but never daring to get closer than ten feet to the aerial being. After twenty minutes the creature began to breathe or pulsate rapidly again, and it tried (and failed) once more to leave the earth. "And so help me," continues Wood, "the thing grew as bright as all get out, except where it was hurt." Yet this strange encounter was to grow stranger.

A large shadow slid over the men, who needed only a glance up to send them running. A second "flying clam" dropped toward Flat Mesa, this one thirty feet across!

"It paid no attention to us, but settled itself over the small one. Four sucker-like tongues settled on the little one and the big one got so dazzling bright you couldn't look at it. Both rose straight up and were out of sight in a second."

The pilots rallied and studied the "froth" left by the smaller creature. It resembled extremely fine aluminum wire, and an "awful stench" filled the atmosphere around it. A thin line of similar froth formed a thirty-foot-wide circle around the clam's landing spot, as if the larger being had dripped a small amount from its rim. The substance slowly dissolved in the strong sunlight. When even the froth was gone, there was nothing left for the pilots to do but climb in their airplanes and leave the mesa.

Wood and his friends kept quiet about their experience for many years. Finally Wood wrote an account and sent it to Ray Palmer's magazine, Flying Saucers, which published it in its October 1959 issue.

Unless you are aware of the theories of "sky animals" suggested by Ivan Sanderson, Vincent Gaddis, Trevor James Constable and others, this is probably the oddest UFO or monster report ever. Constable, a strong proponent of the "sky creature" concept, reprinted Wood's story in his 1975 article "UFOs Are Living Beings." Constable reports that he traced Wood to his new address in "one of the southern states" and contacted him. He was "satisfied that he reported his experience accurately."

While myth and legend has filled the skies with all manner of angels, sylphs, and dragons, these "flying clams" are something else again. If seen at a distance or at night, the self-luminous "clams" would pretty much be archetypal flying saucers, so they seem to belong to the modern mythos of UFOs rather than to any legends of the past. So unless Don Wood's story is a complete fabrication, it seems he and his friends did stumble across some sort of "sky creature" in 1925 – it simply does not work as an alien spaceship, government experiment, weather balloon, etc.

Indeed, as Trevor James Constable says, if true, this is the single best observation ever of a living UFO – the entities Constable dubbed "critters". "Truly that one example is worth a thousand, containing all within itself – what Goethean scientific thinkers call the ur example." The injured creature's "froth" is reminiscent of "Angel Hair," the wispy substance that sometimes falls from the sky only to evaporate into nothingness.

It is rather heartening that the large one (Mother? Mate?) would rescue the smaller one. My question is – what "chewed" a hunk out of the little one? I'm put in mind of Arthur Conan Doyle's 1913 tale, "Horror of the Heights," in which gigantic flying predators suddenly decide that these humans invading their aerial world are good to snack on...

Constable, Trevor James, "UFOs Are Living Creatures," in Saga's UFO Report Vol. 2, No. 4 (Summer 1975), pp. 14-17, 52-54.

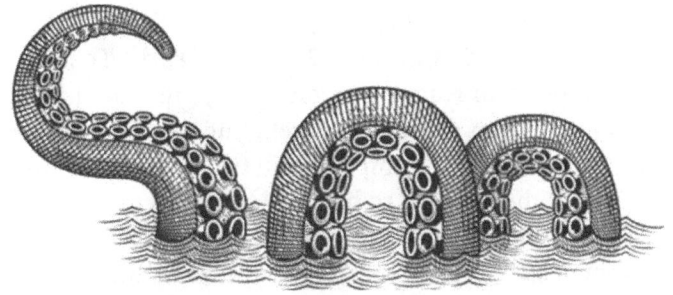

- Children's hand- and footprints on walls and ceiling
- Ghostly footprints on walls and ceiling
- Wolverhampton, UK: Ghosts; footprints on ceiling

Footprints on the Ceiling

Ian Deakin's mother and her family moved into a terraced house in the East Park district of Wolverhampton, West Midlands, UK, in the late 'sixties. One night as Ian's mother and her older sister were preparing to go to bed upstairs, they noticed a man in a sailor's uniform on the landing. They thought for a moment that the figure was their father, who had served in the navy during World War II, but the figure walked toward the bathroom and vanished. Later a younger sister claimed to have felt something like a small child, but unseen, push by her in a hallway.

A conventional haunted house, you say, but the most frequently occurring phenomena therein were quite unconventional: the handprints of a grown man and the footprints of children's shoes, which appeared all over the house, but only on the walls and ceilings. The family painted over these unlikely imprints, but they simply bled through to appear again. Only the application of wallpaper and ceiling tiles hid them, and even then not permanently: "I can recall actually seeing these prints on the walls of the front bedroom after the house was stripped when the remainder of the family moved out in the mid-Eighties," writes Deakin. "No contact has been made with the family that currently resides in the house."

Deakin points out that in the 1920s, Harry Parks Temple, a sailor, drowned attempting to rescue two young boys in a pool in East Park. Tragically, the children drowned as well, but he is considered a local hero. Deakin suggests that Temple is still trying to rescue the children to this day. If so, they appear to have led him on a merry chase up the walls and across the ceilings of this Wolverhampton domicile.

Most human specters walk (though sometimes on surfaces that no longer exist) or at best "waft" along. Few ghosts fly through the air Casper-like or walk up walls and across ceilings like Spider-Man. If such entities have any free will, and if they are not affected by gravity, one wonders why they don't perform such amazing feats more often.

The Wolverhampton account awakened a background radiation of memory of other reports of "footprints on the ceiling," however. I have the notion I've read or heard of such things, but whether in fiction, legend, or actual reports, I can't recall. I'm sure I've heard it mentioned in films -- I vaguely recall an old mystery (Basil Rathbone as Sherlock Holmes, maybe) where as an aside they recall a case in which a pair of acrobats in a hotel did it by having one crouch over while the other lay on his back and "walked" along the ceiling. The phenomenon is central to a Holmes pastiche by French writer Jules Castier called, appropriately, "The Footprints on the Ceiling" (1920).

Carl Sandburg's one-volume Abraham Lincoln reveals that teenaged Abe, honest or not, was a bit of a prankster. "He put barefoot boys to wading in a mud puddle near the horse trough, picked them up one by one, carried them to the house upside-down, and walked their muddy feet across the ceiling." [p. 15]

Should I ever come across footprints on the ceiling, though, I won't count too much on spotting the 16th President of the USA in the area.

Deakin, Ian, "Hello Sailor," in It Happened to Me!: Real-Life Tales of the Paranormal, Vol. 1, edited by Paul Sieveking and Jen Ogilvie (London: Dennis Publishing, 2008), p. 14.

Sandburg, Carl. Abraham Lincoln: The Prairie Years and the War Years One-Volume Edition (New York: Galahad Books, 1993 [1954]).

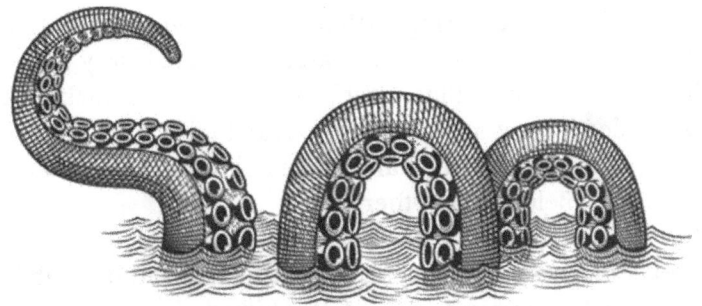

- Haunting: Oregon Trail
- Nebraska: Pioneer ghost story
- Oregon trail ghost

Ghost of the Oregon Trail

Charles Dawson lived in Jefferson County, Nebraska for forty years before realizing that the original settlers of the state were dying off around him. In 1909 he began interviewing old-timers and people who knew personally the first homesteaders of the area. His efforts resulted in a thick volume entitled Pioneer Tales of the Oregon Trail and of Jefferson County (1912). With few exceptions the interviewees were allowed to remain anonymous, including the old pioneer who provided the following story.

From the 1840s to the '70s the main artery of travel across the North American continent was the winding dirt path known as the Oregon Trail. The main jump-off point for the Trail was St. Joseph, Missouri, from which city would-be settlers and their wagons ambled northwest across Kansas and into Nebraska, after which the trail curved slowly back toward the south.

Sometime in the early 1860s the narrator's father established himself in still-wild Nebraska, and he sent word to his son that he, too, should strike out into the wilderness. During one spring in the late 'sixties, the narrator did just that, he, his wife, and "our bunch of tow-headed youngsters" venturing forth in an ox-drawn wagon. The family settled in a bountiful, well-watered area "about half-way between the Old Trail and the Little Blue river" in southeast Nebraska, near the Kansas border. They spent nearly a year building a log cabin and clearing the surrounding land, and in the following spring they planted corn, potatoes, melons, and other crops.

Wild strawberries grew in abundance in some nearby valleys, and one Sunday morning the narrator and his wife hiked off with buckets to harvest the luscious red fruit. A low hillock, in a valley lined with shelflike walls, produced the largest and reddest berries the two had ever seen, and they fell to picking them despite a huge tangle of vines and underbrush that covered the rise.

The narrator's foot caught in something, and he uprooted a human skull. He and his wife dug through the brush and discovered the almost complete skeletons of twelve people, men, women, and children.

The find was not that unusual; of the thousands of people who traveled the Oregon Trail, many hundreds died due to disease, the elements, bandits, Indian raids, wild animals, or accidents. The pioneer couple buried the skeletal remains and returned home by nightfall.

The family ate supper and sat out on the porch. Suddenly, reports the narrator, "there came an uncanny, weird moan or cry, like that of a woman or child in the depths of anguish or despair. Listening in awe, I awaited the repetition of that mournful sound. Soon it came, now in the fringe of trees about the cabin, then in the waist-high corn."

The homesteader took his rifle and, leaving his wife and children to watch from the porch, he "proceeded to search about in the growing corn, around the barn and all through the near-by underbrush." He saw nothing, though he followed the sound from place to place.

The moaning seemed to approach the cabin, and the settler's family jumped inside and barred the door. The homesteader continued his pursuit. "After vain attempts which led me to the roof, around and underneath the cabin, I contracted the same feelings of the rest of the family and called for admittance." The family slept little, for the cries continued until dawn.

The bodiless voice returned night after night, and finally the family grew accustomed to it. Neighbors visited and took turns chasing the noise, but no one ever saw anything that might account for it.

Summer passed. Fall arrived, and with it a bountiful harvest, but the settlers' success was tarnished by the nightly visitations, which wore on their nerves. They spent the winter with the narrator's father some miles away along the Little Blue. Occasionally the narrator visited the cabin to make sure all was well, but he never stayed past sunset.

Spring came again, and the family moved back to begin planting. The moaning began anew the night of their arrival. "Of course, it was annoying, but what could we do?"

As if to bring things full circle, the pioneer couple went strawberry-picking again. As they rested on a boulder after a bout of harvesting, their eyes ran over the craggy, pitted walls of the valley. To their astonishment, they spotted another skeleton. "On closer investigation we found it to be that of a woman, huddled in a crouched, squatting position, back against the wall of a cavern-like place, seemingly as though she had taken refuge here, only to be found."

The couple buried the woman near the rough graves dug a year earlier, and they searched for more bodies. There were no more human remains, but they did find charred wood, wagon-irons, and ox bones, plus a few arrows, indicating that the unknown dead were pioneers who had been slain by native tribesmen.

The narrator waited up that evening on the porch, but the voice did not return – that night or ever again.

"Was this [voice] the spirit of the murdered woman beseeching me to bury her bones beside those we had previously buried, who no doubt had met a similar fate?" asks the homesteader. "I hope so, and if this gave rest to the Soul, let it be the end."

One assumes, like the narrator, that the spirit moaned both from the sheer horror of its manner of death and from a desire to attract the attention of mortals who could lay it to rest. Yet its communications were very uninformative, and it led people on pointless chases, sometimes over and under buildings, as if it were a mischievous elf rather than a soul in torment. One can conclude that we still do not know much about the motivations of ghosts.

Collections of folklore usually contain many supernatural anecdotes, but Pioneer Tales can boast of only this one – entitled, logically enough, "The Ghost Story." Perhaps Theodore Roosevelt was right, as he says in The Wilderness Hunter: "Frontiersmen are not, as a rule, apt to be very superstitious. They lead lives too hard and practical, and have too little imagination in things spiritual and supernatural." [Roosevelt, p. 752] Of course, right after this observation, Roosevelt goes into the account usually called "Baumann's Tale," a chilling proto-Sasquatch legend. But that's another story.

Dawson, Charles. Pioneer Tales of the Oregon Trail and of Jefferson County (Fairbury, Nebraska: Holloway Publishing, 1967 [1912]), pp. 236-243.

Roosevelt, Theodore. Hunting Trips of a Ranchman and The Wilderness Hunter (New York: Modern Library, 1996 [1893]).

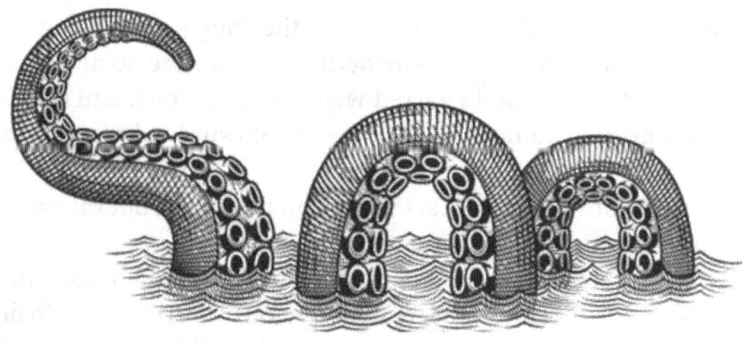

- Giant shrimp in apartment basement
- Shrimp-like monster in basement/laundry room
- Washington state: Monster shrimp

Giant Shrimp in the Laundry Room

In 1948 Virginia Staples lived in an apartment house on Denny

Street, Bremerton, Washington. At that time the apartment buildings in Bremerton were, according to the percipient, old, huge, and crowded close together. Ms. Staples' building possessed a "gigantically huge basement," in which were located a washer, tub, and clothesline. There were wide holes in the walls that the manager claimed led to the sea.

One day as Ms. Staples washed her clothes and hung them up, she suffered that well-known sensation of being watched. She turned to one of the openings in the far wall and saw a bizarre creature as tall as she (5 feet) lurking within. "It had a bright orange colored body and little spidery thin legs and antennae on its head that kept moving back and in and out." The thing crawled toward Ms. Staples, who fled upstairs. She packed her belongings immediately and moved in with her cousin in Seattle. She later visited an aquarium and decided that the closest thing to what she had seen was a "little tiny shrimp."

The experience gave Ms. Staples nightmares for years. She gave her testimony over the phone to Strange Magazine; she cried and almost broke down during her call. However, "a couple of years" before her report (ca. 1990), she worked up the nerve to return to Bremerton, only to find that the U.S. Navy had appropriated the land long before. The apartment building no longer existed.

There is an implication that the Giant Shrimp crawled through a passage from the sea, but even if there existed a crustacean this large, it could not walk on land on "spidery thin" legs. Fortean author Mike Dash suggests explanations from an unconscious desire to leave the apartment building resulting in a frightening vision to a plain old hallucination, but he admits that in the end "we cannot know."

The year 1948 was filled with monster reports of all kinds.

Dash, Mike. Borderlands (New York: Dell Publishing, 2000), pp. 434-437.

"First Person," at www.strangemag.com/firstperson.html; originally from Strange Magazine #6 (1990), p. 5.

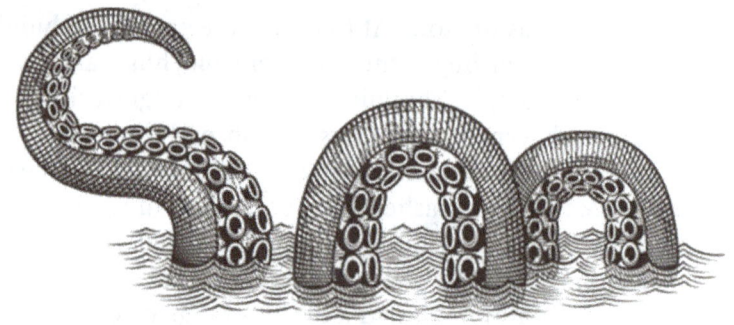

- Crosses of light on windows, 1971
- Glowing crosses appear on windows
- United States: glowing crosses appear

Glowing Crosses of 1971

On August 27, 1971, at about four o'clock in the afternoon, Mabel Davis, a choir member of an African-American church in downtown Los Angeles, was disappointed that she had been unable to find an organist for choir practice. Things had been going so poorly at the church, in fact, that Mrs. Davis had considered resigning from the choir completely. Then, however, her eleven-year-old daughter Patricia said, "Look, Mommy!"

In a large window at the back of the church, "a great gleaming golden cross" appeared. It appeared at around 4:00 pm every afternoon for some weeks following. As the sun was directly in line with the window at that time of day, most people ascribed the image to refraction or reflection. "But it is still a mystery to me," the Reverend Roy Williams told the Los Angeles Times. "I had never seen it before in the six years we've had the church." [Rogo, p. 131]

On September 12, 1971, all the way across the country in Apalachicola, Florida, a cross of light appeared in the window of the First Born Holiness Church. Unlike the LA cross, this visual cruciform varied in size and color. Dr. K. R. Chapman, from the physics department of Florida State University, investigated and found that the window glass was etched with vertical and horizontal furrows that refracted light. Also, a 60-watt fixture hung directly outside the window. Again, however, no one could explain why the image had never shown up before.

Florida became the epicenter of the glowing cross phenomenon. On September 22, the United Methodist Church in Mexico City, Florida, reported a cross of light in one window. No less than three churches in Panama City reported crosses, as did three in Jacksonville. The Nazarene Church in Panama City boasted three crosses on different windows, but the cross at the Paxon Revival Center in Jacksonville went them one better: Photographs of the Paxon cross showed what appeared to be human hands at the ends of the crossbeam.

The phenomenon spread to Georgia, and it increased in complexity. In Brunswick, GA, a cross appeared at Glynn-Brunswick Memorial Hospital – the first apparition outside of a church. Three churches in the same town reported glowing crosses, but at a fourth – St. Andrews Methodist – witnesses reported seeing "a scroll with the Ten Commandments" on one window. [Techter, p. 55] Crosses were reported in Kingsland and Savannah, and in Darien a cross appeared in a private home – the house of Mr. and Mrs. George C. Hall.

In the second week of November, the phenomenon arrived in New York – at 835 Trinity Avenue, apartment 1, the Bronx, to be specific. The cross was first seen in a window by a visitor, the mother of Mrs. Viola Mitchell, who lived in the building. The intriguing thing, however, is the fact that Mrs. Mitchell was a friend of the Mr. and Mrs. Hall from Darien, Georgia! Could paranormal events – even miracles – somehow pass from person to person like a cold or flu?

There were a few more manifestations in New York and Georgia, but the "flap" of glowing crosses faded away by January 1972. The Brunswick Glass Company, which provided the window glass for many Georgia churches, blamed the crosses on "interior patterns of horizontal and vertical lines termed 'finetex obscure.'" [Techter, p. 57] Others have suggested wishful thinking and pareidolia, the propensity of the human brain to find figures and faces in random patterns.

Were the glowing crosses the result of freak refractions and wishful thinking? Were they miracles? Were they something in between?

Psychic researcher D. Scott Rogo theorized that the church members might have created their own miracles via psychokinesis. "If a single psychic can alter the path of a beam of light, why couldn't a group of emotionally charged people manipulate rays of sunlight?" [Rogo, p. 135]

All one can say in the end is that glowing crosses have been reported to this day around the world. See, for instance, the "Crosses of Light" webpage: http://miracles.mcn.org/crossesb.html

Rogo, D. Scott. Miracles (New York: The Dial Press, 1982), pp. 131-135.

Techter, David, "A Flap of Glowing Crosses," Fate Magazine Vol. 25 no. 6 (whole number 267), June 1972, pp. 52-59.

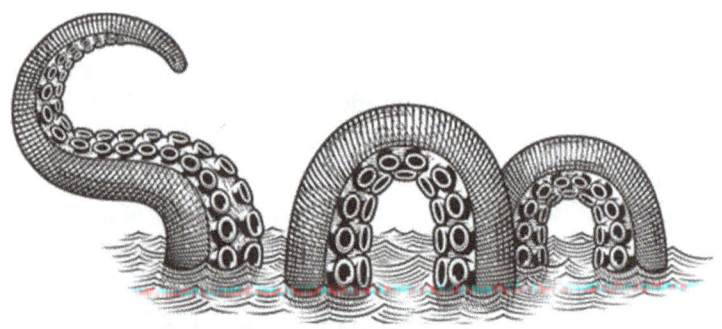

- Glowing apparition/blob in a country lane (Iowa)
- Hughes, Irene, medium – ghost hunt
- Iowa: Ghost hunt
- Medium frightened by glowing apparition
- Psychic frightened by glowing apparition

The Glowing "Something" in the Lane

In 1969, paranormal author Brad Steiger wrote Know the Future Today, the biography of spirit medium and psychic Irene Hughes (1920 – 2012). During the winter of 1969, Steiger suggested that he, Hughes, and other investigators should travel around Illinois, Iowa, and

Nebraska the next summer on a sort of "psychic safari," visiting haunted places.

Angie and Glenn McWane, friends of Steiger's, suggested they investigate a haunted spot in the McWanes' hometown of Iowa City, Iowa. This was the estate and mansion of the Sumter family. Generations earlier the Sumters had been a prominent clan, but by the mid-twentieth century only two aged sisters lived in the decaying mansion amid old mementoes, stained furniture, and a century-high pile of magazines and newspapers. The story went that a strange, glowing "shape" wandered to and fro through the grounds and the house. Neighbors called the police occasionally, but the cops could do little more than sit in their squad cars and watch the glowing thing wander around. The Sumter sisters were not bothered by the apparition – as a matter of fact, according to Glenn McWane, "the sisters would sit calmly and converse with it." [1972, p.35] Eventually one sister died and the other was put in a nursing home. The glowing shape still appeared.

On a warm night in July 1970, before getting permission to enter the estate (and before informing the police of their presence), the ghost chasers pulled up into the entry lane in Steiger's station wagon. A locked wooden gate blocked their way; Glenn, who drove, could barely pull the vehicle out of the road. The grounds and trees were so unkempt, the lane looked like a tunnel through a jungle. The time was about midnight.

Suddenly, someone cried out "What's that?" A "very large, glowing orb of wispy light" appeared down the lane, not far from the front door of the mansion and thus forty to fifty yards away from the vehicle. Glenn killed the headlights; clouds hid the moon and trees hid the nearest streetlight, so the group could agree the phenomenon was self-luminous.

There is a slight discrepancy between Steiger's early description of the apparition versus later ones. In the Irene Hughes book, he states that the object was a "glowing orb," a "strange orb," a "glowing glob." A few years later, in Psychic City: Chicago, he describes the entity as "a glowing, human-shaped thing," "a glowing, man-shaped thing." In his 2003 ghost book he calls it "a very large orb of light." At any rate, the ghost hunters turned to Irene and asked if they should start investigating a day early.

"No," the normally unflappable psychic said. "Not tonight. I have a very bad feeling that it would not be good for us to walk down that lane right now."

The group hesitated as the "orb" drifted toward the house. Hughes yelled out "Let's leave now!", and the startled investigators obeyed.

The next day Mr. Roberts, the caretaker of the house, led Irene through the rooms and halls. The psychic described her impressions concerning the people who lived in the mansion. Steiger asked how accurate Hughes was, and the caretaker said, "I'd have to give her a ninety percent."

On the second night the troupe parked in front of the mansion. "Glenn and I were in the front seat, a police officer between us," Steiger recalls in Psychic City: Chicago [p. 32]. "Irene, two journalists, and a friend were in the back" [in Irene Hughes he adds the caretaker to the back seat]. Even right in front of the house the brush and trees screened out most of the moonlight.

As they sat, taking in the dark scene, a tendril of mist formed in front of the station wagon. Steiger and the formerly skeptical policeman remarked on it first; Glenn claimed that the "tendril" had wafted over to the car from some nearby bushes.

Again, McWane killed the headlights, and the company exited the car. Steiger poked his hand into the thickening mist and found it cooler than the night air. Suddenly the "mist" vanished, and equally suddenly Irene Hughes cried, "There are some people coming through the bushes by the house!"

Steiger admits he saw and heard nothing, but others of the group said they heard the sounds of footsteps and branches cracking. Someone spotted the glowing mist off in the trees, but it vanished again. Irene insisted she had seen solid people, but Glenn McWane, looking in the same direction, saw only the glowing mistiness.

The medium next claimed she heard a woman calling for help – a woman whose leg was broken. "There! There in the bushes. See her head?"

Steiger and McWane saw only a glowing mass. In fact, everyone saw the glowing "thing" at some point; a few heard noises as if of people in the underbrush; but only Irene Hughes saw full-bodied apparitions. Steiger concluded that Irene was just better attuned to psychic vibrations.

"Well, there are plenty of vibrations around here to tune in to," the medium remarked.

A year after the psychic safari, Glenn McWane and a university professor spotted the ghost on the estate grounds. Three nights later Brad Steiger, Glenn, and three companions drove out to the mansion at around midnight. A thick wire, from which dangled strips of red and white cloth, now hung across the lane, blocking the way.

The group switched off the car and left the vehicle, venturing a few yards down the lane. Soon a "column of light about the height of an average human being" appeared, followed the lane up to the mansion, and entered the building. The quintet turned back to their vehicle and were stunned to find a three-tined pitchfork plunged upright into the earth just in front of the grill. "I was becoming concerned that we may have worn out our welcome at the haunted estate." [2003, p. 52]

Three years after that, Steiger and McWane heard the mansion was about to be torn down. They visited the grounds one last time but saw nothing. They then visited a Halloween party at which several police officers were in attendance. The ghost hunters regaled the guests with the tale of the Sumter estate. Two of the officers present became so scornful of the story they drove a squad car to the estate that very night and sat near the entrance. The glowing entity obligingly materialized right in front of them, and they quickly left the vicinity.

The Sumter mansion is long gone. The apparition, whatever it was, seemed to be on good terms with the Sumter sisters. Perhaps it was someone they knew? On the other hand, Irene Hughes seemed frightened by it the first night, and on the second she was plagued by visions.

To this writer, it feels like Irene tried to put words in other witnesses' mouths concerning the phenomena. However, everyone present – and numerous other people of Iowa City, including several police officers – saw the glowing apparition at one time or other.

Irene Hughes, Steiger, and their companions visited many haunted sites during their "safari". The Glowing Thing was by far the most memorable phenomenon experienced. A year later the people of the traveling troupe still discussed it, and it "so impressed itself on the psyches of certain members of our investigative group that for years afterward they reported awakening from nightmares, fearful that the ghost was forming again right in their bedrooms." [2003, p. 47]

    Steiger, Brad. Irene Hughes on Psychic Safari (New York: Warner Books, 1972), pp. 32-42 and passim.
    Ibid. Psychic City: Chicago – Doorway to Another Dimension (Garden City, New York: Doubleday & Co., 1976), pp. 31-33.
    Ibid. Real Ghosts, Restless Spirits, and Haunted Places (Canton, MI: Visible Ink Press, 2003), pp. 47-53.

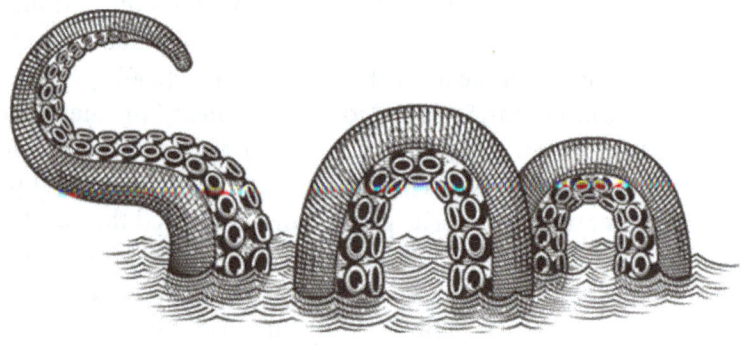

- Spontaneous life?
- Weird science

Gold Bugs?

"It was a beautiful scarabaeus, and, at that time, unknown to naturalists -- of course a great prize in a scientific point of view… The scales were exceedingly hard and glossy, with all the appearance of

burnished gold."
Edgar Allan Poe, "The Gold-Bug" (1843)

When physicist Sumio Iijima was young, he was fascinated by all aspects of nature. He kept and studied pigeons, rabbits, snakes, frogs and other animals to see how they lived and acted. Although he went to college to become an engineer, he switched to physics at Tohoku University (Sendai, Japan). Due to his engineering education, he was assigned to the lab of Professor Tadatoshi Hibi, where he worked on electron microscopes. Although uninterested in such devices at first, he soon realized he had a knack for microphotography. In 1977, at Arizona State University, he perfected a high-resolution electron microscope and became the first person to observe individual atoms.

In 1984, after moving back to Japan, he discovered the "structural instability of ultrafine particles of metals." Basically, an ultrafine particle (nowadays called a nanoparticle) of gold or some other metal – composed of perhaps 50 to 500 atoms – does not sit still like a lump of clay or a crystal. The atoms are more-or-less cohesive, but quantum effects still come into play, and the particle can alter shape – as Dr. Iijima puts it, "the atoms of metals move about like amoeba." [1]

The first video recordings of gold nanoparticles, made for the ERATO ultra-fine particles project, showed what looked at first like a hexagonal crystal. This was an aggregate composed of about 500 gold atoms, 18 angstrom units in diameter. As the camera ran, the particle began changing form, "with all the gold atoms making up the ultra-fine particle moving cooperatively to form various crystalline structures," as the science journal Nature put it. [2]

"The gold atoms move cooperatively to shift kaleidoscope-like into various crystal structures. They have, in fact, been dubbed 'quasi-solids'. A large gold particle may even ingest smaller gold particles." [3]

The atoms rearranging themselves "cooperatively"? Moving around "like amoeba"? And a large particle can "ingest" smaller ones? It sounds almost like gold is alive on the molecular level! This is one of those stories that demonstrate the physical world can be as strange as the paraphysical.

Other "bugs" – two species of bacteria, rather – extract rather than absorb gold. Acidithiobacillus ferrooxidans and Acidithiobacillus thiooxidans feed on sulfides, and upon oxidizing the sulfur content of pyrites and arsenopyrites, the tiny amount of gold held in those minerals is freed. Iron, copper, and other metals can be obtained this way as well. Other processes used to free gold from such low-grade sources require corrosion-resistant materials, high temperatures and high pressures. They also give off toxic by-products, and they are more expensive to boot. The bacteria simply do what comes naturally; their only drawback is that the biological extraction is a bit slow for a gold-hungry industry. [4]

Maybe someday one of Dr. Iijima's cooperating-atom particles will ingest enough of its fellows to reach a size visible to the naked eye – a bug, colloquially speaking, always seeking more gold to absorb. Fortunately, we have the gold-producing "bugs" to counteract them. The treasure-crazed characters in Poe's "The Gold-Bug" might have been on to something, after all.

1. http://www.nanoscienceworks.org/Members/siebo/iijima-sumio/

2. "Japanese Gold in Atomic Motion," Nature Vol. 325 (June 20, 1985), p. 628.

3. Corliss, William, "Restless Gold," Science Fontiers no. 41 (Sept.-Oct. 1985), p. 4.

4. Chiacchiarini, P., et al., "Pre-treatment of a refractory gold sulfide ore by means of Acidithiobacilli cells," Latin American Applied Research: http://www.scielo.org.ar/scielo.php?script=sci_arttext&pid=S0327-07932003000100006

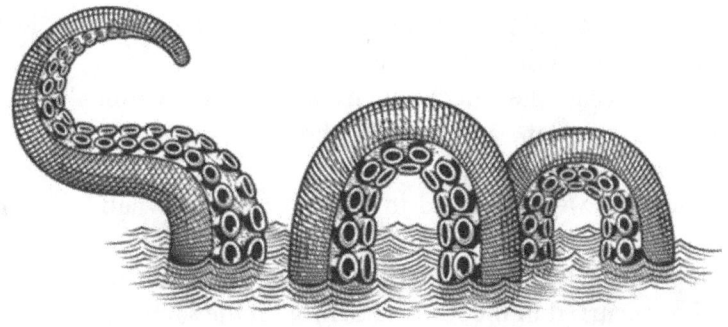

- Egg-shaped object falls from sky, Griffin, Georgia
- Georgia: Golden, burning "egg" falls from sky
- UFOs and burning egg-shaped object in Georgia

Griffin's Egg?

"Serious UFO research groups, who tirelessly sift, sort, and systematize reports, will never forget 1973," writes UFO investigator Leonard H. Stringfield. "Autumn of that year staged the biggest UFO flap since bush pilot Kenneth Arnold captured headlines in 1947 with his sighting of nine 'saucer-like things' over Mt. Rainier, Washington." [1]

Entire books have been devoted to the UFO events of 1973 (such as David Webb and Mimi Hynek's 1973 -- Year of the Humanoids and Kevin Randle's The October Scenario). Many strange and frightening events were reported that year, but there was one occurrence during this period that always struck me as amusing.

A UPI release datelined Griffin, Georgia, September 10, 1973, read in part:

"Sunday night, a Spalding County deputy answered a call reporting an object hovering over a house. The deputy radioed his office that he saw 'two red lights descending slowly to Earth,' and then the lights disappeared.

"Mrs. Hugh D. Beall told local police an 'upside-down cup and saucer-shaped object' hovered over her house. She said the object had gold, red and green lights on the bottom.

"Mrs. Beall said the object, which she said made a 'funny' noise, was too low for an airplane and was just above tree-top level. She said the lights changed colors." [2]

More UFOs were reported in Griffin and in Newnan, thirty miles west.

One wonders what such phenomena had to do with another strange event that occurred in the town of Griffin on the same night:

"A something described as a 'golden egg' fell slowly onto the lawn of the Res Clanton house in the Orchard Hill area, September 10, 1973. Mr. Clanton said that the object 'twisted' as it fell and that there was a sharp report and a cloud of smoke as it touched ground." When a representative from a local college arrived the temperature of the ground read 300 degrees Fahrenheit. He found no remnant of the falling object. [3]

What can you say about the Golden Egg of Griffin, Georgia? As a fan of the half-lion, half-eagles, I'd like to suggest it was the egg of a Cosmic Griffin -- that the "two red lights descending" reported by the Spalding County deputy were the eyes of the space-griff as it searched for its egg -- that the unidentified objects' multicolored lights were its shiny rainbow feathers -- but that would be reaching. Maybe the last word should go to the "egg" witness: "Clanton's opinion was that the 'egg' was 'brimstone from heaven, to show folks they better straighten up fast.'" [3]

1. Stringfield, Leonard H. Situation Red: The UFO Siege. (New York: Fawcett, 1977), p. 19.
2. Ibid., p. 21.
3. Brandon, Jim. Weird America. (New York: E. P. Dutton, 1978), p. 69.

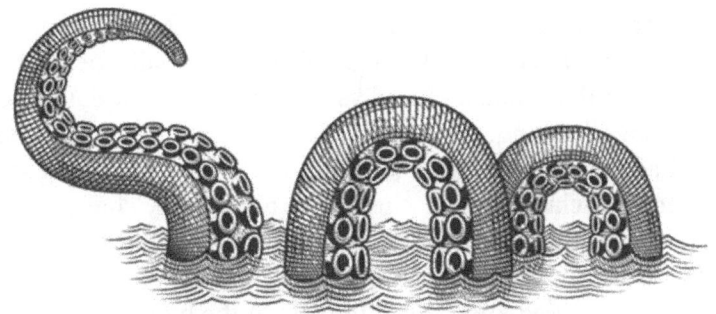

- Arizona: Slaughtered pioneer family's voices heard
- Haunted Old West stage station
- Place memory at western stage station
- Voices and sounds of Indian raid, Arizona

The Haunted Stage Station

Sometime in the mid-nineteenth century a stagecoach station, one of many dotting the American west, was built about thirty miles southwest of Winslow, Arizona, "near the Chavez Hills and the Pass." One fateful evening a white family decided to take shelter at the station until morning. They were slain by Apache Indians during the night, and afterwards the site was abandoned. Ranchers and cowboys visited the station during the ensuing years, however, as it provided shelter and water, as well as grass for their horses.

In his autobiography Cow by the Tail, rancher Jesse James Benton tells how he, his partner Gus, and various cowboys in his employ would bed down in the dusty building when riding in the area. On several occasions, after settling in for the night, they would hear the thunder of hooves, the rattle of wheels, and the squeak of springs. A voice would cry out "Whoa!", then "Hello in there!" Although the cowboys would jump up and open the door, there was never anything to be seen.

One evening they decided to wait up for the phenomenon, which usually started at about 8:30 pm. A search in a three-hundred-yard radius revealed no one in hiding. The men finally bedded down beneath a tree about one hundred yards away. Soon the sounds of two or three dogs barking came from the station. The men rose and approached the building, "and we heard many blood-curdling screams of women and children, the curses of rough men, chains clanking. Screaming and cursing grew louder than ever, mixed with the growling of dogs. Suddenly all were dead quiet."

The ranchers fled and spread the tale of the haunted stage station far and wide. A man named George Perry bet the witnesses he could spend a night in the old station, and he went so far as to chain himself by the ankle to a support post in the crumbling building. When Benton and the others entered the next morning, "[h]is eyes were bloodshot; he was wild-looking, with hair all mussed up; and he had worn a path all back and forth in front of the post he was chained to." He had heard even more horrible noises than the cowboys had, and the entire event repeated itself three times during the night.

"All this were back in the [eighteen] eighties," writes Benton. Actually, it would be 1888 and earlier, as the witness Gus left Arizona forever that year. In 1921 Benton met a family who were taking a trip by automobile through Arizona to see the Grand Canyon, the Meteor Crater, and other attractions. They told the aging rancher that they had stopped and camped near a grove southwest of Winslow, and just as they settled into their blankets, they heard "growling and fighting." Thinking of bears, they packed up to leave, but as they did more noises came from what they thought was "the outlines or ruins of a little house" among some bushes. From their description of the area Benton determined that it was the stage station site, the building having finally fallen to ruin.

"We agreed the old ghosts of that dead family was still there, hanging around the place," concludes Benton. Modern researchers would say that the station haunting was a perfect example of a "place memory," in which tragic events are re-enacted as if a strip of film or tape were running over and over across the years. Even the repetition during Perry's stay is not unknown during such events. This memory had only an auditory factor; many such hauntings have a visual component.

This is my favorite "place memory" story, complete with tragic origin and spectacular "effects". Many hauntings fade away when the buildings they are associated with collapse or are demolished, but these auditory phenomena seem to have outlasted the stage station by many years.

Benton, Jesse James. Cow by the Tail (Boston: Houghton Mifflin Co., 1943), pp. 172-174.

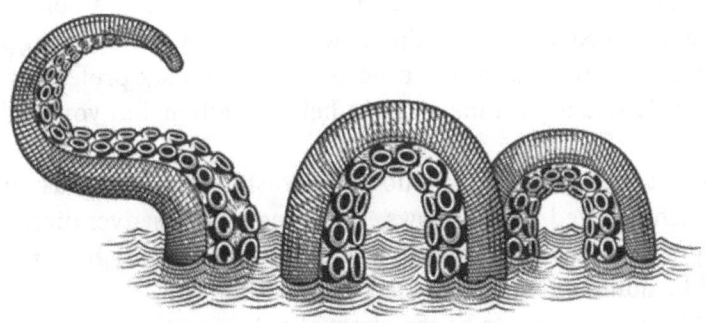

- Headless ghosts
- Headless Horseman
- Sleepy Hollow and other headless specters

Here Comes a Chopper to Chop off Your Head

"I have listed a number of other examples elsewhere of headless horrorsmen. Like Washington Irving's classic figure in The Legend of Sleepy Hollow, these seem to be among the more aggressive of paranormal beings."
-- Jim Brandon, Weird America (1978)

Horsemen and Cyclists

Jan Harold Brunvand, dean of urban folklore, outlines the apocryphal tale "The Decapitated Motorcyclist" in The Mexican Pet. A sheet of metal, blown off a truck by a wind gust, beheads a motorcyclist following behind. "The headless corpse's grip convulsively tightens on the hand throttle ... When he sees the headless cyclist, the truck driver is so horrified that he suffers a heart attack." [1]

Perhaps Mike Marinacci has uncovered the supernatural sequel to this tragic event. He writes of the many ghosts of Ventura County: "Yet another Creek Road spook is the 'headless biker' who rides a big prewar motorcycle." [2] The modern acephalic rider may prefer a vintage motorcycle as a mount instead of a hellish stallion, but you can't beat the classics.

"The Legend of Sleepy Hollow" by Washington Irving, as virtually every school-aged child knows, concerns the misadventures of the gangly schoolmaster, Ichabod Crane, culminating in his encounter with "the dominant spirit" of Sleepy Hollow:

"It is said by some to be the ghost of a Hessian trooper, whose head had been carried away by a cannon ball, in some nameless battle during the Revolutionary War, and who is ever and anon seen by the country folk, hurrying along in the gloom of night ... the spectre is known, at all the country firesides, by the name of the Headless Horseman of Sleepy Hollow." [3]

The house of the Van Alen family, where Irving wrote "Sleepy Hollow," lies in Kinderhook, New York. According to Sharon Jarvis' book Dark Zones, the Van Tassels of the Irving story were based on the Van Alens. Ichabod Crane's rival Brom Bones was actually a fellow named Abraham Van Alstyne, and Ichabod himself was a local schoolmaster named Jesse Merwin. Supposedly the ghost of Merwin has been spotted in the vicinity of the Van Alen house, on State Road 9H.

The concept of the Headless Horseman seems to have been transplanted from Europe to America by Washington Irving. German Legends of the Brothers Grimm (Deutsche Sagen) carries a typical account:

"In the year 1644 a woman from Dresden went out early one Sunday morning to gather acorns in a nearby forest. At a spot on the heath not far from the place called Lost Waters, she heard someone blowing loudly on a hunting horn. This was followed by a heavy falling sound, as though a tree had fallen . . . when she turned around she saw a headless man in a long grey coat sitting on a grey horse." [4]

Translator Donald Ward records the belief that if someone committed a crime for which the punishment would have been beheading, but eludes the law in this life, he or she will become a headless specter after death. [5]

Imported as the concept may be, perhaps there is some phenomenal reality for New York's Headless Horseman. According to Sharon Jarvis: "During the Halloween season, someone in the village -- no one really knows who -- dresses up as the horseman and rides through the streets at night. However, there are reports that sometimes the imitation headless horseman had the misfortune to meet the real one, for the fright of a lifetime." [6]

Headless-horseman-types seem to have been quite common in New England. Louis C. Jones mentions several in his book Things that Go Bump in the Night (1959).

Blemmye and Youaltepuztli

The concept of headless entities is very old and widespread. The Blemmye (plural, Blemmyae) was known to Pliny and other ancient writers. Shakespeare mentions "men whose heads/ Do grow beneath their shoulders" in Othello (Act I, scene iii).

Medieval pictures of Blemmyae look rather silly, and the idea seems to be based on imagining one's breasts as huge eyes and one's navel as a mouth. Yet the headless creatures were known to the inhabitants of Mexico as well, and these are described in frightful fashion.

According to Montague Summers' The Vampire: His Kith and Kin, the Aztec god Tezcatlipoca sometimes manifested himself as a Blemmye-like horror, which was called Youaltepuztli, which means "ax of the night." Sometimes at night a noise might be heard like someone chopping on a tree with an ax:

"Should anyone dare to investigate the cause of the noise he was suddenly caught by Tezcatlipoca who appeared as a decomposing headless corpse in whose mouldering breast were set 'two little doors meeting in the centre [the rib cage?],' and it was the swift opening and shutting of these which produced the sound of a man hewing down the trees." [7]

The Dund and the Skandhahata

Headless spectres are so common in some areas they have generic names for their "species". William Crooke, in Popular Religion and Folk-Lore of Northern India, writes that the sub-continent's Headless Horseman is popularly known as the Dund, which means "truncated".

The Dund actually has his head with him, tied to the pommel of his saddle. He rides at night and calls to people in houses, trying to get them to come outside, "but woe to any one who answers him, for this means death." Certain vampires of eastern Europe were prone to use this same trick. The inhabitants of Bengal, meanwhile, speak of the Skandhahata, a particularly unnerving headless corpse. "He dwells in low moist lands outside a village, in bogs and fens, and goes about in the dark, rolling about on the ground, with his long arms stretched out. Woe betide the belated peasant who falls within his grasp."

Crooke also speaks of the Ghostly Army seen along the Queen's highway near Faizabad: "They say that after dark the road is thronged with troops of headless horsemen, the dead of the army of Prince Sayyid Salar." [8]

Losing Our Heads Elsewhere in the World

Donald Ward, in his translation of Deutsche Sagen, notes that "[h]eadless spirits and divinities were widely known in ancient Egypt as well as classical antiquity . . . The earliest documented reference to a headless spirit in Germany was in a sermon written by Geiler von

Kaysersberg, ca. 1505." Iceland had similar traditions in the Middle Ages. [9]

Headless specters abound in Ireland and Scotland. Like those of India, they have their own name: the Dullahan, or Dubhlachan. "The word Dubhlachan originally signified a dark, sullen person, but over the centuries it has become applied to this unusual phantom," writes British author and anthologist Peter Haining. [10] There are not only headless horsemen but headless coach drivers as well -- and phantom coaches are often pulled by headless horses. Indeed, headless dogs and even bears have been reported in the British Isles.

> He thought he saw a Coach-and-Four
> That stood beside his bed:
> He looked again, and found it was
> A Bear without a Head.
> 'Poor thing,' he said, 'poor silly thing!
> It's waiting to be fed!'
>
> -- Lewis Carroll, "The Mad Gardener's Song"

This weird phantom bruin sparked one of the strangest letter writing campaigns in history, in the pages of the Modern Language Review. In Volume 1, Number 3 (April 1906), one H. Littledale quotes Shakespeare's Puck: "Sometime a horse I'll be, sometime a hound,/ A hog, a headless bear, sometime a fire" (Midsummer Night's Dream, III:I). Littledale suggests "headless" actually meant "leadless"; that is, free from a leash. In Vol. 2 no. 1 (October 1906), Littledale reports having found a second quote in Burton's Anatomy of Melancholy, wherein "my phantasie/ Presents a thousand ugly shapes," including that of "headless bears."

"It seems clear, therefore, that the 'headless bear' was a popular terror," concludes Littledale. A later correspondent discovered a poem about a headless horse.

Headless women are not as often reported as men, but they are not unknown. Perhaps the most famous of these female specters is that of

Anne Boleyn, ill-fated wife of Henry VIII, which haunts the Tower of London: "[In the 19th century] a yeoman warder swore under oath to seeing a bluish form hovering, a shape which then seemed to move towards the Queen's House, whilst in 1933 a guardsman reported seeing a headless woman floating towards him near the Bloody Tower." [11]

In North America the glowing phenomena called ghost lights or will-o'-wisps often get tangled up with headless specters. The Maco Ghost Light, for instance, which haunts the railroad tracks near Wilmington, North Carolina, is thought to be the ghost of a conductor who was killed in a train accident in 1868, the ball of light being his lantern. [12] Louis Jones mentions a similar story from New York state, that of a headless brakeman who swings a red light. [13]

Some psychical researchers believe that a traumatic death confuses a soul passing into the Great Beyond to the point that it remains on the earthly plane. Certainly, losing one's head, whether by cannonball, sword, or freak accident, would be traumatic. Maybe this is why so many ghosts and undead creatures of folklore are described as headless.

Oddly enough, the Saxons of pre-Roman Britain believed quite the opposite: "decapitation was an attempt to prevent the spirit of a powerful and feared individual from haunting the living," according to Fortean Times writer David McGrory. Perhaps, however, the Saxons were wrong in this assumption. McGrory states that a field near Heydon, Cambridgeshire, where many headless skeletons were unearthed in the 1950s, had, "for as long as anyone can remember, been reputedly haunted by spectres of giant warriors." [14]

Pearl-fishermen used to "get rid" of marauding starfish by chopping them up and tossing the pieces back in the sea -- when in fact, each piece grew into another starfish! Perhaps there lay buried around the world many long-forgotten corpses, decapitated with an eye on keeping them down, but which are waiting instead to rise and seek revenge -- and a new head or two!

1. Brunvand, Jan Harold, Mexican Pet (New York: W. W. Norton, 1986), p. 56.

2. Marinacci, Mike, Mysterious California (Los Angeles: Panpipes Press, 1988), p. 87.
3. Irving, Washington, "Legend of Sleepy Hollow," in Sketch Book (New York: Signet Classics, 1981 [1820]), pp. 330-331.
4. Grimm, Jacob and Wilhelm, German Legends of the Brothers Grimm (1812-1814). New edition edited and translated by Donald Ward (London: ISHI, 1981), Vol. I, p. 246.
5. Ibid., p. 412.
6. Jarvis, Sharon, Dark Zones (New York: Warner Books, 1992), p. 155.
7. Summers, Montague, Vampire: His Kith and Kin (New York: University Books, 1960 [1928]), p. 261.
8. Crooke, William, Popular Religion and Folk-Lore of Northern India (Dehli: Munshiram Manoharlal, 1896), Vol. I, pp. 255, 258.
9. Grimm, op. cit, p. 412.
10. Haining, Peter, Leprechaun's Kingdom (New York: Harmony Books, 1980), p. 39.
11. Abbott, G. Ghosts of the Tower of London (Newton Abbott, Devon: David & Charles, 1980), p. 49.
12. Brandon, Jim, Weird America (New York: E. P. Dutton, 1978), p. 174.
13. Jones, Louis C., Things that Go Bump in the Night (New York: Hill & Wang, 1959), p. 53.
14. McGrory, David, "They Might Be Giants," Fortean Times no. 101 (August, 1997), p. 32.

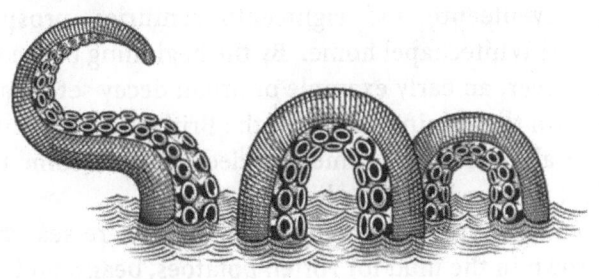

- Jack the Ripper – London serial killer
- London: Whitechapel murders/Jack the Ripper
- Ripper murders – occult, ghost stories, miscellanea
- Unsolved murders – London
- Whitechapel murders, 1888

Jack's Knife Flashes

"Yes, I've followed a trail of blood. From New York westward across the continent. Then to the Pacific. From there to Africa. During the World War of 1914-18 it was Europe. After that, South America. And since 1930, the United States again. Eighty-seven such murders -- and to the trained criminologist, all bear the stigma of the Ripper's handiwork . . ."

-- Robert Bloch, "Yours Truly, Jack the Ripper" (1943)

The compost pile that nurtured the person who would someday be known as "Jack the Ripper" was the East End of London. In the late nineteenth century, England's capital was the largest city on the planet. While the average person, hearing the words "Victorian Era," might imagine evenings at the theater, the Albert Hall, and top-hatted "toffs" escorting genteel ladies along gaslit streets, the reality fell short of the ideal. This was particularly true in the eastern sections of the metropolis: boroughs bearing the ominous names of Spitalfields, Houndsditch, and Whitechapel.

In the seventeenth and eighteenth centuries, prosperous silk weavers called Whitechapel home. By the beginning of the nineteenth century, however, an early example of urban decay set in, and dry rot spread beneath the shining veneer of the British Empire. In 1903 Jack London, of Call of the Wild fame, decided to spend some time in the East End just to see what it was like:

"At a market, tottery old men and women were searching in the garbage thrown in the mud for rotten potatoes, beans, and vegetables, while little children clustered like flies around a festering mass of fruit, thrusting their arms to the shoulders into the liquid corruption, and drawing forth morsels, but partially decayed, which they devoured on the spot." [London, p. 651]

While wandering through these slum lands, Jack London joined up with one of the locals, who led him through a miserable grassy square called Spitalfields Garden, where the homeless came to sleep. "It was a welter of rags and filth, of all manner of loathsome skin diseases, open sores, bruises, grossness, indecency, leering monstrosities and bestial faces," he wrote.

Pioneer criminologist Peter Mayhew, years before the Ripper's time, estimated that eighty thousand prostitutes operated in London, and that "as large as this total may appear, it is not improbable that it is below the reality rather than above it."

The ideal Londoner of Victoria's day would have swooned at the mere concept of prostitution. By choosing victims from this social underworld, the Ripper threw a spotlight on the lowest stratum of the poor, wretched, and "sinful", a class of people that nineteenth century Britons did not want to know existed. Several authors, from crime writer Tom Cullen to Harlan Ellison (Dangerous Visions), have suggested that the Ripper intended this all along. Existentialist author Colin Wilson writes: "The reaction [to the murders] was more than shock; people were stunned and winded, as if by a blow. And a deep, instinctive disquiet stirred inside them." [Wilson, p. 3]

Crime, even murder, was common enough in Whitechapel, Spitalfields, and Houndsditch, but it was quite mercenary: robbery, theft, assaults from drunken laborers, bar fights, prostitution. These crimes were understandable on a purely subsistence level. Then, however, came a different kind of murder. Perhaps Wilson's "instinctive disquiet" was a vague feeling that a new era dawned: a new monster walked the streets, the alien creature with a human face we now call the serial killer.

The Beginning

Some students of the Whitechapel crimes are adamant that the Ripper murdered only five women; the "canonical five," as they are called. It would be very strange, however, for a serial killer to appear full-blown on the stage of life, especially one with as complex and horrible an M.O. as Jack. Several "incidents" that occurred before the Ripper murders may have borne some relationship with the nascent Jack.

A prostitute nicknamed "Fairy Fay" was supposedly stabbed to death near Mitre Square on Boxing Day, December 26, 1887. Tom Cullen among others has mentioned her, but she seems to have been spawned of rumor and misquotes. A woman named Margaret Hames was attacked by unknown assailants at about the same spot as Emma Smith (see below) on December 8 and released from the infirmary on Boxing Day; her experience may have provided the seed for the Fairy Fay story. [Evans & Skinner, p. 3]

On the cold, wet Saturday evening of February 25, 1888, Annie Millwood, a widow of 38 years, appeared in a state of collapse at the Whitechapel Infirmary. She had been stabbed in the legs and lower body by an unidentified man. Little else is known about the case, and the only reason she was mentioned in the newspapers at all was because she died rather strangely a month later. On March 31, while talking to a man named Richard Sage at the Whitechapel Union Workhouse, she dropped dead due to "the rupture of the left pulmonary artery." [Begg and Bennett, pp. 24-30]

It had barely become March 28 – it was half-an-hour after midnight – when a 39-year-old dressmaker named Ada Wilson was stabbed twice in the throat in a house at 19 Maidman Street in the East End. According to Ada, she had answered a knock at the door to find a man there, about five feet six inches tall, with a light-colored mustache and a sunburnt face. He demanded money, and when Wilson refused, he stabbed her.

At least, that was her story. An upstairs tenant, Rose Bierman, attracted by Ada's screams, came to the top of the landing to see Ada, half-dressed, in the entry hall. The unfortunate woman cried, "Stop that man for cutting my throat! He has stabbed me!", as a man fled past her out the door, then she collapsed. The testimony that she was only partially dressed, and that the man was running out from well within the house, suggests that Wilson had turned to prostitution and had made a poor choice of client. At any rate, the man was not apprehended, and Ada was discharged from London Hospital on April 27. [Begg and Bennett, pp. 28-29]

On April 3, 1888, another prostitute, Emma Elizabeth Smith, staggered into a Spitalfields lodging house, claiming that she had been attacked by four men. A blunt instrument -- not a knife, as many reports claimed -- had been forced into her vagina, rupturing the back wall. She died of peritonitis in the London Hospital soon thereafter.

On August 7 the body of Martha Tabram, aka Turner, was found on a landing in the George Yard buildings. She had been stabbed thirty-nine times with a bayonet and a shorter blade. The London Times commented [August 10], "It was one of the most dreadful murders anyone could imagine. The man must have been a perfect savage to inflict such a number of wounds on a defenseless woman in such a way."

August 31, 1888, 2:30 am

Mary Ann "Polly" Nichols had had difficulty since the previous morning scraping together four pence for her "doss", a flea-ridden mattress in a flophouse. In the early hours of Friday, August 31, she met a woman named Ellen Holland on Whitechapel High Street and told her that she had made her doss money three times, but she spent it on gin and "a jolly bonnet."

At 3:40 am, laborers Charles Cross and Robert Paul found her body in Buck's Row, outside a slaughterhouse. Police Constable John Neil was the first of several officers on the scene. His bull's-eye lantern revealed two wounds in the throat, the second of which "completely severed all the tissues down to the vertebrae," according to the Times. Only after the body was taken to the Old Montague Street Workhouse Infirmary were the wounds in the abdomen found: a deep one running vertically and several running across. "There were also three or four similar cuts running downwards, on the right side."

Demonic luck accompanied the killer right from the start. Cross remarked on Buck's Row being unnaturally deserted and quiet at a time when many people were on their way to work. The murder had taken place across the street from several inhabited rooms, some with windows open and with the people inside already awake. Constable Neil could walk his beat in twelve minutes, but this time around he took half-an-hour, and during this interval the Ripper escorted Nichols up Buck's Row, killed her, mutilated her, and escaped without being seen.

September 7, 1888

Annie Chapman, born Eliza Anne Smith, also had trouble getting a bed. She had been feeling ill in general for a week, and she had been involved in one or more rough and tumble fights with Eliza Cooper, a "probable prostitute," over a piece of soap. Annie also suffered from diseases of the lungs and brain that would have killed her in a few months anyway, according to an autopsy performed by Dr. George Bagster Phillips.

Chapman, aka "Dark Annie" and "Annie Sievy" (because she had been living with a man who made sieves) was a small, stout woman, only five feet tall, with brown hair, blue eyes, and a wide nose. At 11:30 pm on the 7th Tim Donovan, the deputy at Crossingham's Lodging House, let Annie into the kitchen temporarily. She left shortly after midnight to get a drink and returned around 1:30 am. She had no doss money, so Donovan turned her out.

September 8, 1888, 5:45 am

John Davis, an aging porter, had been restless since three o'clock. He emerged into the back yard of 29 Hanbury Street -- he and his family lived on the third floor -- and discovered Annie Chapman's body stretched out by the back fence. Two savage slashes had nearly decapitated her. Also, according to the British Medical Association's journal, The Lancet, (September 29, 1888):

"The intestines, severed from their mesenteric attachments, had been lifted out of the body, and placed on the shoulder of the corpse; whilst from the pelvis the uterus and its appendages with the upper portion of the vagina and the posterior two-thirds of the bladder, had been entirely removed. No trace of these parts could be found, and the incisions were cleanly cut, avoiding the rectum, and dividing the vagina low enough to avoid injury to the cervix uteri. Obviously the work was that of an expert -- of one, at least, who had such knowledge of anatomical or pathological examinations as to be enabled to secure the pelvic organs with one sweep of the knife."

On September 27, a letter arrived at the Central News Agency, addressed to "The Boss, Central News Office, London City." Written in red ink, it read:

25 Sept: 1888
Dear Boss

I keep on hearing the police have caught me but they wont fix me just yet. I have laughed when they look so clever and talk about being on the right track. That joke about Leather Apron gave me real fits. I am down on whores and I shant quit ripping them till I do get buckled. Grand work the last job was. I gave the lady no time to squeal. How can they catch me now. I love my work and want to start again. You will soon hear of me with my funny little games. I saved some of the proper red stuff in a ginger beer bottle over the last job to write with but it went thick like glue and I cant use it. Red ink is fit enough I hope ha. ha.

The next job I do I shall clip the lady's ears off and send to the [continued on other side] police officers just for jolly wouldn't you. Keep this letter back till I do a bit more work then give it out straight. My knife's so nice and sharp I want to get to work right away if I get a chance. Good luck.

Yours truly
Jack the Ripper

Dont mind me giving the trade name
[and written at right angles to the above:]
wasnt good enough to post this before I got all the red ink off my hands curse it.

No luck yet. They say I'm a doctor now ha ha

The editor delayed sending it to Scotland Yard for two days because he thought it was a joke. Despite the penchant of serial killers such as Zodiac and Son of Sam to write letters, most modern researchers dismiss the Ripper correspondence as a stream of hoaxes. There is no denying Jack would have gotten writer's cramp producing the hundreds of notes and postcards received by the police, the newspapers, and assorted private citizens. However, the News Agency's letter gave the killer the name by which he would always be known, and, one night after the Yard accepted it from the editor, specifically:

September 30, 1888, 1:00 am

Louis Diemschutz, a peddler of cheap jewelry and shirt studs, had given up trying to push his wares on the patrons of the Crystal Palace. The night was chill, and it began to rain, so he turned his pony cart back east.

His pony clopped along the streets toward the International Workmen's Educational Club, a meeting place for Jews who had fled persecution on the Continent. Tonight's debate was "The Necessity for Socialism Among Jews," but, by the time Diemschutz arrived, much in the way of drink had been imbibed by the International Workmen, and their inebriated singing echoed across poorly lit Berner Street.

Diemschutz guided his cart into the courtyard next to the club building. Just within the gate his pony suddenly reared, and the costermonger checked for any obstacles with the butt of his horsewhip.

He found the body of a woman, her throat cut from ear to ear.

September 30, 1888, 1:45 am

Police Constable Edward Watkins arrived at Mitre Square, part of his nightly beat in the financial district known officially as the City of London. It took only fifteen minutes to make his rounds, and at 1:30 am the square had been quiet and empty. Now, however, his bull's-eye lantern revealed a pool of blood in the southwest corner.

Seconds later Watkins found the body of a woman, shockingly

mutilated. He ran to the Kearley and Tonge Warehouse, which faced the square, and sent the night watchman for help.

The first victim of the "double event" was Elizabeth "Long Liz" Stride, born Elisabeth Gustafsdotter in Torslanda, Sweden, in 1843. A single knife slash had severed her left carotid artery. It is commonly held that the arrival of Diemschutz and his pony cart interrupted the killer, though Diemschutz saw no one. At any event, the murderer struck again only forty-five minutes later.

The second victim, Catharine [sic] Eddowes, had been sobering up in the Bishopsgate Police Station only an hour before she was found dead. She was deemed fit to leave at 1:00 am, at which time she gave her name as "Mary Anne Kelly." This pseudonym came from the fact that she had been living with a casual laborer named John Kelly, but the similarity between this name and that of future victim Mary Jane Kelly is another of those weird coincidences that abound in the Ripper case.

"I shall get a damned fine hiding when I get home," Catharine commented as she stepped into the night.

"And serve you right," retorted P.C. George Hutt.

Catharine wandered off towards Houndsditch, "Good night, old cock," her last known words. She soon walked into the loving embrace of Jack the Ripper.

Jack took his time with Kate Eddowes. Dr. Frederick Gordon Brown required several pages in his post-mortem notes merely describing her wounds:

"The intestines were drawn out to a large extent and placed over the right shoulder... A piece of about two feet was quite detached from the body and placed between the body and the left arm, apparently by design. The lobe and auricle of the right ear was cut obliquely through."

Catharine's lower eyelids were nicked, a slash ran from the bridge of her nose down her right cheek ["This cut went into the bone"], and the tip of her nose was "quite detached." One cut split the upper lip; another paralleled the lower. A triangular flap had been carved in each cheek. Her throat had been slashed over twice, "severed to the bone, the knife marking inter-vertebral cartilages."

The Ripper carried off Eddowes' left kidney, her uterus, and part of her bladder. "I believe the perpetrator of the act must have had considerable knowledge of the positions of the organs in the abdominal cavity and the way of removing them," writes Brown. The killer cut off half the woman's blood-soaked apron and took that, as well. [Sugden, pp. 241-244]

September 30, 1888, 2:55 am

P.C. Alfred Long of H Division stepped into a narrow alley off Goulston Street, Whitechapel, the entryway to the Wentworth Model Dwellings. He found a bloodstained rag -- which later proved to be the missing portion of Catharine Eddowes' apron -- and a message written on the black brick wall in chalk:

> The Juwes are
> The men That
>   Will not
> be Blamed
>   for nothing

Police Commissioner Sir Charles Warren ordered the message wiped away at 5:30 am, lest it stir the embers of anti-Semitism that smoldered throughout the East End. The meaning of the curious message has engendered much controversy over the years, culminating in Stephen Knight's Masonic theory for the Ripper murders, as outlined in his Jack the Ripper: the Final Solution (1976).

The Ripper's luck held during the double murder. Besides P.C. Watkins' fifteen-minute check, and the night watchman nearby, Mitre Square was a popular shortcut through the area, even late at night, as Tom Cullin points out:

"[T]here were three entrances to the square, leading from Mitre Street, from Duke Street, and from St. James's Place, which tripled the Ripper's chances of being caught red-handed by either pedestrians or police. The fact that he was not was one of those weird flukes which caused some people to attribute his crimes to a supernatural force."

[Cullen p. 115]

P.C. Long and another officer named Halse -- who was actually trotting away from the Mitre Square murder site searching for the Ripper -- both passed the Goulston Street doorway at about 2:20 am. Both stated that the apron and message were not there at that time. Long returned on his beat thirty-five minutes later to discover them. This means that the Ripper dawdled somewhere in the area for up to seventy-one minutes before leaving his clues. What's more, he "escaped" from Mitre Square back into Whitechapel, which was already alive with policemen due to the Berner Street crime.

On Sunday morning, the following message, scribbled on a postcard, was sent to the Central News Agency:

I wasnt codding dear old Boss when I gave you the tip. youll hear about saucy Jackys work tomorrow double event this time number one squealed a bit couldn't finish straight off. had not time to get ears for police thanks for keeping last letter back till I got to work again.

Jack the Ripper

October passed without a murderous visitation, but the month was not uneventful. On September 10, sixteen tradesmen formed the Whitechapel Vigilance Committee and offered a reward for the Ripper's capture.

During the early days of October, George Lusk, a building contractor and chairman of the Committee, noticed a "sinister looking black bearded man" watching his house. On the 16th, he received a small box in the mail containing half a human kidney. A letter enclosed with the box read:

From Hell
Mr Lusk
    Sor
            I send you half the Kidne I took from one women prasarved it for you tother piece I fried and ate it was very nise I may

send you the bloody knif that took it out if you only wate a whil longer
    signed   Catch me when
                              you can
                    Mishter Lusk

While the writer at first glance appears to be barely literate, he or she misspells certain words rather oddly: "knif" and "whil" are not spellings a person transcribing phonetically would arrive at. For what it's worth, "Sor" and "Mishter" were words commonly used on the Victorian stage to approximate an Irish accent.

Most detectives and reporters of the period regarded the Lusk kidney as a crude hoax -- the organ having come from a dog, sheep, or anatomy-class corpse. It was sent to Dr. Thomas Horrocks Openshaw of the London Hospital. He determined that it was half of a left human kidney. Major Henry Smith comments, in From Constable to Commissioner (1910):

"Mr. Sutton . . . who was one of the greatest authorities living on the kidney and its diseases, said he would pledge his reputation that the kidney submitted to them had been put in spirits within a few hours of its removal from the body -- thus effectually disposing of all hoaxes in connection with it. The body of anyone done to death by violence is not taken direct to the dissecting-room, but must await an inquest."

Mr. Lusk later received a postcard reading: "Say Boss, you seem rare frightened. Guess I like to give you fits, but can't stop long enough to let you box of toys play copper games with me, but hope to see you when I don't hurry too much. Goodbye, Boss." George Lusk might have had the dubious honor of being the only male stalked by Jack the Ripper.

November 8, 1888, 11:45 pm

Mary Ann Cox, a widow forced by circumstances to take up prostitution, headed toward Miller's Court, a narrow, dingy square in Whitechapel, where she rented a hovel of a room. As she passed the Britannia pub, she saw Irish-born Mary Jane Kelly emerging with a man. The man wore a billycock hat and sported a carroty mustache, and he carried in one hand "a pail of beer." The widow followed the couple -- she had little choice, as Mary Kelly also dwelt in M'Carthy's Rents in Miller's Court -- and when the pair entered No. 13, Kelly began singing an Irish ballad: "Only a violet I plucked for my mother's grave when a boy."

Kelly was still singing when Mrs. Cox went out again at midnight and was still at it when she returned at 1:30 am. Mrs. Cox emerged again just after 3:00 am. Finally, Kelly's room stood dark and silent.

Backtracking a bit: One George Hutchinson, unemployed for several weeks, met Mary Kelly on Thrawl Street at about 2:00 am. Before he could ask her for money, she told him she was broke. Kelly continued down the street, and another man tapped her on the shoulder and said something that made her laugh. The man wore a long dark coat with astrakhan collar and cuffs, a felt hat with an indented crown (the kind that eventually evolved into Stetsons and Panamas), spats, button boots, and he carried a huge gold watch and chain. Hutchinson was surprised to see someone so well dressed out at that hour. For some reason, perhaps jealousy, he followed the couple back to No. 13 and watched the room for forty-five minutes before giving up.

Mrs. Elizabeth Prater, who occupied No. 20, directly above Mary, was awakened sometime between 3:30 and 4:00 am by her cat Diddles. She heard a woman cry out "Oh! Murder!", but, as such cries were common in Whitechapel, she simply went back to sleep. (Hey -- Diddles tried his best.)

November 9, 1888, 10:45 am

John M'Carthy, proprietor of M'Carthy's Rents, sent his assistant, Thomas "Indian Harry" Bowyer, to collect the rent from Mary Kelly, who was six weeks (some sources say three months) in arrears. Bowyer knocked on the door of No. 13 to no avail. He moved to a broken side window, pushed back a coat used as a curtain, and recoiled. He fetched his employer, who also peered in:

"She had been completely disemboweled, and her entrails had been taken out and placed on the table. It was those that I had seen when I looked through the window and took to be lumps of flesh. The woman's nose had been cut off, and her face gashed and mutilated so that she was quite beyond recognition. Both her breasts too had been cut clean away and placed by the side of her liver and other entrails on the table. I had heard a great deal about the Whitechapel murders, but I declare to God I had never expected to see such a sight as this." [The Times, November 10, 1888]

The Ripper had outdone himself. According to Dr. Thomas Bond, Assistant Surgeon at Westminster Hospital and Surgeon for A Division, Metropolitan Police:

"The whole of the surface of the abdomen & thighs was removed & the abdominal Cavity emptied of its viscera. The breasts were cut off, the arms mutilated by several jagged wounds & the face hacked beyond recognition of the features. The tissues of the neck were severed all round down to the bone. The viscera were found in various parts viz: the uterus & Kidneys with one breast under the head, the other breast by the Rt foot, the Liver between the feet, the intestines by the right side & the spleen by the left side of the body." [Sugden, pp. 314-315]

Mary's left thigh had been denuded to the bone, and the killer had removed and taken her heart.

(Dr. Bond's post-mortem notes were re-discovered in 1987 after being lost for nearly a century. They allowed researchers to correct mistakes that have been repeated in nearly every book and article on the Whitechapel crimes. For instance, as Mr. M'Carthy reported above, it was always believed that the killer set Mary Kelly's breasts on the table beside her bed. Also, Kelly was not three months pregnant, as has been universally believed since newspaper stories reported this in 1888. Her uterus was not carried off by the Ripper, but her heart was.)

The Kelly murder seemed to mark the end of Jack the Ripper's reign of terror. Out of the numerous letters received by the police, the press, and assorted "privileged" individuals, the following, received on 21 November (twelve days after the last murder) at Thames Police Court, might be significant:

"Dear Boss, It is no use for you to look for me in London because I'm not there. Don't trouble yourself about me until I return, which will not be very long. I like the work too well to leave it alone. Oh, it was a jolly job the last one. I had plenty of time to do it properly in. Ha, Ha, Ha! The next lot I mean to do with Vengeance, cut of their head and arms. You think it is a man with a black moustache. Ha, ha, ha! When I have done another one you can try and catch me again. So goodbye dear Boss, till I return."

Aftermath

Did the Ripper's career continue beyond 1888? On July 17, 1889, at about 12:50 am, P.C. Walter Andrews discovered the body of prostitute Alice "Clay-Pipe" McKenzie lying on the pavement of Castle Alley in Whitechapel. Her throat had been cut and there were wounds to her abdomen, but they seemed to lack the ferocity of Jack's earlier attacks. Dr. Thomas Bond described the throat injuries as "stabs" rather that ear-to-ear slashes, and Dr. George Phillips described the abdominal wounds as "superficial". The same doubts were held for the case of Francis Coles, whose body was found very early in the morning of Friday, February 13, 1891, by P.C. Ernest Thompson. Dr. Phillips "did not think that the attacker had demonstrated any skill and he did not believe that he was the perpetrator of the 1888 murders." [Sugden, pp. 352-353]

If one continues in this vein . . . some researchers believe Jack traveled to the United States and resumed his bloody career, starting when a New York prostitute named Carrie Brown, nicknamed "Old Shakespeare" from her habit of quoting the Bard, was killed in the East River Hotel on April 24, 1891. "From New York westward across the continent," as Robert Bloch wrote back in 1943.

> Since every Jack became a gentleman
> There's many a gentle person made a Jack.
> -- Shakespeare, King Richard III

There have probably been as many people accused of being the Ripper as there have been people doing the accusing. It would take another volume just to list them all. Here are some of the more extreme theories, along with examples of Saucy Jack's influence on society right up to the present.

The Freemason Conspiracy

This interpretation of the Ripper murders is too long and complicated to go into here. It was the subject of the movie and graphic novel From Hell, written by Alan Moore; the full story is told in Jack the Ripper: The Final Solution, by Stephen Knight. Briefly, this theory has it that Sir William Gull, Physician Ordinary to the Queen, was the Ripper, aided by a coachman named John Netley. Gull deliberately targeted the Canonical Five, because they were privy to a scandal that encompassed the highest in the land: Edward, Duke of Clarence, had secretly married a commoner – a prostitute – who had borne him a daughter. Gull's brother Masons, many of whom held high positions in the government and law enforcement (including Police Commissioner Sir Charles Warren), were supposedly bound by their oaths to aid and protect even so heinous a fiend as the Ripper. If you're really paranoid about Freemasons, you might look up the works of Michael A. Hoffman II, a conspiracy writer who has blamed the Masons for the President Kennedy assassination and the Son of Sam murders, among other things.

The Medium and the Murderer

Robert James Lees (1849-1931) was a clairvoyant and medium, at one time the leader of the Christian Spiritualists. On a more mundane level of existence, he was also a journalist for the Manchester Guardian, as well as the author of several books.

Supposedly, at the tender age of nineteen, he conducted a séance for Queen Victoria herself, during which the late Prince Albert spoke through the teenage spiritualist. After this Lees became the queen's favorite consultant concerning things occult and spiritual.

Lees' greatest claim to fame, however, stems from the story of how he fingered Jack the Ripper for the police. According to the tale, one day in 1888 Robert James Lees had a startling vision of the Whitechapel murderer slaughtering a hapless victim. He was so disturbed he went straight to the police and told them of his precognitive warning. The police, having been inundated with cranks, false informants, and self-styled psychics, laughed at the medium and sent him home.

The next day, Lees learned that the Ripper had struck again. The news upset him so much that his doctor suggested a tour of Europe to steady his nerves. True enough, the spiritualist was not bothered by visions during his vacation, but business needs required him and his family to return to England.

One day after his return, Lees and his wife were riding a London omnibus. At Notting Hill, a man climbed aboard.

"Looking up, he perceived that the new passenger was a man of medium size," reports a newspaper article from 1895. "He noticed that he was dressed in a dark suit of Scotch tweed, over which he wore a light overcoat. He had a soft felt hat on his head." [Harris, p. 172, quoting the Chicago Sunday Times-Herald, April 28, 1895]

Lees pointed the man out to his wife, saying, "That is Jack the Ripper!" His wife laughed at this, but the medium was adamant. In fact, when the "Ripper" left the 'bus at Oxford Street, Lees jumped out and followed him. After few blocks Lees ran across a constable and pointed out the man as the Whitechapel killer. The bobby laughed at him (you'd think he'd be used to that by now) and threatened to run him in.

Perhaps "Jack" heard the exchange, because he hailed a cab and was ferried swiftly away along Piccadilly.

After the November 9th murder, the police began to listen to the spiritualist. Lees had a vision of the killer's home, and he led the detectives across the city to the very address. To their shock, it proved to be the house of a very eminent physician and surgeon.

The police knocked, and, somewhat embarrassed, explained their unexpected visit to the lady of the house. Surprisingly, the woman said she had her own suspicions concerning her husband: He had been out during the time of each murder, and sometimes he came home with blood on his clothing. Usually his behavior was loving and saintly, but occasionally he became angry and sadistic, striking his wife and son.

The policemen and Lees confronted the doctor himself. He confessed to blacking out occasionally and waking later to find blood on his clothing and gloves. Investigation within the premises turned up damning evidence, and the surgeon agreed that he harbored some "Mr. Hyde"-like second personality.

The word was giving out that the doctor had died. He was given a fake funeral and incarcerated in an asylum. Mr. Lees received a pension from a grateful Victoria.

Most modern researchers dismiss the Lees story as a hoax. Enquiries made by the Society for Psychical Research at Scotland Yard and the Home Office failed to uncover any documents related to Lees' involvement in the hunt for the Ripper, or to any kind of pension granted him. [Begg, et al., p. 256]

The original story, as mentioned, first appeared in the Chicago Sunday Times-Herald. It was attributed to a Dr. Benjamin Howard of London. Dr. Howard later wrote a letter absolutely denying he ever told such a story. [Beggs, et al., p. 255] Mrs. Emily Porter, on the other hand, Lees' great-niece, often heard "Uncle James" recite the tale while he was alive (he died when she was twenty). [Knight, p. 195]

Stephen Knight uncovered a Ripper letter, received July 25, 1889, that began "You have not caught me yet you see, with all your cunning, with all your 'Lees' with all your blue bottles." This seems to indicate that the Ripper (or whoever wrote the letter) knew of the medium's involvement. However, more recent examinations of the letter show that the word in question is "tecs" (short for "detectives") rather than "Lees". [Evans and Skinner 2001, p. 147]

Ripper researcher Melvin Harris considered the story -- at least the part about the Ripper being apprehended -- to be a hoax. However, Harris admitted that R. J. Lees truly believed he had visions of the murders, and that he did go to the police, because Lees made references in his diary to the matter:

"Tuesday 2nd October. Offered services to police to follow up East End murders -- called a fool and a lunatic. Got trace of man from the spot in Berner Street.

"Wednesday 3rd October. Went to City police again -- called a madman and a fool.

"Thursday 4th October. Went to Scotland Yard -- same result but promised to write to me." [Harris, p. 179]

At the end of the day, the truth probably lies somewhere between the extremes of "R. J. Lees, Ripper-Hunter" and complete fiction. Something similar could be said about most unsolved mysteries.

The Black Magician

Several researchers have suggested that the Ripper was a practitioner of Black Magic, including occultist Aleister Crowley, crime writers Simon Whitechapel and Leonard Gribble, and teacher/radio broadcaster Melvin Harris. This is the theme of "Yours Truly, Jack the Ripper," Roger Zelazny's Night in the Lonesome October, Kolchak: The Night Stalker, and other stories and movies.

In 1994 Melvis Harris, a leading authority on the Ripper murders, published a book entitled The True Face of Jack the Ripper (1994). In it he lists thirteen "essential points" that must be met for a suspect of the 1880s to be the Ripper. Only one man, in his opinion, fits all thirteen points: an English soldier, doctor, and self-professed Black Magician named Robert Donston Stephenson, better known to his contemporaries as Dr. Roslyn D'Onston.

In an unpublished article entitled "Jack the Ripper," the infamous Aleister Crowley wrote:

"After the last of the murders, an article appeared in the newspaper of W. T. Stead, the Pall Mall Gazette, by Tau Tria Delta, who offered a solution for the motive of the murders. It stated that in one of the grimoires of the Middle Ages, an account was given of a process by which a sorcerer could attain 'the supreme black magical power' by following out a course of action identical with that of Jack the Ripper."

Crowley claimed to have studied the astrological aspects of the Ripper murders. He noted that Saturn or Mercury hung on the eastern horizon at the approximate time of each murder. He continues: "Mercury is, of course, the God of Magic, and his averse distorted image the Ape of Thoth, responsible for such evil trickery as is the heart of black magic, while Saturn is not only the cold heartlessness of age, but the magical equivalent of Satan. He is the old god who was worshipped in the Witches' Sabbath."

"Tautridelta" also published an article entitled "African Magic" in the November 1890 issue of Lucifer, the Theosophical journal. Here is an interesting excerpt concerning the typical necromancer:

"The very least of the crimes necessary for him (or her) to commit to attain the power sought is actual murder, by which the human victim essential to the sacrifice is provided . . . Yet, though the price is awful, horrible, unutterable, the power is real."

This could easily be the creed of the Ripper. "Tautridelta" was later determined to be Dr. Stephenson; a letter Stephenson sent to the police was almost word-for-word the same as one of "Tau"'s essays. [Harris, pp. 111, 212] The article published in the Pall Mall Gazette ran under the title "Who Is the Whitechapel Demon?" In this essay he explained that a necromancer needed "a certain portion of the body of a harlot" and that the Ripper murders marked the points of a profaned cross over London.

D'Onston/Stephenson was a slippery critter. He dropped out of the world completely from 1891 to 1896. "The missing five years baffle us. There is not the slightest trace of the man until 1896." [Harris, p. 129] Eventually he disappeared as thoroughly from history as the Ripper himself. In 1904, after publishing a book called The Patristic Gospels, "He simply vanished without trace. Despite repeated searches no death certificate can be found within the British Isles or anywhere else." The last man to see Dr. D'Onston/ Stephenson was his publisher, Grant Richards, who called him "a weird uncanny creature." [Harris, p. 139] (Update: Ivor Edwards, author of Jack the Ripper's Black Magic Rituals, recently tracked down Stepenson's grave site. Dr. Stephenson died in 1916 -- supposedly.)

Beyond the Grave

The spots of the original Ripper murders appear to be haunted, according to ghost hunters like Elliott O'Donnell. When O'Donnell visited Whitechapel in 1895:

"They told me that in the streets where the murders had been committed appalling screams and groans uttered by no living human being were sometimes heard at night, and that in Bucks Row, a huddled-up figure, like that of a woman, emitting from all over it a ghostly light, was frequently to be seen lying in the gutter." [O'Donnell, quoted in Underwood, p. 128]

When Peter Underwood visited the murder sites in 1961, he found that most East Enders - usually dismissive of the supernatural - considered all the sites to be haunted: "Isolated screams were common, but although such sounds could have a natural explanation, these originated from the actual sites of the murders ... The sound of heavy panting was also repeatedly reported from deserted streets and empty corners; and inexplicable footsteps, usually running away from the hearer." [Underwood, p. 131]

Imitators, Disciples, and Copycats

Certain disturbed minds that learn the details of the Ripper crimes decide of their own free will to become like him. Peter Kurten, the Dusseldorf Ripper of the 1920s, lived with a seriously dysfunctional family and ran away often as a youth. He went to jail for robbery at the age of 14. By his own account, while in jail "I read the tale of Jack the Ripper several times. When I came to think over what I had read, when I was in prison, I thought what pleasure it would give me to do things of that kind once I got out again." [Rumbelow, p. 261] He certainly followed up on these thoughts: at one point the police believed that four different homicidal maniacs were loose in the Dusseldorf, Germany area. "They" were all a quiet little man named Peter Kurten.

Son of Sam killer David Berkowitz claimed to have been inspired to some extent by Ripper letters he had seen in a book. The Zodiac Killer and the Yorkshire Ripper also seem to have been conscious imitators of Jack.

Some killers may even have imitated Ripper crimes to throw off the bloodhounds, as it were. In 1910 Hawley Harvey Crippen poisoned his wife, Belle Elmore, and ran off with his lover, Ethel LeNeve. All well and good. But Crippen went to the trouble of dismembering Belle, and, upon the discovery of her mutilated remains, rumors flew for a while that the Ripper was back. Serial poisoner Dr. Thomas Neill Cream famously cried "I am Jack the –" on the scaffold just as the trapdoor dropped. Perhaps he thought the execution would be delayed as the police looked into this possibility, but Cream held his tongue a bit too long.

Hoaxers

A case as sensational as the Ripper crimes will always draw out hoaxers, jokers, and doofuses bent on alarming the public by pretending to be the killer in person or via various media. Certainly most of the hundreds of Ripper letters received by the police were hoaxes.

One might say that these jokers have questionable taste but are otherwise harmless. However, that is not always the case. "In Kilkeel, County Down, a certain Miss Milligan, just twenty-one years of age, died, supposedly from the effects of shock, a fortnight after a knife-wielding practical joker pounced out at her declaring himself to be Jack the Ripper." [Sugden, pp. 280-281.]

Ripper Cults?

If the "Black Magician" Jack truly had powers granted by the "Dark Gods", certainly there would arise those who would emulate him. From 1973 onward the "cattle mutilation" scare began in the American Midwest. "The most striking nature of the outbreak was the nature of the mutilations. Ears, eyes, lips, udders and tails would be removed and occasionally internal organs were surgically extracted in a purposeful, even ritualistic manner . . . In one case the intestines had been drawn out through a hole in the cow's side and piled neatly by its head (recalling a similar gesture by Jack the Ripper)." [Michell and Rickard, p. 44] UFOs, Satanists, Bigfoot-type monsters, and other odd entities were blamed for the mutilations.

Christopher O'Brien, in The Mysterious Valley, quotes a researcher into unusual phenomena and cults: "What if they succeeded in creating a 'thought form,' a very powerful entity brought into being by sheer force of will, couched in ritual and agreement among these occultists, who were impressively powerful and proficient themselves. Perhaps things got a little out of hand when the 'thought form' became too powerful to control and began demanding 'blood sacrifice.'" [O'Brien, p. 154] Such a being could easily be the sort of "dark god" the black magician Ripper worshipped.

Of course, many authorities do not believe the animal mutilation phenomenon even exists, or rather, that ordinary animal deaths are given a veneer of mystery by uninformed locals and tabloid reporters. However, more blatant "cults" have been documented:

May 23, 1981 to November 5, 1982 – "A serial slayer, predictably dubbed 'Jack the Ripper' by newsmen, was stalking young women in Chicago and environs, discarding their mutilated corpses like cast-off rubbish." It was not a single killer but a murder-cannibal cult of four young men, Robin Gecht, brothers Andrew and Tommy Kokoraleis, and Edward Spreitzer. Beginning with 28-year-old Linda Sutton on May 23, 1981, the cultists were thought to have abducted and killed as many as eighteen women until Thomas Kokoraleis was arrested on October 20, 1982, and the other three on November 5. The killers would drag each victim to a "shrine" in an upstairs bedroom in Robin Gecht's house; torture, rape, and kill her; and cut off one or both breasts, with "each celebrant 'taking communion' by eating a piece before the relic was consigned to Gecht's trophy box." [Newton, p. 32]   Andrew Kokoraleis was executed via lethal injection on March 16, 1999; the other three cannibal cultists are imprisoned in various Illinois correctional facilities.

Children of the Ripper

Former London policeman Donald Rumbelow points out that the Ripper's influence has not diminished over the years. In November 1972 a young woman, "known for her casual sex relationships" was found dead in her London apartment, a stocking around her neck. A yellow, lemon-scented household cleaning fluid had been sprayed all over her body. On the wall, written in the same cleaning fluid, was the word "Ripper".

In 1974, 21-year-old Terence Collins killed a 79-year-old woman in a Surrey graveyard by beating her with a tombstone (!). He ran screaming into the streets and ended up in an antique store.

"He then went into an antique shop and said that he wanted a swordstick, sharpened to a fine point, and a black cloak with a red silk lining, 'Like the one that Jack the Ripper wore,'" Rumbelow reports. "When he was arrested and questioned the next day he told the police: 'Sometimes I think I am the devil; sometimes Jack the Ripper or a vampire or something like that.'" On March 12, 1974, he was found guilty of manslaughter and sent to Broadmoor.

Not long after this, 18-year-old Thomas Hopkins assaulted a 67-year-old woman in Manchester. "[W]hen detectives searched his home they found documents relating to Jack the Ripper and a tea caddy containing photographs of Hitler. One of the documents read: 'Jack the Ripper. I have returned from the dead. I will kill again." On June 4, 1974, he was sentenced to life imprisonment.

In 1978, a 15-year-old boy committed a Ripper-esque mutilation murder. His step-father, who like to stab pictures of naked woman, had told him all about the Whitechapel crimes and had encouraged him to "stab the teenage victim 'like Jack the Ripper.'" He was acquitted. We are not told what happened to the step-father. [Rumbelow, pp. 247-250]

Mother of Jack

Finally, an article in INFO (publication of the International Fortean Organization), demonstrates that there are those who actually want the Ripper back among us:

May 29, 1989: "Two women lured a man to their apartment so that a third woman could kill him with a hatchet (he took a blow to the forehead, but lived and escaped) . . . Her [the third woman's] motive was to cannibalize the victim in a ritual intended to bring Jack the Ripper back to life. She believed her son was Jack in a previous life." [Shoemaker, p. 29]

Begg, Paul, Martin Fido, and Keith Skinner. Jack the Ripper A to Z. (London: Headline Book Publishing, 1994).

Begg, Paul, and John Bennett. Jack the Ripper: The Forgotten Victims (London: Yale University Press, 2013).

Cullen, Tom. When London Walked in Terror (Boston: Houghton Mifflin Co., 1965).

Evans, Stewart, and Keith Skinner. Jack the Ripper: Letters from Hell (Gloucestershire, UK: Sutton Publishing, 2001).

Ibid. Ultimate Jack the Ripper Companion (New York: Carroll & Graf Publishers, 2000).

Harris, Melvin. True Face of Jack the Ripper (London: Michael O'Mara Books, 1995).

Knight, Stephen. Jack the Ripper: The Final Solution (New York: David McKay Co., 1976).

London, Jack, People of the Abyss (1903), in Jack London Omnibus (New York: Octopus Books, 1985).

Michell, John, and Robert J. M. Rickard. Phenomena: A Book of Wonders (New York: Pantheon Books, 1977).

Newton, Michael. Encyclopedia of Serial Killers (New York: Checkmark Books, 2000).

O'Brien, Christopher. Mysterious Valley (New York: St. Martin's Press, 1996).

O'Donnell, Elliott, Haunted England (1948), quoted in Underwood, op. cit.

Rumbelow, Donald. Jack the Ripper: the Complete Casebook (Chicago: Contemporary Books, 1988).

Shoemaker, Michael T., "Doubly Damned," INFO Journal no. 77 (Spring 1997).

Sugden, Philip. Complete History of Jack the Ripper (New York: Carroll & Graf, 1995).

Underwood, Peter. Jack the Ripper: One Hundred Years of Mystery (London: Javelin Books, 1987).

Wilson, Colin, "Introduction", in Rumbelow, op. cit.

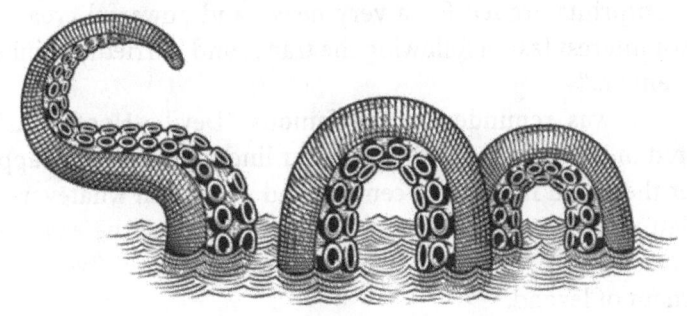

- California: Mysterious footprints and creature
- Destructive creature in woods
- Devil's Hoofprints/strange footprints
- Footprints of unknown being (not Bigfoot)

The Juggernaut of Josepho Canyon

Josepho Canyon is located in the Santa Monica Mountains, north of Sunset Boulevard in western Los Angeles. In 1956 the canyon was an unspoiled wilderness with tall trees and beautiful ferns, its length traversed by a small stream. Raymond Bayless, professional artist and writer on psychical phenomena, and his wife were picnicking one summer day in the canyon and afterwards decided to take a stroll along the stream. They came across what appeared to be footprints in the sand of the bank, each a perfectly circular depression about three inches wide, "just as though a round fence post had been pushed into the ground."

The creature, or whatever it was, might have simply dropped from the sky, as the prints began in the middle of the sandy bank, crossed the stream, passed over a relatively wide clear area, and entered the brush beyond. "It" had passed quite recently as well, because only now was water seeping into the crater-like prints. The "thing" had smashed its way through the underbrush like a tank, snapping limbs up to a half-inch in diameter. "When I saw that fairly large branches had been broken off," Bayless writes in his autobiography, "and that the depth of the footprints argued for a very heavy and powerful creature, we both lost interest fast in following the tracks and hurriedly climbed out of the canyon."

Bayless was reminded of the famous "Devil's Hoofprints" that appeared in Devonshire in 1855. Similar lines of tracks have appeared all over the world in the past century and a half, but whatever caused them left marks in snow or mud without disturbing the environment in the least. This "creature" left a trail of destruction worthy of the Juggernaut of legend.

Bayless was certain the prints were not those of a horse, cow, or other hoofed animal. Although he had encountered psychic and ghostly phenomena as far back as 1938, this canyon Juggernaut puzzled him thoroughly. He finally classed it "with those unnatural events which are known as Fortean phenomena," which is not very enlightening.

No one else reported an encounter with the entity, but a year after this ill-fated outing, Regal Pictures released a science fiction movie entitled Kronos, starring Jeff Morrow and Barbara Lawrence. Kronos is a blocky robotic being from outer space whose four columnar legs are simply huge metal pistons that pound the earth as it travels across the Mexican countryside, its goal – Los Angeles. A smaller version of Kronos would fill the role of the Baylesses' creature quite well. Perhaps director Kurt Neumann or screenwriter Lawrence Goldman heard rumors of something strange in the woods outside the City of Angels.

In Brazil there are reports of an entity called pe de garrafa, which means "Bottle Foot." As Bernard Heuvelmans writes, "There is not the slightest doubt that tracks which look as if they were made with the bottom of a bottle do exist. They have been seen by witnesses whose veracity is above suspicion." [Heuvelmans, p. 389] As a boy I drew many pictures of ghosts, Yeti, and sea serpents, and I was frustrated that I didn't know what these Devil's-Hoofprint-makers looked like. I envisioned everything from a classical demon to a weird wagon-wheel-shaped thingy that rolled across the land, each "spoke" a hoof setting briefly to earth.

Now I'm not sure I would like to see one. At the very least I would keep out of its way.

Bayless, Raymond. Experiences of a Psychical Researcher (New Hyde Park, New York: University Books, 1972), pp. 192-194.

Heuvelmans, Bernard. On the Track of Unknown Animals (New York: Columbia University Press, 1995 [1955]).

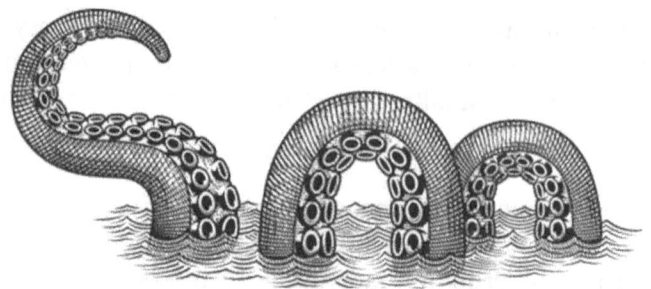

- Dogmen – Wisconsin
- Gettysburg (PA) ghosts
- Legend trips
- Mothman – first appearance
- New York: Staten Island: Legend trip
- Pennsylvania: Legend trips
- West Virginia: Mothman sighting
- Wisconsin: Dogmen sighting

Legend Trips

In 1989 folklorist Patricia Meley interviewed teenagers in Columbia, Pennsylvania, about "legend trips" – an activity which consists of driving to spots where crazy people, ghosts, or monsters are supposed to lurk, just for something to do in a rural community (one informant dismissed Columbia with "This town sucks;" another's goal in life was to "get the hell out of this town").

Legend trips require between three and ten participants, though Meley heard of one with twelve young men crammed into a station wagon. This puts the activity in a different category from "lover's lane" horror stories like "The Hook." As Meley points out: "my informants were adamant about this point: no one ever went to the legend trip sites to drink or neck." [Meley, p. 17]

The site of a "legend" is normally well out in the country, but there are exceptions. A 35-year-old from industrialized Harrisburg put his two cents in:

"[A]s a teenager, he and his friends walked to a city graveyard to see 'Fidget Widgets,' creatures that he described as 'outer spacemen.' Teenagers at the Harrisburg Middle School report going to the same cemetery to see the Fidget Widgets, but they claim the scary creatures are video game characters." [Meley p.24]

Various things reported in the Columbia area by the local teens included floating blue lights, "half-cat, half-fox" animals that love dashing in front of cars; houses that move or vanish entirely; winds that come out of nowhere, capable of pushing a car off the road; and various ghosts and homicidal hermits. "A group of teenagers referred to 'the night we saw the gas cans.' but when pressed for details, they could not tell me why the gas cans frightened them." [Meley, p. 8] Oh, and one must not forget that the "Gates of Hell" are to be found on Toad Road, York County; "teenagers foolish enough to enter the gates are never seen or heard from again."

Numerous fortean incidents have resulted from legend trips. They are the staple of urban legends and horror movies. Expectation no doubt plays a part in many apparent manifestations, passengers having been primed by hearing the story behind the ghost, murders, creature, or escaped psychopath as the trippers roll out to the abandoned house or haunted forest. Some incidents, however, seem to blindside innocent travelers.

The most interesting legend trips, in my opinion, involve a sort of "quantum entanglement": The witnesses don't merely see something frightening and drive home, shaking and talking, they seem to run into "it" or other odd phenomena multiple times before the trip is over, as if they have been "marked" somehow.

Mothman

The prototype Mothman encounter, on November 15, 1966, is a case in point. The story has been recounted many times, but in a nutshell four young people from Point Pleasant, West Virginia, Roger and Linda Scarberry, with their friends Steve and Mary Mallette, were driving around the abandoned munitions factories of the "TNT Area" outside of Point Pleasant just for something to do, when they spotted a tall, shambling figure near the North Power Plant. The figure turned out to be a vaguely humanoid creature, about seven feet tall, gray, with huge wings jutting from its shoulders. It had no discernable head, but huge red glowing eyes were seemingly set into its broad shoulders.

The teenagers roared away in Roger's black '57 Chevy, bouncing onto Route 62 and heading back to Point Pleasant. The winged entity followed them. They saw the creature on a hillside ahead of them; it took to the air and followed them at speeds exceeding one hundred miles an hour. The lights of the town seemed to drive it off.

The quartet stopped at a fast food restaurant called Dairyland and decided not to call the police – yet. Incredibly, they drove back into the country. At the entrance to the C. C. Lewis farm, the two couples noticed a dead dog by the side of the road. As Roger turned the car around, the winged creature appeared again, "springing" over the vehicle! (There is the eerie implication that the dog had been placed by the road in the hopes that someone would stop to investigate.)

This time the young people did drive to the sheriff's office. Deputy Millard Halstead accompanied the quartet back to the TNT Area. On the way, Linda Scarberry saw the creature out in a field.

Back at the power plant, Deputy Halstead and the teens did not see the entity, but they noted strange clouds of dust, odd shadows sliding over the abandoned buildings, and an unidentified, high-pitched noise. The Scarberrys spent the night with the Mallettes at the latter's trailer, as Mary felt extremely nervous.

Although this carload of young joyriders was admittedly searching for other teens to hang with, in a dark, lonely, abandoned industrial complex, their entry into a "legend trip" was abrupt and unexpected. Certainly none of them ever heard of a giant bug-eyed apparition of the type that appeared before them on that cold November night.

Here are a few other cases of legend trips that went "boink".

The Cross on the Car

In the 1960s, on Staten Island, New York, Kim Kowalcyzk and his friends would spend certain nights "borrowing" the family cars and spending several hours cruising around, looking for excitement. One night in July 1969 it was Kim's turn to sneak off in his father's

Oldsmobile station wagon. "It had no roof rack. (This is relevant to the story.)"

Kim and three friends went driving around, but nothing happened to alleviate their boredom. Eventually one teen suggested visiting a graveyard well out in the wilderness (as much as there was on Staten Island), at the end of a lonely dirt road. Kowalcyzk followed his directions, and yes, they found an old cemetery, lit by a single streetlight, out in the middle of nowhere.

Kim's passengers acted goofy in the burial ground, pretending to be zombies and the like. One of them tried to climb onto the car and knocked off the side mirror. That was it for Kowalcyzk. He ordered everyone back so they could leave.

One boy dragged a large wooden cross to the station wagon. "It was one of those temporary markers used for graves before the headstone is put on the grave. It was faded, dirty, and some of the paint was missing." [Wilder, p. 55] He wanted to bring it with them, but Kim, predictably, refused. The youth swung the cross around and hurled it into the darkness.

As the quartet drove around the island, Kim's passengers wanted him to "burn rubber." The station wagon did not have the power or speed to spin its wheels like that, even when Kim's companions got out to lighten the load. When they clambered back in, another souvenir hunter wanted to put an old dirty tire on the roof, which Kowalcyzk also vetoed. This was also a significant act, as the legend trippers saw the roof of the vehicle while wrestling with the tire.

Yet another fine fellow suggested pulling up behind a closed bar on the west side of the island. He said they threw the empty beer kegs out back, and they could take a few. Kim followed his directions but soon discovered that a) the bar was not closed, b) the kegs were quite full of beer, and c) the angry bartender was now chasing them in a van. Kim roared along (as much as the Buick could roar) as the others rolled the kegs out the back, one by one. The bartender finally gave up.

Kim screeched to a stop on a street with no houses. There was a scrape on the roof and a bang on the hood. "There, on the hood of my father's car, was the wooden cross that everyone saw my friend throw away more than an hour before. We had driven miles, made sharp turns, sudden stops, and drove quite erratically to evade the angry bartender. Yet somehow the cross held on?" [Wilder, p. 57] There was no rack, as mentioned earlier, for it to catch on, and besides, they had seen nothing on the roof when trying to put the old tire up there.

The boy who took the cross in the first place now decided to keep it, quite against popular opinion. He thought it was an omen, and maybe it was. After stopping at a hamburger joint, Kim started back home. Just as they drew up behind a slower car, writes Kowalcyzk, "the entire area lit up, as bright as day but with a strange orange glow. Then there was an explosion louder than anything I have heard to this day." A shock wave shoved the station wagon and the car ahead into the opposite lane. It turned out that an oil tank in New Jersey had exploded.

Despite this apocalyptic ending to the night's drive, the boy with the cross kept his prize. After taking it home and cleaning it, he received one more shock: His grandmother's name was inscribed in the wood.

The elder Mr. Kowalcyzk never knew what happened to his Buick.

This legend trip may have held long-reaching consequences for Kim Kowalcyzk. Years later he founded the GhostBreakers Paranormal Researcher Organization in New England. Was the Cross on the Car his inspiration?

Four Teens and Four Terrors

In 1991, a bipedal, werewolf-like creature began stalking the areas around Elkhorn and Delavan, Wisconsin. Local artist and writer Linda Godfrey was given the chance to write a "human interest" story for a Delavan newspaper, The Week, about the monster, which had been dubbed the Bray Road Beast. This she did, and soon a flood of upright canid reports poured out of her phone and email, resulting in several books on "Dogmen" (a term Godfrey prefers over "werewolves", which carries too many B-movie connotations). [Godfrey 2012, pp. 31-41] It was only a matter of time before the lupine beasts started multiplying.

In the summer of 2003, Katie Zahn and three friends, all fifteen or sixteen years old, decided to drive from their hometown of Janesville,

Wisconsin, out to the Avon Bottoms Wildlife Area, almost on the Illinois border. Supposedly there was a haunted bridge in the forested floodplain. If that was not enough, there had once been, according to legend, a government facility in the woods where scientists had created "animal hybrids" that broke loose, killed their creators, and still roamed the area.

The traveling troupe consisted of two girls, two boys, and a Rottweiler. The boys were to sell the dog to someone they were to meet in a field – the same field where the secret laboratory (and the hybrids) had once been located. (There is no mention of seating arrangements in the car.) They also intended to do some target practice with their BB guns, so their schedules were full.

At the field, the boys wandered off with their weapons. Katie and her friend waited by a tree near a stream. As the girls milled around, Katie noticed a paw print in the mud. "It was bigger than my hand, about seven or eight inches," she told Linda Godfrey.

Next the girls heard a howling from the woods or the field, the latter being shrouded in high grass. They thought it might be an injured dog, but before they could search for it, the boys came sprinting back across the field. Something followed the duo only a few yards behind, a shaggy, bipedal beast taller than the boys, one of whom stood a good six feet.

"It was chasing them but not that fast," Katie explained. It ran hunched over and seemed "wobbly" on two feet. The beast had a bushy tail, wide shoulders, and small eyes. It skidded to a stop as the quartet jumped back into their car, and it simply stood there as the boys fired BBs at it. Finally, the teens drove away.

Yet they did not leave the area. As they rolled through the forest, they decided seeing the unknown beast was cool. They drove on to the haunted bridge and stepped out of the car, ready to jump back in if they saw the creature.

One particularly bizarre touch came as Katie studied her surroundings. "We were walking around and I noticed this old cardboard box with four gorillas on it," she said. [Godfrey 2006, p. 127]

The teens wandered farther from the bridge and looked down at the stream that ran beneath it. Three hairy creatures knelt by the water, drinking from their palms as humans would rather than lapping. They had narrow, doglike heads and pointed ears. Their necks were thinner than the first creature's, and they were generally less massive, but their shoulders still seemed very wide.

The canids spotted the teenagers and started across the stream, walking on long, doglike hind legs. They seemed more at ease with bipedal locomotion than the first creature. Naturally, the human visitors rushed back to their vehicle. The dogmen stopped as the humans fled. Katie Zahn believed they just wanted the intruders to leave.

Four teens, four hairy anthropoid animals on a box, and four hairy anthropomorphic animals in the woods? Coincidence, or did someone somewhere think this adventure should have a touch of the symmetrical?

Ghosts of Gettysburg

This account breaks the rule of at least three people on a trip, but it is simply too good to pass up.

The three-day battle around Gettysburg, Pennsylvania, resulted in the greatest loss of life during the U.S. Civil War, and the battlefield that saw so much violence and death is considered one of the most haunted areas on earth. Sometime in the 1990s historical authors Jack Bochar and Bob Wasel visited Gettysburg for the first time, intending to write a book on the area but uninterested in the "spooky" aspects. "In fact," they admit, "the whole idea of haunts was quite unbelievable and only 'weird' people would believe such nonsense." [Bochar and Wasel, p. ix]

On a beautiful October afternoon, they drove to Gettysburg and spent most of their time looking over monuments and going on tours. As a result, they did not reach the battlefield park proper until 8:00 pm – after dark.

As they turned a corner, the pair were startled to see seven young men in uniform standing at the side of the road. The visitors could not tell what kind of uniforms the men were wearing, but they stood sharply at attention and saluted the passing vehicle. The writers turned around quickly, but when they passed the same point in the road, there was no sign of the young men.

Bochar and Wasel rolled on through the dark, wooded battlefield. They thought they heard gunfire, so they stopped and shut off the engine. Yes, they definitely heard the sounds of muskets and even cannon. They assumed it was some sort of reenactment, though it seemed that would be difficult to stage at night. They drove about one hundred yards and stopped again, this time leaving their vehicle.

The gunfire had ceased, but as they walked around, they grew conscious of a third set of footfalls accompanying their own. They returned quickly to the car and continued on to General Lee's (aka State of Virginia) monument.

They again left the car to study the statue of Lee, and for a minute or two all seemed serene. Suddenly, as Jack Bochar read an inscription on the monument, Bob Wasel dashed back to the car and jumped in.

Understandably puzzled, Bochar followed. Wasel seemed terrified. "Didn't you hear it?" the latter demanded. "Didn't you hear that? The loud crashes through the woods right next to us? It was so loud, how could anyone not hear it?"

To Bochar, the night had been unbrokenly cool, serene, and quiet.

Refusing to admit to paranormal occurrences, the pair drove on to the boulder-strewn hill called Devil's Den. On the whole trip, they realized, they had not seen another car. At Devil's Den they parked (with the windows rolled up) and tried to make sense of what they had seen and heard.

Strange noises from right outside made them jump. "As they looked in fright, a hideous-looking goat had its face pressed up against the window, saliva dripping out of its mouth, staring intently at them. Still shaking by the fright, Jack quickly picked up the camera on the front seat, turned on the flash, and snapped the shutter, after which the goat was gone." [Bochar and Wasel, p. xiii] The two visitors did not say another word but simply drove away from the battlefield.

Queries as to any reenactments that night brought only one answer: "There was no reenactment and besides, they do not allow firing of weapons on the battlefield." All of their photographs came out – except the one of the goat, which was completely black.

Frightening though the trip had been, the two visitors went on to write several books on Gettysburg and its history.

Bochar, Jack, and Bob Wasel. Haunted Gettysburg (Gettysburg, PA: Americana Souvenirs & Gifts, 1996).

Godfrey, Linda S. Hunting the American Werewolf (Madison, WI: Trails Books, 2006).

Ibid. Real Wolfmen: True Encounters in Modern America (New York: Tarcher/Penguin, 2012).

Keel, John A. Strange Creatures from Time and Space (Greenwich, CT: Fawcett, 1970).

Kim Kowalcyzk bio: http://ghostbreakers.com/Bios.html

Meley, Patricia M. "Adolescent Legend Trips as Teenage Cultural Response," Mid-America Folklore (Vol. 18, no. 1, Spring 1990), pp. 1-26.

Sergent, Donnie, Jr., and Jeff Wamsley. Mothman: The Facts Behind the Legend (Point Pleasant, WV: Mothman Lives Publishing, 2002).

Wamsley, Jeff. Mothman Behind the Red Eyes (Point Pleasant, WV: Mothman Press, 2005).

Wilder, Annie. Trucker Ghost Stories (New York: TOR 2012), pp. 54-58. "The Cross on the Car" was originally online at Paranormal.About.com (Your True Ghost Stories) for November 2012 (link broken)

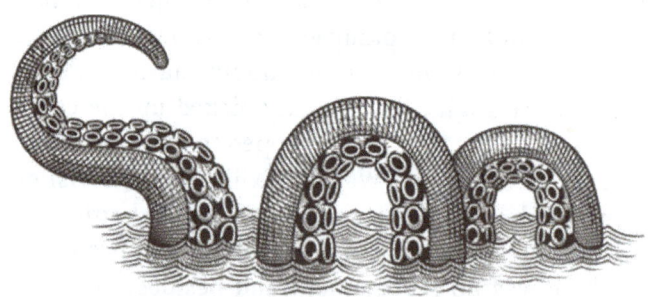

- Alaska: Lemmings fall from sky
- Lemmings fall from sky/disappear
- Sky falls: Lemmings

Lemmings from Heaven

In 1949-50, nature writer Sally Carrighar lived in Alaska, gathering material for a book on northern animals. She focused her attention on the small, plump rodents known as lemmings. Lemming populations grow explosively every few years then their numbers dwindle to the point of near-extinction. During their population spurts, northern predators live almost exclusively on them. Despite their ecological importance, little was known of these bob-tailed rodents.

"In every far Northern country, on every continent," writes Ms. Carrighar, "the primitive people call lemmings 'mice from the sky.'" As she mingled with the Inuit (Eskimo) inhabitants of the village of Unalakleet (on the shore of the Norton Sound in western Alaska, about the 64th parallel), she soon learned why: Several of them claimed to have seen lemmings drifting down from on high, "falling in bigger and bigger circles that turned same way as sun" (that is, clockwise when looking at the ground). Even those who did not witness actual falls were familiar with lemming footprints that started from nowhere and led away to the nearest grass or hiding place. Reggie Joule, a native bush pilot Carrighar held in high esteem, claimed to have seen such tracks on the roofs of cabins at Point Hope, where he grew up. "I think lemmings fly," was his final word on the subject.

One day in April 1950, Frank Ryan, the native postmaster of Unalakleet, told Carrighar that lemmings had just landed at (appropriately enough) the end of the local airstrip. The nature writer hurried out and found fifteen spots where the rodents had apparently coasted in. "The blacktop was covered with less than an inch of new, light, soft snow – too shallow for any lemming to tunnel under it without thrusting up a ridge on the surface." The tracks continued "more deeply" on from the landing points, as if the animals had been nearly weightless in transit. They were definitely lemming tracks, because mice left tail marks between their footprints and there were none here. The tracks were so new and sharp, even the imprints of long, dragging hairs on the animals' paws were visible.

"In each case the tracks led off the blacktop to a clump of grass, where the lemming evidently had burrowed down among the roots." [Carrighar, p. 27]

The naturalist tried and failed to think of an explanation for her flying lemmings. They possess nothing like a flying squirrel's membranous "wings". A powerful wind might have scooped them up by their long, fluffy fur, but "the snow was as light as eiderdown and it lay as level as it had fallen." An owl might have dropped one struggling lemming, "but hardly fifteen in a space about twenty yards square."

While certainly an odd story to the man on the street, reports of small living things falling from no visible source are numerous. The books of Charles Fort are full of them. Even the apparent loss of weight (until touching the earth) is not unusual – see "Clavaux Stone Falls." It is rare for mammals to be the subject of sky falls, however. Fish, frogs, snails and other so-called lower life-forms are much more common.

Ms. Carrighar had the misfortune to spend her year in Alaska during a population crash of the lemmings. Despite the sky fall, not even the native children could find any. Carrighar even convinced the Coast Guard to ferry her out to St. Lawrence Island to seek them, but no one could locate any at all. She left Alaska for the winter and returned the next spring.

Or do lemmings sometimes vanish as strangely as they appear? During her 1950 hunt for live lemmings, Sally Carrighar visited the small village of Shishmaref, located on a mere sandbar, a few acres in size. She and her Inuit assistant found lemming burrows easily and dug into a dozen or more. Even as she admired the intricate construction of the tunnels, Carrighar wondered where the animals were. It was summer, food was plentiful, trails in the grass had been used quite recently, but not a lemming was to be found. "Since this was a small, narrow island, the only direction the lemmings could have taken was toward the sea. They could only have crossed the wide, smooth beach." [Carrighar, p. 33]

When she finally did obtain five lemmings in 1951 (one of which eventually produced two litters), Carrighar had two habitats built in a large house she occupied in Nome, one on the first floor, one on the second. She studied the animals for several months – then they, too, began to disappear. One, kept upstairs, ended up in a drip-pan beneath an oil heater on the first floor (it died from its oily bath). The writer slowly transferred the lemmings downstairs, and finally there were four left topside. "What became of the final four never was known. I had heard them regularly, running about, spinning their wheel, chirring – and then from a certain day on there was silence." [pp. 164-165] An Eskimo youth helped her take apart the whole room and sift through the soil, grass, and sticks of the animals' environment, to no avail. "They were just gone – a fact to be added to the rest of the lemming mysteries." Perhaps Ms. Carrighar underestimated the abilities of small animals to escape captivity, but the consensus still seems to be – lemmings are strange little critters.

There is one legend associated with these rodents that almost everyone has heard: their "suicidal" tendency to march to the sea and drown. This myth was helped along by the 1958 Walt Disney film White Wilderness. (When the lemmings being filmed refused to march over a cliff into the sea, off-screen grips with push-brooms shoved them over the edge!)

A more scientific view is that when the lemming population explodes, the animals are forced to migrate to find food. Sometimes they wander over cliffs or into rivers in their marches. Even this idea is not accepted by many modern biologists, who believe the whole legend to be greatly exaggerated.

Naturalist Dennis Chitty, who studied the animals for nearly fifty years, seems to think there is something odd about lemmings. The notes that he and his fellow naturalists took between 1935 and 1949, such as the following, make interesting reading:

"Bake Lake. Lemming were abundant in the summer of 1943. In November they migrated, presumably toward Eskimo point. In May 1944 they were practically non-existent. Numerous carcasses were seen lying in the glare ice on the lakes as if they had frozen to death." [Chitty, p. 8]

Chitty admits that lemmings that move out onto sea ice will die from starvation and exposure, thus they "in a sense are committing suicide."

Carrighar, Sally. Wild Voice of the North (New York: Doubleday, 1953).

Chitty, Dennis. Do Lemmings Commit Suicide?: Beautiful Hypotheses and Ugly Facts (New York: Oxford University Press, 1996).

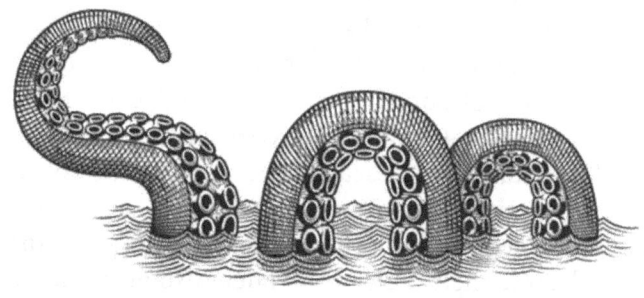

- Colorado: Wailing spirit/La Llorona
- La Llorona in Colorado
- Men chase wailing spirit
- Wailing woman and mysterious "buzz" in Colorado

La Llorona in las Colonias

In the spring of 1954, when she was fifteen years old, Joann Baca, her husband Alfonso, her brother-in-law Jose, and her cousin Isidro traveled from Las Vegas (New Mexico, not Nevada) to Avondale (near Pueblo, Colorado) to labor in the fields along with scores of other Hispanic workers. During their three-month stay they lived in a set of barracks-like houses they called Las Colonias ("the settlement"). One night in April, at about 12:30 am, a loud wailing sound echoed up from a river about half a mile away. "It woke everyone up, not just in our house, but in all of the surrounding houses," as she wrote to author Judith Beatty. Everybody in Las Colonias rushed outside. The wail did not fade; if anything it grew louder. "It was so loud that it made our ears ring."

Joann's husband and several other men piled into a car with a mounted spotlight. As the rest of the laborers watched, the carload of men drove down to the river. When they reached the bank, they determined that the noise came from the opposite shore. They drove across at a shallow point only to realize that the wailing now came from the settlement side. They crossed back only to find that the noise emanated from the far side again. Once more they drove through the shallows. "This happened about four times, I think," Mrs. Baca recalls. Eventually, as if tiring of the game, the wailing simply stopped. "All of us knew right away it was La Llorona."

La Llorona, the Wailing or Weeping Woman, is a major figure in the folklore of Mexico and the southwestern US. Supposedly she is the ghost of a woman who drowned or otherwise slew her own children, and now she wanders the earth, weeping and searching for her dead offspring. La Llorona stories vary in credibility from urban legends (including phantom hitchhiker tales) to frightening personal accounts.

There are many folktales of noisy apparitions or creatures that are heard ahead of a percipient at first, but, when the witness reaches the spot, are heard behind. Some researchers believe this indicates that the phenomena are subjective, i.e., the noise – whether hallucinatory or telepathically induced – being "in your head," therefore you can't get any closer, as a visual afterimage always floats at the same apparent distance in front of your eyes. In this instance, however, many witnesses watched (and listened) from a fair distance away as the carload of searchers chased the wailing from one side of the river to the other.

Although the wailing noise stopped, something else unusual occurred that night. A strange but totally different noise manifested itself at a small, unused chapel standing near the settlement. "You know the sound of a football game, when you're in a very big group of people, and it sounds like the buzzing of bees? This is the sound that came from the chapel in the pitch black night." The buzzing lasted about half an hour, then it too stopped. There was no sign of anything out of the ordinary at the chapel the next morning.

The migrant workers at Las Colonias unanimously agreed that the wailing noise was the cry of La Llorona. No one could explain the "buzzing" from the abandoned chapel.

Most of the tales from Beatty and Kraul's book about the Wailing Woman come from Santa Fe, New Mexico, or farther west. The Colorado story stands alone in its setting. This implies that the migrants "brought" this creature of folklore with them. On the other hand, no one saw the pale, sorrowful spirit described by legend. The workers heard a bizarre sonic apparition and identified it with an entity they already knew. They had no cultural pigeonhole for the "buzzing", so it is mentioned only as an anomaly. According to John Keel and other fortean writers, however, many religious manifestations and UFO sightings are accompanied by a buzzing, as if of a swarm of bees.

Beatty, Judith S., and Edward Garcia Kraul. La Llorona: Encounters with the Weeping Woman (Santa Fe, NM: Sunstone Press, 2004 [1988]), pp. 60-61.

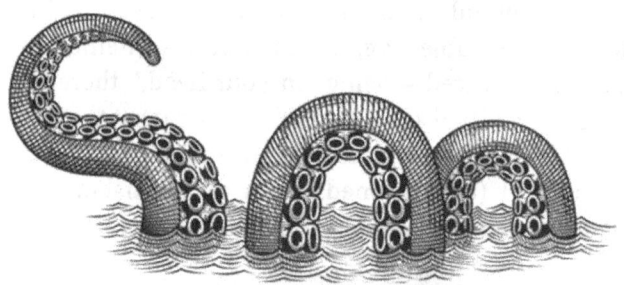

- Hvcko capko: Seminole Indian mystery animal
- Oklahoma: Wolf-like quadrupedal cryptid
- Seminole Indian legendary animal
- "Wolf crossed with deer" cryptid

Long Leggity Beasties

One evening in 1951, Mrs. Lawrence Laub of Calumet, Oklahoma, went out to check on her cattle. As she passed over the summit of a hill, she saw a strange creature.

"I know how this sounds and I know this is impossible," she said later, "but it looked like a cross between a wolf and a deer."

Jerome Clark writes: "The animal, standing on four thin deer-like legs but with huge pads for feet, had long hair slightly lighter in color than a German shepherd dog's. It was larger than a dog or a wolf and had small pointed ears and a bushy tail." [1]

Mrs. Laub threw a stick at the thing. It merely looked at her for a long moment, completely unafraid. The woman returned to her house with the animal watching her steadily all the way. Her husband told her that he had seen a similar creature two years previously, and neighbors reported strange tracks on their lands.

This short tale, anomalous even among stories of Bigfoot and other cryptids, has often been repeated by cryptozoological authors. There is a South American "maned wolf" that is actually a kind of fox with extremely long legs. It would look a lot like the Lawrences' beast, but it is certainly not larger than an actual wolf. Perhaps this gangly creature was Hvcko capko, or Long Ears, as described in the book Oklahoma Seminoles:

"It resembles a horse, with a horse's tail, but has a head more like that of a wolf, and enormous long ears. It is extremely ugly, and like Tall Man [Sasquatch] it smells like stagnant muddy water. Willie commented that the creatures frequent rocky areas, where they are often observed watching people as they pass. One man, he said, recently saw two of them near New Tulsa." [2]

The long-legged creatures sound similar, even to their pastime of watching people, but the Calumet thing had pointed ears, not long, floppy ones. Perhaps someone cropped them, in the manner of a Doberman Pinscher...

    1. Clark, Jerome, "'Manimals' Make Tracks in Oklahoma," in Fate Vol. 24 No. 9 (September 1971), p. 65.
    2. Howard, James H., and Willie Lena. Oklahoma Seminoles: Medicine, Magic, and Religion. (Norman: University of Oklahoma Press, 1984), pp. 212-213.

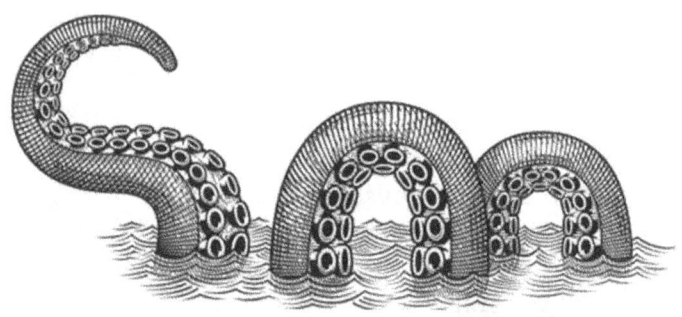

- Giant walks through small town
- Nine-foot-tall man walks through small town
- Pennsylvania: Giant walks through town
- Spaceman in shiny suit walks through town

A Long, Tall Drink of Water

On August 19, 1973, at about 8:00 pm, the small town of Buffalo Mills, Pennsylvania, played host to a most unusual pedestrian. A "human-like being" standing approximately nine feet tall and wearing an outfit "of some odd shiny fabric, and of unusual design," strode silently and determinedly through the streets of the city. Though many people saw him, no one tried to stop him, and he marched through Buffalo Mills and on into the Twilight Zone. [1]

"A few months earlier" a similar strangely-dressed being appeared in Tres Arroyos, Argentina, according to fortean author John Keel. This entity, approximately seven feet tall, stepped into a bar, marched straight to the men's room in front of the gaping customers, and entered. After several minutes passed with no sign of activity, the owner peeked in. Though there were no other doors or windows, the tall stranger had vanished. [2]

Pennsylvania suffered a flat-out invasion of UFOs, Men-in-Black, Bigfoot-like creatures, and unidentified animals in the fall of 1973. The weirdness of the phenomena matched the quantity: the Bigfeet (if that's what they were) appeared in the same areas as the UFOs; people who shot them or hit them with cars said they would simply disappear in a flash of light; they left three-toed prints totally unlike classic Sasquatch footprints; one young man who ventured too close to a pair of hairy apparitions started howling like an animal and later delivered apocalyptic prophecies. The tall walker in his shiny suit was like a herald in colorful bunting, announcing the strange phenomena's arrival.

A tall-walking stranger was also reported in the wilds of northern Wisconsin in the late nineteenth century. Most able-bodied men in the northern settlements spent the winters working in lumber camps while the women and children remained in town. "One winter," report college professors and folklorists Robert Gard and L. G. Sorden, "a person of fabulous height, enveloped in a long black cape, walked through a street of West Algoma every night at midnight." [3] The tall man walked through town, to the end of the boardwalk, and beyond into the pitch black wilderness, every night at the same time. A local youth crossed paths with him once by accident; the apparition's face was "colorless" and "expressionless", but the boy was too frightened to notice anything else. When the townsmen returned home in the spring, the night walker stopped appearing, and he was never seen again.

1. Gordon, Stan. Silent Invasion (Greensburg, PA: Bulldog Design, 2010), p. 94.

2. Keel, John A. Eighth Tower (New York: Signet Books, 1975), p. 121.

3. Gard, Robert E. and L. G. Sorden. Wisconsin Lore (Ashland, WI: Heartland Press, 1987 [1962]), p. 43.

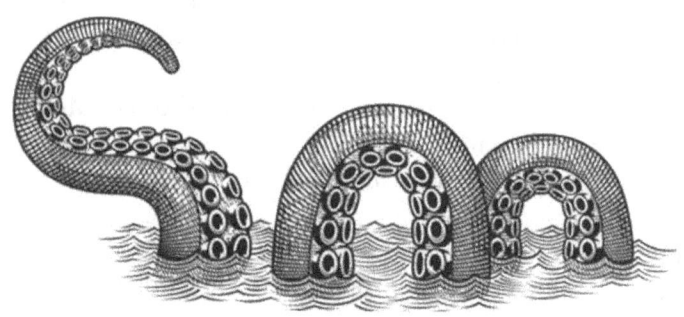

- Hawaii: Faceless woman haunts drive-in theater
- Hearn, Lafcadio – Mujina (faceless spirit)
- Japan: Faceless spirit
- Mujina – faceless spirit of Japan
- Noppera-bo – faceless spirit of Japan

Losing Face in Japan and Hawaii

Born in Greece, raised in Ireland, and working as a journalist in the United States, Lafcadio Hearn felt dissatisfied with life until he moved to Japan in 1890. In his book of Japanese supernatural lore, Kwaidan ["Weird Tales"] (1904), Hearn writes of a frightening, faceless being he calls Mujina.

It seems that a strange and frightening creature haunted the Akasaka Road in Tokyo during the nineteenth century (the Meiji Period). Few people would travel it at night due to something called a Mujina.

"The last man who saw the Mujina was an old merchant of the Kyobashi quarter, who died about thirty years ago," writes Hearn.

One night on the road, between a moat and an imperial palace, the merchant happened upon a young woman who wept bitterly, her face hidden by her hands and voluminous sleeves. Fearing she meant to drown herself, the merchant asked what the trouble was. The O-jochu [honorable damsel] merely continued weeping, despite the traveler's insistence that he wished to help her and that "this is no place for a young lady at night!"

"Then that O-jochu turned round, and dropped her sleeve, and stroked her face with her hand; -- and the man saw that she had no eyes or nose or mouth -- and he screamed and ran away."

That was not the end of the merchant's story. He fled along the road, which was pitch black in this era before streetlights. Eventually he spotted the flicker of a lantern. It proved to be the light of a soba-stand (soba being buckwheat noodles, similar to vermicelli). The terrified man ran up to the soba-peddler and blurted out his strange story – or most of it:

"I saw ... I saw a woman -- by the moat; -- and she showed me ... Aa! I cannot tell you what she showed me!" ...

"'He! Was it anything like this that she showed you?'" cried the soba-man, stroking his own face -- which therewith became like unto an Egg ... And, simultaneously, the light went out." [Hearn, p. 80]

The word mujina more properly refers to the Japanese badger, or sometimes the raccoon dog (which in turn is more properly called tanuki). These are mischievous, magical animals like the famous kitsune (fox spirit). The faceless entity is actually called Noppera-bo ("No Face"). The implication is that a badger spirit took on the form of a Noppera-bo to frighten people.

One expects tales of goblinesque creatures from long ago and far away, but stories of a Noppera-bo surfaced in the mid-twentieth century – not in Japan but in Hawaii, according to author, journalist, and university professor Glen Grant.

Professor Grant was always fascinated by Japanese obake stories ("Weird Things") told by the Issei (Japanese immigrants to Hawaii) and Nisei (second generation, born in Hawaii). After his years of investigating such stories, it was not that difficult for him to believe such entities existed. He could not understand, however, why Japanese spirits would manifest themselves to non-Japanese tourists and

Polynesians. Yet that was precisely what happened at the Waialae Drive-in in Kaimuki, a neighborhood of Honolulu, starting May, 1959 – specifically, in the ladies' restroom.

The typical encounter ran thusly: "Around midnight, a young woman goes into the restroom to freshen her lipstick. Standing at the mirror, combing her long, black hair is another young woman; the view of the face, however, is obscured by her beautiful, silken hair. As the first girl approaches the one at the mirror, she catches a reflection of the face – only, there is no face. Beneath the luxurious hair is a smooth, fleshy orb without evidence of mouth, eye, nose or ear." [Grant, p. 4]

Journalist Bob Krauss suggested the faceless woman was a spirit from the cemetery that bordered the drive-in. At first the theater owner denied the rumors, saying that his employees worked well into the night and had never seen anything. He was less argumentative as attendance skyrocketed; people actually hoped to see the strange being. According to Krauss a similar being had been seen at the Jarrett Intermediate School nearby.

The reports faded over the years and were forgotten by the 1970s. In November 1982, however, a radio talk-show mentioned the Noppera-bo of the Waialae Drive-in, and immediately phone calls poured in from people who claimed to have encountered the faceless woman.

"One caller insisted that in 1980 she had gone into the restroom at the drive-in and had seen another girl combing her long, red [not black] hair in the mirror. She had evidently never heard about the resident ghost and therefore unhesitantly went up next to her to use the sink. Then she discovered that this red-headed girl had no face!" [Grant, p. 5]

As one might expect, the woman fled screaming. She returned with friends, but, predictably, the faceless creature had disappeared.

The Mujina or whatever you wish to call it was in fact reported by unfortunate patrons of that restroom until the drive-in was finally demolished to make way for a housing project in 1986.

Grant, Glen. Obake: Ghost Stories in Hawaii (Honolulu, HI: Mutual Publishing, 1994).

Hearn, Lafcadio. Kwaidan: Stories and Studies of Strange Things (Tokyo: Charles E. Tuttle Co., 1986 [1904]).

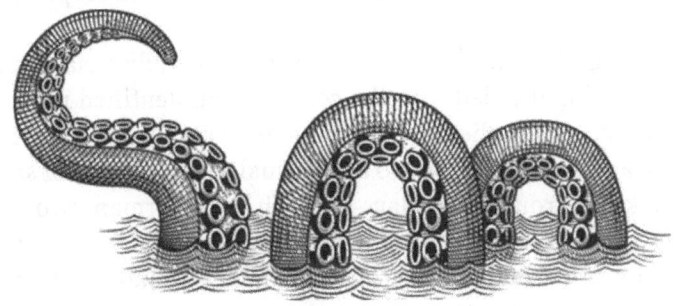

- Canada (NW Territories): Wilderness ghost
- Ghost protects corpse from animals

"Marche!"

On March 15, 1853, Augustus Richards Peers, a trader and post manager for the Hudson's Bay Company, died unexpectedly at the age of thirty-three. He was stationed at that time at Fort McPherson, Peel's River, in the Mackenzie River district of Canada's Northwest Territories, and had let it be known that he did not want his body buried there should something happen to him. He was, however, buried on the banks of Peel's River.

In the autumn of 1859, the former Mrs. Peers and her new husband, Alexander Mackenzie, decided to fulfill the late Mr. Peers' wish. The new head of Fort McPherson, a Mr. Gaudet, was to convey the body by dogsled three hundred miles to Fort Good Hope. From there Roderick MacFarlane, an official with the Hudson's Bay Company, was to convey it another five hundred miles south to Fort Simpson.

Mr. Peers' body, preserved by the marshy soil and cold environment, was placed in an overlarge coffin and strapped to a dog sled. "It was an extremely difficult and awkward load for men and dogs to conduct and haul over the rugged masses of tossed-up ice which occur at intervals along the mighty Mackenzie River," writes MacFarlane, but Gaudet managed to reach Fort Good Hope by March 1, 1860.

MacFarlane's team consisted of an Iroquois Indian named Michel Thomas, driving the sled with the coffin; an unidentified man driving the sled carrying supplies and camping gear; and MacFarlane himself, on foot, leading the way. Due to an unusual accumulation of snow and ice, it took the group seven days to reach Fort Norman, two hundred miles away. At Fort Norman the unnamed man left the party, to be replaced by a new native driver named Michel Iroquois. Nicol Taylor, the Trader-in-Charge, also joined the group, having been a good friend of the late Peers. Six new dogs were acquired to replace the exhausted teams.

The men made camp at night on bluffs above the river banks. The dogs were left near the bank, but the sled bearing the coffin was dragged up with the men – usually. On March 15 -- by coincidence the seventh anniversary of Peers' death -- the sledding party found themselves among steep, rocky cliffs. As evening approached, they were barely able to drag themselves and their provisions up the craggy walls. As the dogs had never shown any interest in the coffin, it was, this time, left down near the river.

After spending ten or twelve minutes chopping firewood and clearing brush, the travelers heard the dogs barking. "While I was talking to Mr. Taylor on the subject, we all distinctly heard the word 'Marche!'." (This is the word we know as "mush" from many a cartoon and movie, meaning not only "go" but also "go away," i.e., someone was ordering the dogs to back off). MacFarlane and Taylor ran to the top of the cliff, but no one was visible. "The dogs were clustered round the body-train at a distance of several feet and were apparently excited by something." After much coaxing the men got the dogs to clamber up the rocky slope and spend the night by their encampment.

On March 18, the company had to travel two hours in total darkness before finding a camping spot, and even then they had to retreat farther than usual from the river to find a stand of pine. They managed to bring up the dogs and the provisions sled (it having grown very light by now), but the body sled was too heavy, so they left it by the riverbank.

After wandering far afield gathering firewood, MacFarlane returned to camp and was informed by the other men that they had heard another human cry, twice repeated, from the river. The men investigated and found no one. However, they decided to double their efforts, and they finally dragged the body sled up to the campsite.

The next morning, they discovered the footprints of a wolverine on the bank where the sled had been resting. "Had we left the body on the spot, he would undoubtedly have made havoc with the remains."

The company reached Fort Simpson on the 21st with no other incident. Peers was buried at last on the 23rd.

Chief Trader Ross, it seems, was not only a close friend of the late Augustus Peers, he also "had an excellent memory and could easily mimic anyone's voice." He called out "Marche!" in Peers' voice, and the company agreed that it sounded like the cries they had heard.

MacFarlane gave a written statement concerning the incident to a Colonel Butler of Plymouth, who sent it to Lord Halifax, the British politician and collector of ghost stories. MacFarlane later sent a letter clarifying a few points in his narrative.

In both wilderness manifestations, there was the possibility of the body being attacked and eaten by a wild animal or even the dog team. "If it be granted that the spirits of the dead are sometimes allowed to re-visit former scenes and their discarded bodies," MacFarlane writes, ". . . what more natural course would his spirit have taken in order to prevent the desecration of these?"

Much of this account rides on one man's memory of the voice of someone dead seven years, as well as his skill at mimicking him using a single word. On the other hand, this tale has one of the creepiest build-ups I've ever read in a ghost story, reminding me of the 1951 film The Thing, with the dead Peers among the sled dogs rather than James Arness' vegetable monster. The ending is rather anticlimactic, but real accounts rarely lead to satisfying conclusions.

Lindley, Charles, Lord Halifax. Lord Halifax's Ghost Book: A

Collection of Stories of Haunted Houses, Apparitions, and Supernatural Occurrences (Secaucus, NJ: Castle Books, 1986 [1936]), pp. 93-105.

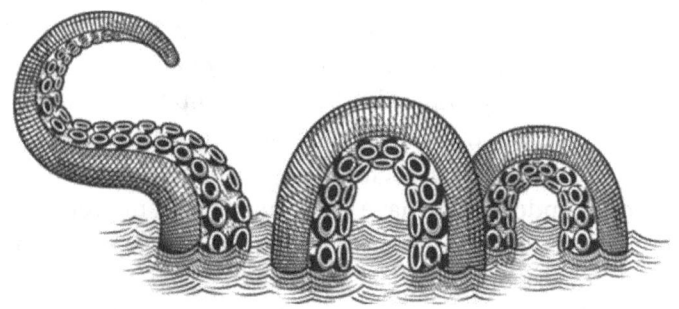

- Desert, airmen disappearing in, 1924
- Iraq: Vanishing airmen, 1924
- Missing Pilots, 1924
- Vanishing Airmen, Iraq

Missing Pilots of Iraq

One of the most iconic missing person stories can be found in Charles Fort's Wild Talents, chapter 17:

"Upon July 24, 1924, at a time of Arab hostility, Flight-Lieutenant W. T. Day and Pilot Officer D. R. Stewart were sent from British headquarters, upon an ordinary reconnaissance over a desert in Mesopotamia [Iraq]. According to schedule, they would not be absent more than several hours." [Fort, p. 953]

Fort's source was the London Sunday Express, Sept. 21 and 28, 1924. The plane did not return, but searchers soon located it in the Iraqi desert. It had not crashed, it still held fuel, and it had not been hit by gunfire. "So far as can be ascertained," proclaimed the Sunday Express, "they encountered no meteorological conditions that might have forced them to land." The two airmen, however, were not to be found. Fort continues:

"In the sand, around the plane, were seen the footprints of Day and Stewart. 'They were traced, side by side, for some forty yards from the machine. Then, as suddenly as if they had come to the brink of a cliff, the marks ended.'" [Fort, p. 954]

This account has been repeated in the books of Frank Edwards, Daniel Cohen, Brad Steiger, and other paranormal/Fortean authors. In 2005, TV producer and freelance writer Paul Chambers took a crack at the mystery, and the results were downright embarrassing.

Chambers looked up newspapers like the London Times and the Daily Mail. These publications stated authoritatively that there had been a sandstorm at the time of the airmen's flight, which forced them down. Furthermore, the plane was damaged in landing, resulting in the airmen's desire to strike out on foot, and the shifting sands simply blurred out their footprints beyond the forty yard mark.

Chambers then turned to the Index for the Times. "After only seconds of searching I was presented with an entry for 12 March 1925. It had the headline 'Missing RAF Officers' Bodies Found'." The article itself read: "In view of the time of day and the season during which they were subjected to exposure, there is no reasonable doubt that death ensued from heat exhaustion." [Chambers. p. 43]

Thus, a famous case of disappearing people itself disappears, the final answer having been found, not in some old diary or obscure journal, but in no less a source than the London Times. Hopefully future researchers will keep the story of the lost airmen in mind when writing new books of true-life mysteries and not simply repeat what they have read before.

Chambers, Paul, "The Vanishing," in Fortean Times no. 194 (April 2005), pp. 40-44.

Fort, Charles. Complete Books (New York: Dover Publications, 1974 [1941].

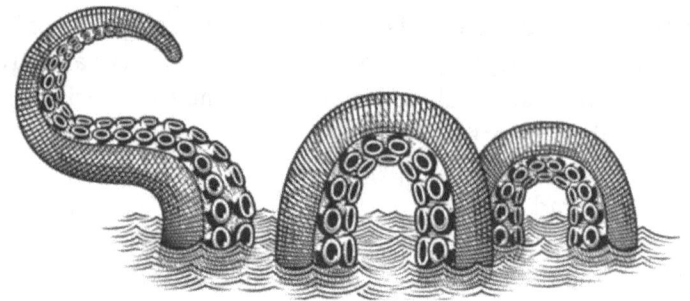

- Animals foretell disaster
- House with history of strange deaths
- Mice flee house before death/disaster
- New York: Mice flee house before deaths

Mrs. Massey's Migrating Mice

Broadway columnist Danton Walker was the sort of person who "goes everywhere and knows everybody." His interviews and articles appeared in The Billboard and The New Yorker, and he finally worked his way up to his own column in The New York Daily News, which in the 1950s had the largest newspaper circulation in the USA. After years of interviewing important names in music, theater, radio, and motion pictures, he realized "that nearly every man jack of 'em had some experience that might, by a slight stretch of nomenclature, be called a 'ghost story,' and from then on I made a point of drawing them out on the subject." [pp. 9-10]

For the following story Walker interviewed Dorothy Massey and "personally knew several of the people involved." Walker regretted that he did not have permission to print the others' names.

Raymond Massey, star of Things to Come, Abe Lincoln in Illinois, Arsenic and Old Lace, and many other movies, grew tired of living out of hotels due to his film commitments. In the early 1940s he and his wife Dorothy decided to purchase a brownstone mansion in New York City, "in the East 80's." The first one they examined seemed to have a "chill like a tomb," so they bought the one across the street.

Someone did buy the first house, however. After a few months Dorothy met the new owner, a socially prominent and wealthy woman. The woman liked the house except for the fact that it was infested with mice.

One day Mrs. Massey happened to look out a second-floor window and saw movement across the street. The mice were climbing out of their neighbor's basement. "They came out in groups, in a panicky sort of way, confused and scurrying along the gutter. Then one or two got brave and made the bold dash across the street to my house. I immediately ran to the phone to call the exterminator." [p. 28]

The mice kept invading until a local plumber brought in a pair of cats. A few days later the Masseys found out their neighbor had committed suicide.

Sometime later an executive in a large oil company bought the house for his mistress, "a former 'Follies' beauty." Soon thereafter Dorothy Massey, while adjusting a Venetian blind, noticed that mice were once more abandoning the house across the street for her own mansion. She called the exterminator again. A few days later the death of the oil executive made the headlines.

Now Mrs. Massey watched the house across the way every morning. The Masseys knew nothing about the next occupant except that he was a successful businessman. Eventually, however, the mice fled the house yet again. The Masseys waited for news, and soon enough they read it in the New York Times. A "prominent businessman," flying back from Canada in his private plane, crashed into the Hudson River and drowned. "Neither of us knew the man but we both instantly recognized his home address – the house across the way!"

Not long after that, Dorothy received a shock of another sort. The Masseys had never successfully gotten rid of all the mice that took sanctuary in their mansion – until one morning when Dorothy watched them flee her basement and scamper back across the street! The only bad thing that happened to the Masseys, however, was that their furnace blew up. "No one was hurt, and we were fully protected by insurance."

In the mid-1940s the Masseys moved to Connecticut. They heard no more about the house or the mice, but Dorothy researched the mysterious residence and learned that it had been built by one of the most prominent lawyers in the country. The lawyer didn't live there long, and after leaving the place he entered a hospital for a physical check-up. Suddenly he fled from the attendants and jumped into the Hudson, apparently trying to drown himself. He was rescued and lived for many years, but he could never explain why he decided one day to jump in the river.

Animals often sense approaching death or disaster, and there is the obvious comparison to "rats fleeing a sinking ship." However, the "mouse house" itself seemed to be a factor in these rodent panics, eventually "infecting" the mansion across the street. "'I don't know what the house across the way had to do with it, if anything,' Mrs. Massey concluded, 'but looking back, it is a bit disturbing, isn't it?'" [p. 30]

I myself came across this story many times as little more than a rumor or urban legend. I was surprised and pleased to find the original tale in Walker's book, which I bought for certain other accounts.

Walker, Danton. Spooks Deluxe: Some Excursions into the Supernatural (New York: Franklin Watts, 1956).

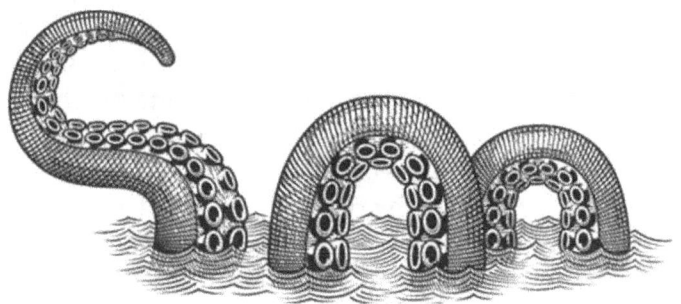

- "Night the Ghost Got in" based on real events
- Ohio: James Thurber's ghost story
- Thurber, James – ghost story

The Night the Ghost Got in

Humorist James Thurber's first major literary triumph came in the form of autobiographical essays published together as My Life and Hard Times (1933). "The Day the Dam Broke" and "The Night the Bed Fell" are gems of mass hysteria to rank with the Orson Welles War of the Worlds broadcast. As to "The Night the Ghost Got in":

During the Nineteen-teens, the Thurber family – father Charles Thurber, mother Mary "Mame" Thurber, and boys James, Robert, and William – lived at 77 Jefferson Avenue, Columbus, Ohio (called Lexington Avenue in My Life and Hard Times). On the cold night of November 17, 1915, Thurber's father and younger brother (Robert) were out of town. James, taking a late bath (about 1:00 am on the 18th), had just climbed out of the tub when he heard heavy footsteps. He ventured to the head of the back staircase wearing only a towel.

"The light from the bathroom shone down the back steps, which dropped directly into the dining room," he writes in "Night the Ghost Got in." "I could see the faint shine of plates on the plate-rail; I couldn't see the table. The steps kept going round and round the table; at regular intervals a board creaked, when it was trod upon." [Thurber, pp. 227-228]

Thurber listened to the puzzling noise for about three minutes and finally woke his older brother William (called Herman in My Life). He dragged his sleepy sibling to the top of the stairs, but the footsteps had stopped. William, naturally, wanted to go back to bed, but Thurber insisted "There's something down there!"

"Instantly the steps began again, circled the dining-room table like a man running, and started up the stairs toward us, heavily, two at a time. The light still shone palely down the stairs; we saw nothing coming; we only heard the steps." [Thurber, 229]

The brothers rushed to their respective rooms and hid. Their mother Mame heard the footsteps and assumed burglars had broken in. The police were called, and they ransacked the house seeking a human prowler, resulting in a comedy of errors. The ascent of the stairs by the unseen jogger was the last of the manifestation, however.

The Thurber household eventually settled down (as much as it ever did). The Thurbers did not see or hear anything else of a ghostly nature before moving away in 1917.

In a 1957 letter to Columbus Dispatch reporter Bill Arter, Thurber explained that the previous inhabitants of 77 Jefferson had moved out due to strange noises in the house. "The corner druggist to whom I related my own experience, described the walking and running upstairs before I could describe it myself. They were undeniably the steps of a man. It was quite an experience to hear him running up the steps toward us, my brother and me, and to see nothing whatever." [Bernstein, p. 49] Thurber's essay gives the impression that on one and only one night, for no apparent reason, "footsteps" invaded the Thurber home, which would seem quite odd. However, if the noises were known to previous tenants, they become a more "ordinary" haunting.

Like most writers, Thurber partially fictionalized the essays depicting family members and other people known to him. Burton Bernstein, in his book Thurber, goes so far as to say "most of his reminiscence dealt with 'imaginary people.'" [p. xi] For instance, the cantankerous, attic-dwelling grandfather who believes he's still fighting the Civil War is based on Thurber's grandfather William Fisher, but Fisher did not live in the Thurber house, being a respected businessman until the day he died.

On the other hand, Harrison Kinney's 1995 book on Thurber suggests there is more truth to My Life and Hard Times than is often supposed. Thurber's account of the panic that struck Columbus, Ohio in "The Day the Dam Broke" is quite accurate (Bernstein mentions that essay only once). Not only James, but William and Mame Thurber always insisted on the truth of "The Night the Ghost Got in." (William's support is particularly interesting, because the older Thurber brother hated James' depiction of the family and still said unflattering things about the humorist twenty-five years after James' death.) Even absent brother Robert wrote to biographer Kinney, "It's true that my father and I were in Indianapolis the night they heard the ghost, as Jamie writes. They really did call the police, too." [Kinney, 140]

Mary Agnes Fisher (Mame) Thurber, mother of James, had quite a sense of humor. She sometimes threw shoes down the hall at night, not to frighten burglars as "Aunt Gracie" does in "The Night the Bed Fell," but to cause further chaos when other family members thought there might be intruders. Mame's nephew Earl Fisher suggested decades later that "She could convince the boys that they had heard a ghost, whether they had or not." [Kinney, 140] On the other hand, Mame was quite serious in her belief in the occult: Kinney's book reprints some rather desperate-sounding requests to schedule James' eye surgeries at specific times, when the astrological signs would be favorable.

In the last months of his life Thurber developed an elaborate back story of a jeweler who came home to find his wife in bed with another man and who subsequently ran crazily through the house before shooting himself. The writer suffered from many mental and physical problems by that time, however, so the story was probably apocryphal.

In 1984, the ghost house was restored as a museum and christened The Thurber House. Guest writers could live and work in the attic room, where once stood the infamous old bed of "The Night the Bed Fell." In 1988, Patricia DiPerna, one such writer, saw something passing behind the attic windows as she exited her car in the parking lot – "a hefty, somewhat stooped, black torso shadow, apparently dressed in a raincoat with the collar turned up." She also heard occasional "clatterings" in the kitchen cupboards when no one was there. The Thurber ghost marches on.

Bernstein, Burton. Thurber (New York: Ballantine Books, 1975).

Kinney, Harrison. James Thurber: His Life and Times (New York: Henry Holt and Co., 1995).

Thurber, James. "My Life and Hard Times," in Thurber Carnival (New York: Dell, 1962), pp. 227-233.

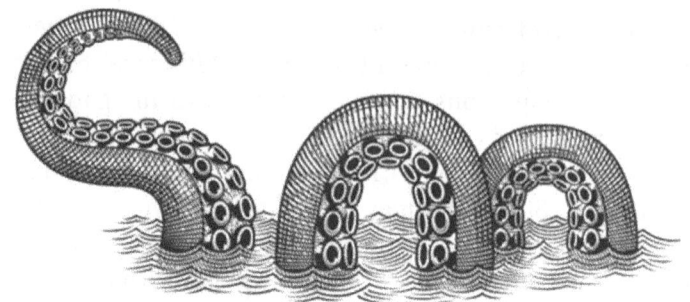

- Ghostly pushes
- Ghostly slaps
- Haunted staircase: Birmingham, England

Nudge, Nudge

Last night I saw upon the stair,
A little man who wasn't there.
He wasn't there again today
Oh, how I wish he'd go away.
"Antigonish", William Hughes Mearns (1899)

A letter entitled "Pushy Ghost" [Fortean Times no. 190] – a haunting that consists entirely of a single "push" on a staircase – started me thinking. [1]

On that favorite Fortean date of June 24, in 1924, archaeologist Thomas Lethbridge visited the island of Skellig Michael off the southwest coast of Ireland. He ascended a hill to see the ruins of an ancient monastery and decided to pick his way down to a rubbish dump about 100 feet below. On the way he was overcome with the idea that someone or something wanted to push him off the cliff, so he climbed back up. He then hiked down to a grassy expanse called Christ's Saddle. "Something made me think of turning round and I was about to do so, when without a sound and with no apparent feeling, I was suddenly flung flat on my face on the grass. There was no gust of wind, no person, no animal, nothing." [2]

This fall impressed Lethbridge mightily. Perhaps it was the reason he turned to the investigation of dowsing and psychic powers by the 1950s. The latter certainly led him to devise a theory that most paranormal phenomena resulted from people's interactions with "fields" in forests, buildings, and streams, and with the images "recorded" on them. Colin Wilson refers to Lethbridge's "push" so often in his book Mysteries, perhaps it influenced his own theories about "Faculty X".

John Aubrey (1626-97), in Chapter 10 of his book Miscellanies, writes of an odd event in the life of one John Borograve of Hamel, Hertfordshire, who, "when he was a young Man, Riding in a Lane in that Country, had a Blow given him on his Cheek (or Head): He look'd back, and saw that no body was near, behind him; anon, he had such another Blow; I have forgot if a Third. He turn'd back and fell to the Study of Law; and was afterwards a Judge."

This "smack" or "push" from nowhere easily slides across the paranormal spectrum to Charles Fort's attacks by "invisibles". When we think of an immaterial being affecting the physical world, we usually think of poltergeists with their furniture-moving and dish-breaking. The world can be affected with much less effort, however. A shove at the top of the stair or on a crowded train platform, a yank on a steering wheel on a busy highway, and the life of a brilliant scientist or a potential world leader might be nipped in the bud. Or perhaps the victim is "pushed" in a new direction psychologically. Lethbridge drifted from archaeology to psychic phenomena. John Borograve became a judge.

Maybe there exist beings that can only build up energy over months or years and release it in one well-placed "punch". History might be guided, not by conspiracies or aliens, but by the occasional psychokinetic nudge in the right (or wrong) direction.

1. A real estate agent from Birmingham, John Rice undertook the sale of a Victorian house with a steep staircase. "The vendor warned me always to hold the handrail firmly." One day while waiting for a prospective buyer, he was descending the stairway, not using the

handrail, when, about five steps from the bottom, "I felt a distinct push in my back. I literally leapt down the hall." A surveyor, after examining the house, returned the key to Rice and shakily admitted that something had pushed him as well, and in fact he had "descended almost the whole flight of stairs on his back." The vendor of the house could only suggest that an older relative of his, found dead at the base of the stairway, might have something to do with the "push". Or was this another victim? (Rice, John F., "Pushy Ghost," in Fortean Times No. 190 (Jan. 2005), p. 79.)

2. Lethbridge, Thomas. Essential T. C. Lethbridge, edited by Tom Graves and Janet Hoult (London: Routledge and Kegan Paul, 1980), pp. 16-17. See also:

Wilson, Colin. Mysteries (New York: G. P. Putnam's Sons, 1978), p. 63.

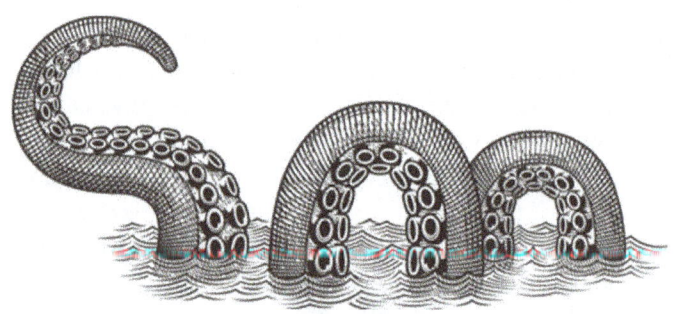

- Bierce, Ambrose – "Mysterious Disappearances"
- Boy or man's voice still heard after vanishing
- Boy or man walking to well vanishes
- Indiana: Oliver Lerch disappearance
- Man/boy pulled into the sky
- Pennsylvania: Man pulled into the sky

Oliver Lerch's Trail

"HERE is the shortest story that I know of: St. Louis Globe-

Democrat, Nov. 2, 1886 -- a girl stepped from her home, to go to a spring."
    --Charles Fort, LO!, chapter 16

As David Paulides of Missing 411 fame collected more and more accounts of people going missing in national parks and forests, certain patterns emerged. There is a growing number of reports of people disappearing while actually talking on their cell phones: the person at the other end hears the gabble of a confused voice and a rushing of wind as if the caller is suddenly moving at great speed – later the victim's phone is found on the ground. If they were snatched up and carried off somehow, while babbling into the phone, why is the phone still at the point of their last known position?

Someone finally suggested that the missing people might be going – up. That would explain the phones – they fell straight down when the victims dropped them. The implications, however, are simply mind-numbing. Can a human being just rise into the air?

On Christmas Eve of 1889, relatives and friends gathered at the Lerch farmhouse in South Bend, Indiana, to celebrate the holidays with a hearty Christmas dinner. At about 11:30 pm, Bradley J. Lerch, the head of the house, asked his 20-year-old son Oliver to take a pail and fetch more water from the well. He took the bucket and stepped out into the cold, but moments later family and guests heard him cry for help. The gathered people spilled into the yard, some with lanterns. The young man's footprints were plain in the snow, but after about 75 yards they stopped completely in the white expanse, as if he had abruptly ceased to exist.

Stranger was to come, however. Oliver's voice cried out, "Help, help, it's got me!" The startled group realized his call came from overhead! Though the people strained their eyes, they could make out nothing in the dark night.

Oliver continued crying out "Help me, help!", but his voice slowly faded, as if he were rising higher and higher into the air. Eventually his desperate appeals passed beyond audibility.

Over the next few days neighbors searched the farmlands and

forests, climbed onto roofs and up into trees, and even checked the well, but Oliver Lerch was never seen again.

The Lerch disappearance is one of the most famous – and most frightening – of human vanishings on record. It is strange, then, that authors who have written on the subject can't seem to get their basic details to agree.

In Frank Edwards' Strangest of All and Morris K. Jessop's Case for the UFO, the boy's name is Oliver Lerch, but in C. B. Colby's Weirdest People in the World, where I first came across it, and John Keel's Our Haunted Planet, the boy's last name is "Larch". Well, what's one letter off, more-or-less?

Brad Steiger's Strangers from the Skies: "It was on Christmas Eve, 1909, that 'they' took 11-year-old Oliver Thomas up into the sky." Wait -- what? Young Oliver Thomas of Rhayader, Wales, sent out to get a pail of water, started screaming for help. The gathered family and guests rushed outside, only to hear his voice echoing down from high above. His footprints made a trail across the yard for about 75 feet, then they stopped abruptly. "There was only one conclusion that the authorities were able to render: Oliver Thomas had inexplicably vanished -- straight up." [Steiger, pp. 33-34]

Finally, and perhaps inevitably, we reach way back to American literary celebrity Ambrose Bierce and his story "Charles Ashmore's Trail," one of the vignettes that form "Mysterious Disappearances." It seems that the family of Christian Ashmore lived on a farm in Quincy, Illinois, in the nineteenth century:

"On the evening of the 9th of November in 1878, at about nine o'clock, young Charles Ashmore left the family circle about the hearth, took a tin bucket and started toward the spring. As he did not return, the family became uneasy, and going to the door by which he had left the house, his father called without receiving an answer." [Bierce, p. 89]

The father and Charles' sister clambered out in the snow to look for the lad, following his footsteps, but: "the trail of the young man had abruptly ended, and all beyond was smooth, unbroken snow. The last footprints were as conspicuous as any in the line; the very nail-marks were distinctly visible."

Charles Ashmore was never seen again, but as the days passed, Mrs.

Ashmore heard her son's voice at the point where his footprints ended. It sounded distant, but distinct; as the days passed, however, her son's cries grew weaker and weaker and finally stopped. (The last detail was grafted onto the story of David Lang. See "The Difficulty of Crossing a Field...")

So how did Charles Ashmore of Quincy, Illinois, become Oliver Lerch of South Bend, Indiana?

The Lerch version appeared in Fate Magazine (September 1950) under the title "What Happened to Oliver Lerch?", by Joseph Rosenberger. It is this version that most later writers took as a source. Joe Nickell, a researcher known for exploding numerous modern myths, tracked down Mr. Rosenberger and interviewed him. Rosenberger admitted the tale was false, written out of a need for money. "Every single bit is fiction. I wrote the damn piece way back when, during the lean days." [Shoemaker, p. 21; Paijmans and Aubeck, p. 43]

The strange thing is, the confession of a hoax is itself a hoax. Theo Paijmans and Chris Aubeck, checking many back issues of newspapers and magazines, discovered several references to the Lerch story before 1950. The original version was apparently one that appeared in the New York Sunday Telegraph, December 25, 1904, written by an Irving Lewis. This early and elaborate version gives a list of names at the end, witnesses to the tragedy that signed an affidavit as to the truthfulness of the matter. As you might guess, further research failed to prove that any of these witnesses – or the Lerch family itself – ever existed. Presumably "Irving Lewis" lifted the story idea from "Charles Ashmore's Trail."

Often when seeking the reality behind an old tale of the paranormal, the details fade and dissipate, leaving only emptiness behind. Sometimes, however, the demise of one story leads the ascendancy of another – possibly stranger – account.

After the Lerch story appeared in Fate, an H. M. Cranmer wrote in to tell of a similar disappearance that occurred in Hammersley Fork, Pennsylvania, 25 years before Oliver's (non) vanishing. Robert Lyman, Sr., a historian, businessman and folklorist from the Black Forest region of northern Pennsylvania, gave the full story of the "Levitation into Limbo" in his 1971 book, Forbidden Land.

There were two "Hammersley Hotels" in the Hammersley Fork area, one owned by Jake Hammersley and the other by his son Uriah. Jake's hotel faced the area's largest public road, which ran east-west, more-or-less paralleling Kettle Creek, which lay to the south. The farm of Uriah Kelly lay just west of the hotel, also facing the road.

On a warm September evening in 1865, a dozen or so men sat around Jake's front porch, smoking and talking. Men were beginning to gather in the area for the winter work of cutting down pine trees. As they gossiped and joked, they noticed a stranger ambling down the road.

The man seemed to be intoxicated; he walked erratically like a drunk, and as he passed in front of the hotel, the loungers heard him mumbling out loud. It was not that strange a sight in an area where workers were temporarily idle, so Jake's guest continued their conversations.

The drunk wandered west until he reached the halfway point between the hotel and the Kelly farm, about 40 rods (660 feet) from the gathered men. "This was the site where one of the strangest of all strange events happened," writes Lyman.

The stranger suddenly yelled out "Let me go, damn you, let me go!" Then he started rising up into the air. The watchers from the hotel jumped from the porch and ran toward him. Several workers from the Kelly farm came running from the opposite direction. "A score of persons watched him going up in the air screaming, until he went out of hearing and out of sight. No one could see anything carrying him away." [Lyman, p. 57]

Despite what the 20 witnesses saw with their own eyes, they and others searched the area. On one side of the road were cornfields – there were no footprints. On the other side, forty feet down, was Kettle Creek – no trace of anyone on the bank or on a large sandbar out in the middle. [Jessup. p. 104]

No one ever learned who the stranger was, but that was not so unusual. "Lumberjacks came from as far away as Maine and Nova Scotia," according to Lyman. "Nothing was more common on the roads than unknown 'woodhicks', drunk or sober."

How is this account any more acceptable than that of Oliver Lerch or Charles Ashmore? The witnesses were long deceased by the time Robert Lyman began his research, but their sons and daughters still lived. "There are many in the Black Forest today who heard the story from men who were living at the time. Owen G. Metzger, president of the Citizens Trust Co., Coudersport, said it actually happened. And so did Frank Howland, Commissioner's Clerk for many years." The descendants of the Hammerleys and the Kellys were familiar with the event, as were the families and friends of the other witnesses.

The number of witnesses is also important. Lyman admits that no one would have believed the story if only one or two people had been present. "In this case it was observed by as many as 20 persons and reported by such reliable men that I accept it as fact. It is the most amazing true event ever recorded in our Black Forest."

All of which doesn't prove its reality, but at least the unwilling aeronaut's launching site has stayed put over the years.

Just hope, one day when you are out jogging or hiking, that you don't find yourself upwardly mobile in a startlingly unexpected fashion...

Bierce, Ambrose, "Mysterious Disappearances," in Ghost and Horror Stories of Ambrose Bierce (New York: Dover Books, 1964), pp. 86-91.

Jessup, Morris K. Case for the UFO: Varo Edition (Clarksburg, West Virginia: Saucerian Press, 1975 [1955]), pp. 101-104.

Lyman, Robert, Sr. Forbidden Land: Strange Events in the Black Forest (Coudersport, PA: Leader Publishing, 1971), pp. 56-58.

Paijmans, Theo, and Chris Aubeck, "Nightmare Before Christmas: The Strange Disappearance of Oliver Lerch," Fortean Times no. 335 (Jan. 2016), pp. 42-47.

Shoemaker, Michael, "Three Discoveries in Fortean Folklore," INFO Journal no. 66 (June 1992), pp. 20-21.

Steiger, Brad. Strangers from the Skies (London: Universal-Tandem, 1966).

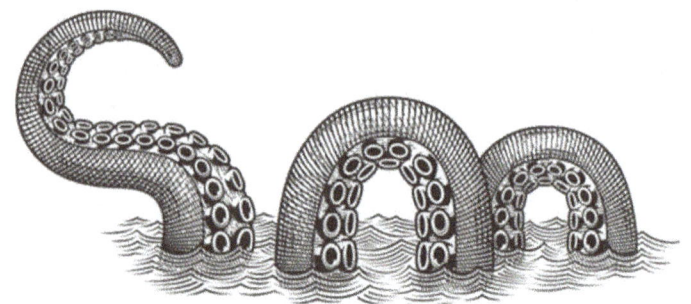

- Bighead – huge headed creature
- Huge headed humanoid
- Ohio: hairy humanoid

On the Track of – Bighead?

The Kline property in Richland County, Ohio, consisted of several acres lying between Ohio State Road 95 and a CSX railroad branch. Wooded hills stretched out across the country beyond the train tracks. On July 8, 1978, at about 11:00 pm, 17-year-old Eugene Kline and his friend Ken O'Neal (also 17) were hiking along the tracks when they heard something thrashing through the brush about fifty feet ahead and to their left. A flashlight revealed a truly unnerving sight: a seven-foot-tall creature with red eyes – and "a head much bigger than its body"! [Clark, p. 65] O'Neal ran for the Kline house, but Eugene appeared to be "transfixed" for an agonizingly long moment. Finally, however, the spell broke and he ran, too.

The boys could not give many details beyond the thing's macrocephalic peculiarity. They did agree that it made a growling noise. On July 9, however, several residents of the small town of Butler (population 1300) purportedly shot at the monster, which had been dubbed "Bighead". One dog was so terrified of the creature, it hurled itself through its owner's picture window and ran wildly through the house in its attempts to escape the thing.

A policeman named Fred Horne supposedly found imprints in wet, unmown grass made by something "bigger than a cow or a deer," and even collected unusual hair samples on the Kline property. When Ron Schaffner of the Ohio UFO Investigators League questioned Butler Police Chief Phil Stortz in September, however, Stortz denied those statements.

On July 10, at about 10:00 pm, a carload of young adults from Mansfield pulled up to a railroad crossing at Bellville, a couple of miles northwest of Butler. They all saw a "huge black apparition with red eyes" in a "slumping" position by the tracks." [Schaffner, p. 1] When interviewed separately, the frightened witnesses' stories all matched.

On the night of July 12, Roger Kline, head of the Kline household, and his daughter Theresa were pitching hay in their barn. A passing freight train started blaring its horn at long and short intervals. Roger returned to the house, but Theresa found it odd the train kept sounding its horn and decided to investigate. She barely started toward the tracks when she came upon the glowing-eyed entity. This time it gave out a "high pitched scream." It was also accompanied by a foul smell. The young woman threw her flashlight at it and ran. No one thought to locate the train, so we will never know if the engineers were sounding off for Bighead on the tracks.

There were supposedly several other sightings of the creature, but details were not forthcoming. Even Police Chief Stortz admitted listening to half-a-dozen reports off the record.

After a reign of terror lasting a week or so, Bighead shambled back to whatever limbo it emerged from.

The Richland County Sheriff's Department acted rather hostilely toward the Bighead stories and witnesses. The lawmen insisted the whole sequence was a hoax, or, at best, that people saw some animal straying from the nearby Mohican State Forest.

That August two Cuyahoga Falls photographers, John and Jerry Nettles, arrived in Butler and went in search of Bighead. On the 27th they found and photographed a bear. Most witnesses insisted they had not mistaken a bear for Bighead.

Investigators Ron Schaffner and Earl Jones were impressed by the Kline children when they interviewed them in September. The brother and sister still seemed nervous when recalling their encounters. Eugene especially was familiar with domestic animals and wildlife, and he had noticed that the usual small animals were nowhere to be seen the week Bighead haunted the vicinity. Also, the local dogs barked for no apparent reason, and the local cattle seemed nervous.

If Eugene made up his encounter, he must have regretted it, as he had to endure much ridicule at school.

In many ways this series of reports is reminiscent of numerous other Bigfoot/ Sasquatch/ Big Hairy Monster stories of the seventies. The glaring difference is the description of the creature's head being larger than its body – and Sasquatch-type humanoids usually have quite hefty bodies! It is difficult even to visualize "Bighead" -- I can only think of some grotesque, oversized Mr. Potato-Head.

There are Native American tales concerning a monster called "The Great Head" or some variation thereof, but that entity is literally a colossal, disembodied head.

A unique story in the already strange field of cryptozoology, the Bighead tale is usually buried among Bigfoot reports when mentioned at all.

"Bighead Causes Stir in Butler Vicinity." Columbus (Ohio) Dispatch, Sunday, July 16, 1978.

Clark, Jerome. "A Summer Full of Monsters," Saga's UFO Report Vol. 6, no. 6 (January 1979), pp. 65-66.

Schaffner, Ron. "Richland County 'Bighead'," originally published in Creature Chronicles, later posted online at:
http://bfro.net/GDB/show_article.asp?id=323

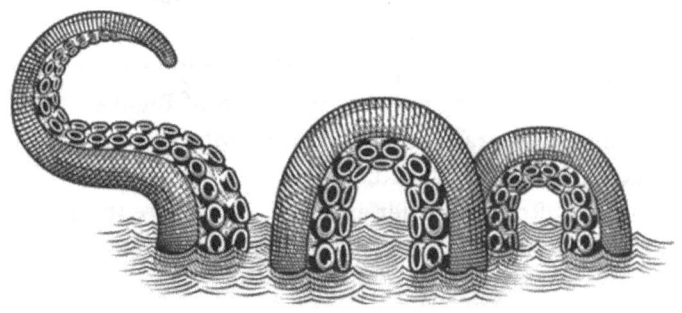

- Bogey-beast, Yorkshire, England (Padfoot)
- Leeds, Yorkshire: Bogey/phantom animal
- Padfoot, phantom beast of Leeds, Yorkshire
- Yorkshire: Bogey/phantom animal

Padfoot, the Yorkshire Bogey-Beast

"A phantom donkey with shaggy hair and 'eyes like saucers' is supposed to have haunted Leeds, England, for many years and earned the nickname 'Padfoot'. It was said to be missing one, possibly two legs."
John A. Keel, Strange Creatures from Time and Space

William Henderson, a nineteenth century British folklorist, describes Padfoot, a "bogey" that haunts the area around Leeds, in Yorkshire:

"He is described as about the size of a small donkey, black, with shaggy hair and large eyes like saucers; and he follows people by night, or waylays them in the road which they have to pass. A certain Yorkshire woman, called Old Sally Dransfield, the carrier from Leeds to Swillington, is a firm believer of the Padfoot. She declares that she has often seen it – sometimes rolling along the ground before her, like a woolpack – sometimes vanishing suddenly through a hedge. My friend, the Rev. J. C. Atkinson, of Danby, speaks of the Padfoot as a precursor of death . . . it was somewhat larger than a sheep, with long smooth hair. It was certainly safer to leave the creature alone, for a word or a blow gave it power over you." [Henderson, p.273]

The Reverend Sabine Baring-Gould, author of many books of history, religion, and folklore (and of the hymn "Onward Christian Soldiers") adds some notes to Henderson's account.

"A man in Horbury has lately seen 'the Padfooit. [sic],'" he writes. "He was going home by Jenkin, and he saw a white dog in the hedge. He struck at it, and the stick passed through it. Then the white dog looked at him, and it had 'great saucer e'en;' and he was so 'flayed' that he ran home trembling and went to bed, when he fell ill and died. The 'Padfooit' in this neighbourhood is a white dog like a 'flay-craw.' It goes sometimes on two legs, sometimes it runs on three."

Baring-Gould compares Padfoot to a Church Grim, which was a dog or boar buried alive "under the cornerstone of a church, that its ghost might haunt the churchyard, and drive off any who would profane it." In Sweden (the Kyrkogrim) and Denmark (the Kirkegrim) the animal used was a lamb, buried under the altar. A similar creature was the "grave-sow", the apparition of a pig buried alive in a churchyard.

You will note a bit of poor information transfer creeps in during the century between Henderson's and Keel's books: When I first read about "Padfoot" at the age of eleven, the image of a weird, three-legged donkey with saucer-eyes haunted me for years. The original source mentions ghostly dogs, sows, lambs, a "woolpack" – but no donkey. Padfoot is "about the size of a small donkey," he doesn't look like a donkey.

Henderson, William. Notes on the Folk-Lore of the Northern Counties of England and the Borders [Publications of the Folk-Lore Society, Vol. II] (London: W. Satchell Peyton and Co., 1879), pp. 273-274.

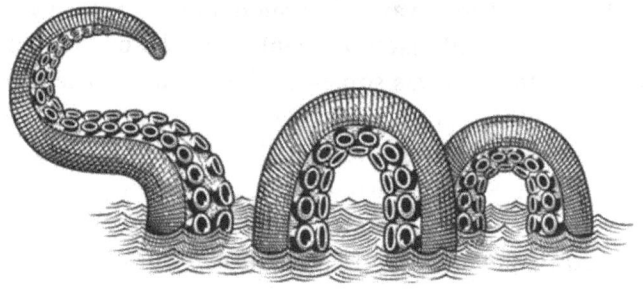

- Crossroads, snake-like entity seen near
- "Ouroboros" serpent encounters
- Pennsylvania: Giant phantom snake
- Snake-like creature haunts school/crossroads

The Pennsylvania Ouroboros

While Annie Whitney and Caroline Bullock collected folk-lore from Maryland and Pennsylvania in the 1920s, along with the usual witch and haunted house stories they received this truly eerie and unusual report from a local named William Johnson.

When William Johnson was a boy in Somerset County, Pennsylvania, the schoolhouse stood in the middle of a field in such an out-of-the-way location (even for a country school) that students lost much of each morning merely walking there. When Johnson was about sixteen (circa 1886), a new building was erected at Jenner (specifically "16 miles west of Johnstown, in Somerset Co., Jenner township, at the Cross roads"). One gray-haired old man warned that the crossroads were haunted; apparently, he was right. No sooner was the building completed than a terrifying entity manifested itself:

"Every month in the dark of the moon, an immense snake would appear. While its head and tail seemed to be hidden under the school-house, its long scaly body, over a foot in diameter, was laid across all public highways leading to the place. He [Johnson] said they often had evenings at the school-house, and spelling schools and the like, and had to get over the serpent before entering the house." [Whitney and Bullock, p. 193]

Johnson said the scales on the creature were "sharp" rather than slick, and that if anyone touched it in stepping over, he or she would "stick" to it and get thrown to the ground.

Not everybody could see the thing, but everyone could feel it, and even those blind to it were thrown down if they stepped on it. The creature was so long its body ran across several people's properties. One such landowner, a man named Frame, became so frightened that he sold his holdings and moved away. The purchaser, Joe Leverson, raised a large family on the "snake" property with no problems. The local children lost their fear of it as well. Occasionally men who had bolstered their courage with drink would attack the serpent with fence stakes or other weapons, to no avail. Along with Leverson, Johnson provided other witnesses' names, such as Joe Boyer and Jeremiah Mowery, a preacher, lifting his tale out of the "friend of a friend" category.

No one ever saw this bizarre apparition's head or tail-tip. It seemed to be a single, endless loop of serpentine body. Its immense size – the implication is that it must have been a mile or more long – calls to mind the colossal serpent Jormungandr from Norse mythology, which encircled the world.

William Johnson moved away from the area at age thirty. The "snake" still appeared at that time, around the turn of the twentieth century. No one he knew had any explanation for the entity. (I tried hard not to write "They could make neither head nor tail of it." I'm wondering now how old that phrase is – perhaps it evolved from encounters such as this?)

An old drawing of a dragonlike creature with a long neck and tail can be found in T. H. White's translation of The Bestiary. Both neck and tail terminate in small, doglike heads, and the front head holds the tail-head in its jaws. The text explains: "This is called an AMPHIVENA (Amphisbena) because it has two heads ... With one head holding the other, it can bowl along in either direction like a hoop."

This medieval monster sounds like the ancestor of the good old American Hoop Snake, a fabulous reptile that bites the end of its tail and rolls after its prey like a loose bicycle tire. The Bestiary in turn lifted its information from older sources like Physiologus and Pliny. (In an odd echo of the trouble people had in crossing the Pennsylvania entity, Pliny reported of the Amphisbena that "a pregnant woman will miscarry if she steps over it." [White, 177])

These legendary creatures, along with the aforementioned Jormungandr, are all permutations of the Worm Ouroboros, the serpent with its tail in its mouth, a universal symbol of wholeness, totality, and the cycles of nature. Yet it seems such things can be more than legends or symbols.

We might take a science-fictional turn and suggest that the Pennsylvania Ouroboros was a multi-dimensional being. Such a creature could project part of its body into our universe while the rest of it remained in a higher spatial dimension. Or we could draw upon occult lore. The trouble people had in merely stepping over the Ouroboros, along with its circular outline, remind one of the "magic circle" used for protecting oneself from or caging a spirit. Also, the spirit power of serpents in general is an ancient and universal belief. Perhaps in some primordial time the two were one: the Magic Circle personified as a huge curled snake, protecting or imprisoning what lay within its coils.

A sign like that would warn me away, certainly.

White, Terence H. Bestiary: A Book of Beasts (New York: Capricorn Books, 1960 [1954]).
Whitney, Annie Weston, and Caroline Canfield Bullock, "Folk-Lore from Maryland," in Memoirs of the American Folk-Lore Society, Volume 18, 1925, pp. 192-193.

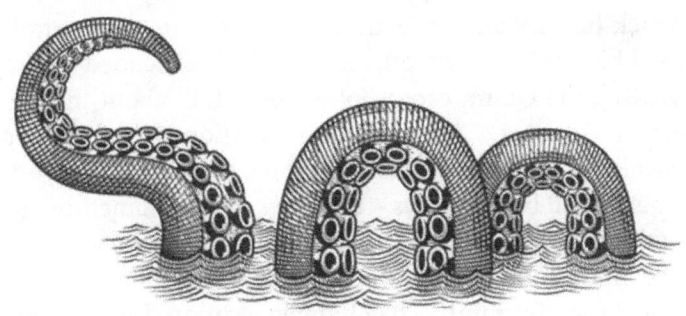

- Arch/trilithion/stone doorway shows other times/dimensions
- Arizona: Mysterious stone doorway
- Mysterious events occur near stone arch
- People and animals vanish through stone arch in the desert

The Portal in the Desert

In the mid-1950s Tacoma resident Ron Quinn, fresh out of the US military, and his brother Chuck, only 23 and 26 respectively, decided to go treasure hunting in Arizona. On March 20, 1956, they left Washington, their destination a tiny desert town called Arivaca, near the Tumacacori Mountains, thirty or so miles south of Tucson. They made camp in the hills nearby, and several weeks after their arrival, after sunset, they noticed "two large balls of blue-green light" descending behind the mountains. The lights appeared again the next evening. They were certain the glows were not airplane flares. The brothers made friends with a cowboy from the Arivaca Ranch named Louie Romero, who informed them that the lights had been seen since 1939.

One day the Quinns happened upon an elderly Native American whose truck had a flat. After they ferried him to a gas station and remounted his tire, the old man, named John, befriended the brothers. When visiting the Quinn camp, John would talk about the legendary treasures of the area. Chuck Quinn mentioned finding a strange archway, like a doorframe made of stone, near Peck Canyon. John seemed perturbed by this news – then he spoke of something far more amazing than Spanish gold.

In the mid-nineteenth century three young men of John's tribe went on a successful hunt. They happened upon the stone arch and, feeling jubilant, took turns jumping through the opening. One who jumped through did not emerge on the other side. Terrified, the others ran back to their village and told what happened.

People journeyed to the plateau to see the arch. Rocks and inanimate object thrown in popped out normally, but a live rabbit tossed through by an old woman vanished. John's own grandfather threw in a lizard which disappeared.

John had visited the arch many times, but nothing odd happened – except once, in 1948 or '49. He was riding past the archway as black storm clouds piled up, and he was shocked to see that, when looking through the "doorway", the sky was blue and cloudless. He dismounted and looked nearer, and, sure enough, though the same mountains appeared to stand behind the opening, they stood in a bright daylight scene with a clear blue sky. John rode off quickly.

The Quinns, accompanied by fellow treasure seekers Roy Purdie and Walt Fisher, returned to the site – a grueling trek up narrow canyons and steep hillsides to a wide plateau. "The archway stood perhaps seven feet in height by five in width," writes Quinn. "Its columns measured approximately 15 inches in diameter. It was made entirely of volcanic andesite." They threw stones into it, but nothing happened. Ron Quinn stuck his arm through, but Purdie warned him back. The arch appeared to be a natural formation, one of several geological oddities on the plateau.

Other strange events in the Arivaca area may or may not have been related to the arch:

Louie Romero and several other cowboys, out on a roundup, set up camp north of Arivaca Ranch. Late in the evening they heard the rumble of many horses' hooves and the neighing of a huge herd. They expected hundreds of wild equines to roar through their camp, but just as the pounding and noise reached them, it ceased as if turned off by a switch. They found no hoofprints in the morning.

Two cowboys out looking for a bull separated to cover more ground. As one studied the area with binoculars, a rock hit his hat. He looked around but saw no one. When he turned away another rock hit his shoulder. It couldn't have been his companion pulling a prank, because he was visible through the field glasses hundreds of yards away.

Only a few minutes later the same cowboy, descending a slope, spotted other riders in the distance. Through the binoculars, the strangers looked to be Spanish Conquistadors, complete with armor and weapons. The whole procession eventually shimmered like a mirage and faded away.

In 1957, three new treasure seekers made camp near Carreta Canyon. One evening they heard what sounded like rain on their tent. They emerged to find hundreds of tiny stones falling out of the clear sky onto their tent and truck – a classic fortean sky fall. The stones were warm to the touch, a detail often mentioned in such cases. They showed a whole sack full to Quinn and his fellows. "Most were the size of a pea, reddish brown, and resembled hematite, an iron ore."

After two years the Quinns returned to Washington. The call of treasure was hard to resist, however, so a year after that they moved to Tucson permanently, where it was easier to chase down the latest rumors. Upon hiking up to the "portal", however, they found that the arch lintel had collapsed. By the end of the century even the columns had toppled, leaving only stumps.

Yet perhaps that wasn't the end of the portal. In late 2003, two brothers, Mike and Jeff Kauffman, explored the plateau of the arch and found the structure's remains. On a later visit, however, they discovered a second arch, several hundred yards from the first – one never spotted by the Quinns or anyone else during dozens of explorations in the area. "It stood about 12 feet high and resembled a snake resting on a single column. The round opening below was approximately six feet in height." Perhaps it wasn't there before . . .

Ron Quinn believed both arches to be natural formations, somehow charged with an energy that distorted time and space. He thought most of the area's strange phenomena were the results of this distortion – hearing a horse stampede of another era or seeing Spanish soldiers of the 16th century through a hole in time. As for the strange lights and falling rocks – well, odd things happen in the desert. Oh – and he and his brother did end up finding a substantial amount of lost treasure.

Quinn, Ron, "The Mysterious Plateau," Fate Magazine Vol. 59, No. 3 (whole number 671), March 2006, pp. 18-25.
Ibid. Searching for Arizona's Buried Treasures: A Two Year Odyssey (Tucson, AZ: BZB Publishing, 2006).

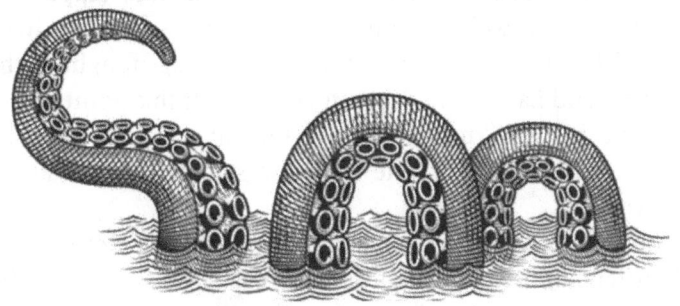

- Animal ghost
- Ghost dog
- New Jersey: Ghost dog
- Terhune, Albert Payson: Phantom dog story

Rex of Sunnybank

Albert Payson Terhune was famous for his books about dogs. The Terhunes and their many canine companions lived at Sunnybank, an estate near Pompton Lakes in northern New Jersey. Most of his animals, like Lad, Lady, Wolf, and Bruce, were thoroughbred collies, but in 1916 there lived at Sunnybank a dog named Rex. Rex was an unlikely cross between a collie and a bull terrier, "a giant, a freak, a dog oddly out of place among a group of thoroughbreds," as Terhune writes in Lad: A Dog. The two breeds did not mix well; although slavishly devoted to Terhune, Rex was unpredictable in many ways. He was larger and more muscular than even the big collies, with short, fawn-yellow hair and powerful, "killer" jaws.

Although Lad: A Dog was a partially fictionalized account of life at Sunnybank, Terhune's autobiographical Sunnybank: Home of Lad states that the story of Rex in Lad was essentially accurate. During a late blizzard in March 1916, Rex and a young collie, Wolf, slipped out the kitchen door and made their way into the nearby forest. Later the collie Lad slipped out as well and followed their trail. Apparently Rex injured (and angered) himself in the woods, because upon his return he attacked Lad for no apparent reason. The dogs fought at the edge of the estate, and Lad, being thirteen years old at this point, was losing. Terhune and his wife rushed out into the snow to help him, and Rex turned savagely on them. The writer was forced to kill Rex with a hunting knife.

In the fall of 1917, a no-nonsense businessman, Henry A. Healey, "a high official of the so-called Leather Trust," visited Sunnybank. He had seen Rex numerous times over the years. On this particular evening Healey and Terhune spent hours before the living room fire, just sitting in easy chairs and talking. Late in the night, as Healey put on his coat to leave, he remarked "I wish some animal cared for me as much as Rex cares for you," and described how the dog lay beside Terhune's chair, looking up at the writer. Terhune burst out:

"Good Lord, man! Rex has been dead for more than a year. You know that."

The businessman seemed dazed. He did know that, yet somehow he had forgotten. "Just the same," he finished, "I saw him lying on the floor beside you all evening!"

During the summer of 1918, the Reverend Appleton Grannis, an old college chum of Terhune's, spent a week at the estate. He had not visited for many years, and had never seen or heard of Rex. Neither did he know Healey. One blazing afternoon the Reverend and Terhune sat in the dining room drinking cold beer. The writer sat with his back to the tall windows opening onto the yard.

Eventually the men stood up to leave the room. The clergyman asked about the dog that had been "out there on the veranda looking in at you" for nearly an hour. He was certain it wasn't a collie, and he went on to describe Rex perfectly, down to "a crooked scar across his nose." "Which dog is he?"

Terhune could only stutter that he didn't know.

The writer also mentions a patch of the hallway "just to the left of the door of my study," where Rex always slept. Rather than walk straight into the room, both humans and dogs had to make a detour of several feet to avoid the animal. After Rex's death, the collie Bruce, whose "domain" was the study, would carefully step around Rex's "spot" on the way in or out. Terhune often tested this aversion before guests, "Ray Long and Sinclair Lewis and Bob Ritchie, among others." Bruce inevitably circled around the spot in the hall.

Bruce avoided Rex's "spot" for years to come, but no one else reported seeing Rex himself.

Terhune knew of no earlier ghost stories at his estate. In Sunnybank, he writes that he had no previous interest in ghosts and did not know anything about psychic phenomena. The fact that Rex looked markedly different from Terhune's thoroughbreds brings up an interesting point, however: There might have been other ghost dogs at Sunnybank, for all we know, but since they would have been collies, visitors would not have given them a second thought!

Taking a stab at rationality, the writer suggested that Healey might have "seen" Rex due to a "throwback of memory," and that Grannis somehow might have mis-seen a collie as a dog of a different size, color, and fur-type – "The sunlight may have been in the man's eyes." The impression from his narrative is that he didn't think much of either explanation.

This is not a spectacular ghost story, but it is interesting due to its association with Terhune's dog tales. Not so famous today, they were a world-wide sensation in the early twentieth century, read and adored even by soldiers in the muddy trenches of World War I. We shouldn't make too much about Healey's "forgetting" Rex was dead, though these curious cases of micro-amnesia seem to allow some phenomena to operate (as in phone calls from then dead, wherein the percipient "forgets" that the caller has recently died).

Terhune, Albert Payson. Lad: A Dog (New York: E. P. Dutton & Co., 1947 [1919]), pp. 263-283.
Ibid. Sunnybank: Home of Lad (New York: Grosset & Dunlap, 1934), pp. 120-130.

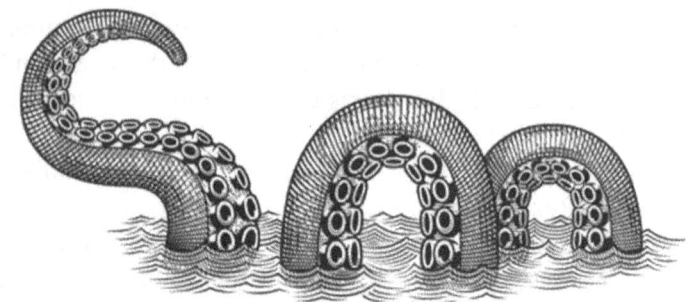

- California: Naked ghost by road
- Child saved by naked ghost
- Naked ghost by the side of the road
- Roadside ghost appears nude

The Roadside Ghost

On June 6, 1994, 24-year-old Christene Skubish began the seventy-five mile drive from Placerville, California, to Carson City, Nevada, to visit a friend. In the car with her was her three-year-old son, Nicky. Somewhere among the hills and curves of Highway 50 they disappeared from the road.

Deputy Rich Strasser of the El Dorado County Sheriff's Office, having small children of his own, followed the missing persons report closely. On June 10 he learned that Christene's family planned to search the long stretch of road themselves. Strasser decided to check gas stations around Placerville to learn if anyone remembered seeing the woman, as the only 24-hour stores on that trip were in Placerville itself.

At about 3:00 am on Saturday the 11th, Deborah Hoyt and her husband were driving west on Highway 50, returning home from Lake Tahoe. On a treacherous stretch of the highway known as Bullion Bend, eighteen miles outside Placerville, Deborah, looking out the passenger's side window, saw a naked woman lying on the shoulder of the road. The woman lay on her right side, her face toward the road but an arm over her head so that no features could be seen. Her legs were held together and slightly bent, the body about halfway to a fetal position. "I just started screaming and screaming," Mrs. Hoyt said later.

The Hoyts found a ranger station farther down the road and called for help. Sheriff's deputies and Highway Patrol cars crept along the highway but found nothing. Despite this, Deborah Hoyt was adamant about seeing a naked body.

Deputy Strasser heard about the Hoyt report around 5:00 am. He felt it might have something to do with the Skubish case, so he rolled out to Bullion Bend himself. By this time it was light enough to see small objects on the road, and Strasser spotted a small child's shoe on the asphalt. He stopped and walked along the shoulder, noting the embankment dropped away at a very steep angle. A few minutes later he discovered a car half hidden by the trees.

Christene Skubish had apparently fallen asleep at the wheel and veered off the road. Her car bounced almost onto its side for a moment, hitting a tree and losing most of its roof. It finally ran into a second tree and lay there, a total wreck, for five days.

Strasser clambered down and found mother and child in the wreck. Christene, still strapped in, appeared to have died quite recently. Nicky lay naked on the passenger's seat, having removed his clothing during one of the hot June days. The boy looked to be in worse shape than his mother, "emaciated, like the pictures you see of starving children in third world countries," in Strasser's words. At first he reported both dead, then he realized the toddler was breathing shallowly. He called for a rescue team, and the paramedics who responded took the child to the University of California Davis Medical Center.

By chance Christene's family came upon Strasser and the wreck before even the rescue team. Strasser had to restrain the dead woman's sister from climbing down to the crash site. In the end, though they mourned Christene's passing, they celebrated Nicky's miraculous survival. Deputy Strasser received the Sheriff's Department's Medal of Valor and later moved on to the Special Weapons and Tactics division.

Did Mrs. Hoyt see a crisis apparition -- Christene's spirit, trying to draw attention to her dying son? Journalists and humorists of the nineteenth century made many jokes about the absurdity of "ghost clothing" and other ghostly inanimate objects. Yet this report of a nude ghost is almost unique.

There is also a mystery surrounding Christene Skubish's physical remains. A medical examination revealed that Nicky's mother died at the moment of impact, a fact that astounded Rich Strasser. The temperature in that wooded region had varied from the nineties Fahrenheit during the afternoon to the forties at night, yet after five days there was no sign of decomposition, nor were insects or maggots associated with the body. In fact, "rescue personnel noted a strange, sweet odor in the air surrounding Christene's body." (Kovach, p. 26)

Some people suggested that Christene managed to crawl from the crash site up to the highway, where she was spotted by Debora Hoyt. Hoyt maintained that the woman she saw was naked. It seemed extremely unlikely that Christene could remove her seatbelt, then her clothes, crawl up the near-vertical slope to the highway -- then crawl back down again, dress again, and belt herself back into her wrecked vehicle. A moot point, as she died on impact five days earlier.

Others pointed to Nicky Skubish as the "ghost", but by that fifth day the toddler could not even move. "The doctors who saw Nicky said if I hadn't found him when I did, he would have died within another hour," as Deputy Strasser put it.

Although rare in ghostly tales, I have read of astral projection cases in which the person leaving his or her body perceives him/herself as naked. Five days after death, however, one would certainly classify Christene's appearance as a ghost instead of an astral traveler. The amazing preservation of her body and the "sweet" aroma surrounding it put one in mind of stories of saints and their "odor of sanctity." Perhaps we should call the Skubish case a miracle and leave it at that.

Kovach, Sue. Hidden Files: Law Enforcement's True Case Stories of the Unexplained and the Paranormal (Chicago: Contemporary Books, 1998), pp. 22-28, 200.

Unsolved Mysteries television series, "Highway Vision."

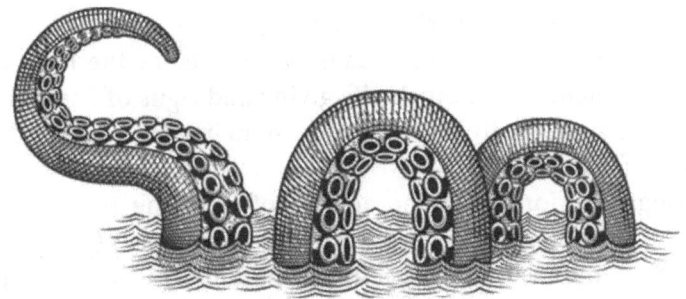

- Disappearance: Roanoke Colony (North Carolina)
- North Carolina: Roanoke colonists vanish
- Roanoke Colony disappearance

The Roanoke Colony

However much the civilization, character, and society of the USA owes to the English, the fact remains that England started late in the race to colonize the New World. This was due mainly to the superiority of Spanish naval power and Queen Elizabeth's desire to keep the peace in an era when Britannia definitely did not rule the waves. The few expeditions England sent across the Atlantic kept well to the north of Spanish holdings, and the results of these surveys did not encourage colonization. As historian David Stick put it, the Conquistadors wrested gold and treasure from the Incas and Aztecs, "while Canada seemed to yield only cod fish." [Stick, p. 22]

Nevertheless, men like Humphrey Gilbert, Francis Drake, Martin Frobisher, and Walter Raleigh pushed for an English foothold in the Americas, and in 1584, a charter was granted to Walter Raleigh to search out land that might be settled profitably.

On April 27, 1584, two ships sailed from Plymouth, Devonshire, one under Philip Amadas and the other under Arthur Barlowe. On July 4 they reached the North American mainland, but they were forced to sail 120 miles north along what are now the Carolinas before they could find anything like a bay or river mouth.

Once they anchored, three days passed before the local natives approached them. After much gift-giving and signs of friendship, the Englishmen were finally introduced to Wingina, the chief of this seaside land of Wingandacon.

Though caution ruled the actions of both the natives and the English, and though a few awkward moments arose (Wingina tried frequently to induce the Europeans to join raids against enemy tribes), the first extended contact between Englishmen and native North Americans went well. "Wingandacon" was a prosperous country (at least where natural resources were concerned), so when Amadas and Barlowe returned to England, the Elizabethan era's supreme historian, Richard Hakluyt, wasted no time in writing a book, the Discourse of Western Planting, outlining the need for an English presence in the New World. (Among his reasons: the many unemployed workers of England could be sent there.)

The Queen agreed to Hakluyt's plan for colonization. Thus, it was that in April 1585 a fleet of seven vessels departed England, their goal Wingandacon, re-named "Virginia" in honor of Elizabeth I, the Virgin Queen. [Note that "Virginia" referred to a vast chunk of North America; Roanoke and the Outer Banks lie off the coast of present-day North Carolina.] Sir Richard Grenville, a knight and naval commander, was in charge of the expedition.

The course to America usually led south to Africa and then west to the West Indies, following the currents, eventually reaching the Gulf Stream off the coast of Florida. Not long after embarking, however, a storm scattered the fleet, sinking one vessel. The Tiger, Richard Grenville's personal vessel, dropped anchor off Puerto Rico hoping the ships would regroup. After a week, the Elizabeth, a second ship of the expedition, did show up. The Englishmen took on water and supplies, built a thirty-foot boat from the local trees (necessary to ply the shallow waters of the Carolinas), and sailed on. They reached the Outer Banks of North Carolina on June 26.

The Tiger ran aground, losing most of her cargo. This was a poor reception for Grenville in America. He was surprised and pleased, however, to find thirty Englishmen waiting for him on the island of

Croatan. The Lion, another ship of the fleet, had deposited them ashore and left to plunder Spanish ships.

Grenville led fifty men onto the mainland. They visited several native villages and were received in friendship. There was one unfortunate incident, however: Someone stole a silver cup from the Englishmen, and Grenville stormed into a village called Aquascogoc, demanding its return. When the natives did not comply, in the words of the Tiger's log, "we burnt, and spoyled their corne, and Towne, all the people becoming fledde." [Stick, p. 83]

Eventually the Englishmen sailed north to Roanoke Island, where they were greeted by Granganimeo, King Wingina's brother. It was decided the English settlement would be constructed not too distant from Wingina's village.

On August 5, four months after leaving Plymouth, John Arundell sailed for Britain to report on the expedition's progress. On August 25, Grenville himself departed on the Tiger. He would not have left unless work on the fortifications were well under way, so the Roanoke colony was becoming a reality.

Ralph Lane, a military officer and former Member of Parliament, sent two letters, dated September 3 and 8, back to England on a third ship. Like Amadas and Barlowe, Lane praised the natural riches of the New World, the abundance of copper ore, and "the goodliest soile under the cope of heaven." Who could resist it?

Three hundred men were supposed to remain at the colony. Strangely, only one hundred seven were left to populate the settlement. Perhaps this was due to the Tiger's supplies being lost; no one knows.

Grenville planned to return by next Easter with more supplies, tools, weapons, and men. Meanwhile, Ralph Lane, the interim leader, and 106 men had the next seven months to survive.

It was too late in the year to plant crops, but Wingina's subjects supplied the colony with fish and corn. Thomas Hariot, a scholar, teacher, and linguist, and John White, a naturalist and artist, helped in communicating with the natives and learning about the surrounding countryside. Unfortunately, the only intelligence obtained by these wise men that interested Ralph Lane was the rumor that a mountain range to the west abounded in gold.

Most of the diaries, letters, and notes of the first Roanoke colony were lost within a year, so the specifics of their activities are unknown. They did, at least, survive the winter. As spring approached, Lane mounted an expedition up the Chowan River with thirty men on small boats. The Englishmen passed into the territory of Menatonon, an old and crippled but powerful chieftain. Lane sensed the elderly leader knew much about the country and its inhabitants, so with typical European arrogance, he took the aging chief prisoner.

Menatonon did reveal quite a bit of information about the lands bordering the Atlantic. He might have anyway if Lane had visited in friendly terms; we cannot know. Unfriendly tribes certainly existed. It was now March, however, and Lane expected to be reinforced by several hundred men with guns and cannon. In the English soldier's mind, a show of force would defuse hostility across the board, while diplomacy was chancy and time-consuming.

Menatonon spoke of a huge bay to the northeast (Chesapeake Bay), which Lane decided would make the perfect spot for a permanent colony. He planned an expedition to seek out this bay – but then the old chief told him of the mountains of gold at the headwaters of the Roanoke River. So, Lane and his thirty men sailed back down the Chowan and up the Roanoke.

Somehow Menatonon's people warned the tribes ahead of Lane that the conquerors were approaching: Though the Englishmen found villages, the inhabitants – and their food – were gone. The expedition ran low on supplies, but gold fever was strong in them. At a point about 160 miles upriver, when they were weak with hunger, the native warriors set upon them. The Englishmen suffered no casualties, but they retreated, their only food on the trip back a stew made from two guard dogs they had brought along.

Easter had come and gone by the time they returned to Roanoke. There were no relief ships to be seen.

Wingina, the chief who had welcomed the Amadas/Barlowe expedition, may have had second thoughts regarding his new neighbors. He undoubtedly knew what had happened with

Menatonon, and feeding the Europeans was putting a strain on his own people.

Ralph Lane claimed that Wingina entered into a conspiracy with several nearby tribes, their goals being to starve out the invaders and finally slay them, but Lane needed someone to blame for not achieving his objectives. At any rate, Lane arranged a meeting with Wingina and some lesser weroances (local chiefs), and as soon as everyone was seated, hidden soldiers emerged to shoot the tribal leaders.

At this same time, Sir Francis Drake finished a series of daring raids against Spanish holdings in the Caribbean, and he grew curious as to how the Roanoke venture was proceeding. On June 8, 1586, an astounded lookout spotted Drake's twenty-seven ships off Cape Hatteras.

Drake offered the colonists a choice: He would leave a ship, experienced sailors, guns, powder, clothing, and a month's supply of food, or he would ferry the whole population back to Europe. The colonists were not timid; they chose to stay, confident that Richard Grenville was on the way. As men and supplies were being transferred, however, a fierce Atlantic storm scattered Drake's fleet.

The storm lasted three days. Some vessels were blown so far out to sea, they could only flee before the wind back to England. The Francis, the ship to be left with the colonists, was never seen again. Several smaller boats and most of the supplies were lost.

The colonists changed their minds. Even after the storm a boat almost capsized in the angry waters of the Outer Banks, and all the diaries, letters, and reports of the colony were jettisoned as the sailors struggled to keep afloat. The battered fleet departed on June 18, in such haste that three colonists out foraging for food were left behind, their fates unknown.

Sir Richard Grenville had not been idle, but he had trouble raising money for another expedition. After he did set sail, he could not resist the call of the buccaneer, and he spent some weeks chasing down Spanish cargo ships.

At least Grenville sent one vessel, loaded with supplies, on ahead. It arrived off the North Carolina coast only days after Drake's fleet departed. The supply ship sailed up and down the coast for a few days, but the crew saw no one. Finally, it left.

Two weeks after this, Grenville himself arrived at the Outer Banks. He and his men found no one at the Roanoke fort. Reportedly they found the hanged bodies of an Englishman and an Indian – possibly one of the three forgotten soldiers and a native friendly with the treacherous invaders.

The men of the relief ships searched for days, then they left, too.

And here comes a footnote of history that magnifies the strangeness of Roanoke. "When his men stormed Santo Domingo and Cartagena, Drake rescued a very large number of slaves and Indians from Spanish clutches," writes historian Karen Kupperman. David Beers Quinn, in The Roanoke Voyages, 1584-1590, puts the number of these "liberated" persons at up to five hundred. In order to make room for the returning colonists, it is believed that Drake deposited the slaves and natives ashore. Remember, the supply ship Grenville sent ahead arrived at the Outer Banks only days after Drake left, and Grenville's main force showed up two weeks after that. "Neither relief expedition mentioned anything about the three men Lane left behind or about the several hundred former captives Drake is thought to have deposited in Roanoke." [Kupperman, p. 93] Slaves, prisoners, Indians or not – they really had no place to go. Even the native captives would have been of Caribbean origin – as out of place here as the Europeans.

Ian Morfitt, in a Fortean Times article, suggests that the prisoners might have crept off across the country, eventually becoming the Melungeons, a mysterious race of people in eastern Tennessee. [Morfitt, p. 27] It seems unlikely that such a huge group could have organized and marched off into the unknown lands of North America so quickly. For that matter, it seems unlikely that they would have dispersed in all directions, been assimilated into the local tribes, or been annihilated to the last man (leaving no bodies or signs of violence) in a few days. The fate of this multitude "is one of the many mysteries surrounding the entire Roanoke enterprise that remain to this day." [Kupperman, p. 93]

Grenville did not wish to give up Roanoke. He left fifteen men with enough provisions for two years at the fort, basically to "hold" most of North America in the name of England until new settlers could be sent. The prospects for these "interim colonists" looked bleak.

On January 7, 1587, Sir Walter Raleigh and the artist John White drew up a document, "The Governour and Assistants of the Cittie of Ralegh in Virginia," outlining plans for a permanent settlement in America, with White as its governor. This time entire families were to sail for the New World; as an incentive each household was to receive 500 acres of land when circumstances would allow. One hundred fifty men, plus their wives and children, signed on.

On April 26 a ship named the Lyon (not to be confused with the Lion), accompanied by two smaller vessels, sailed from Plymouth. The voyage started poorly; one ship foundered off Portugal, and when the Lyon stopped at St. Croix for supplies, many colonists ate "green apples" and drank from a stagnant pond, both of which made them terribly ill. On July 22, however, the two remaining ships reached the Outer Banks.

The plan was to build the "Cittie of Ralegh" on Chesapeake Bay, but when White and forty men went ashore to check on the Roanoke fort, Captain Simon Fernando of the Lyon refused to pick them up again. He had no interest in colonizing, it seemed; he wished only to sail off and plunder Spanish treasure ships.

There was nothing White could do; the sailors obeyed Fernando. Thus, Roanoke became the "Cittie of Ralegh."

White and his men inspected Roanoke. There was no sign of the fifteen men left the previous year, though they did find one human skeleton. According to Governor White's journal, "wee founde the forte rased downe, but all the houses standing unhurt." Construction began immediately on new fortifications and houses for individual families.

No native peoples were seen for the first week – until a man named George Howe went out by himself to catch crabs. Then a group of warriors appeared and slew him. Fortunately, White numbered among his personnel Manteo, a Croatan Indian who had been to England. With Manteo acting as ambassador, the Englishmen convinced the Croatan tribe that they came in peace, and that they hoped both parties could forget the violence of the past.

Eventually Manteo's people revealed that the fifteen men left behind had been attacked by Wingina's tribesmen. Two had been killed, but the others had sailed off in a small boat. Thus we can add thirteen more men of Roanoke whose fates remain unknown.

White sent word to other tribes that the Englishmen wished to dwell near them in peace, yet at the same time a group of colonists set out to attack the warriors who killed George Howe. This was so out of character for White that some historians believe the assault was launched without his knowledge. To make matters worse, the Englishmen attacked the wrong group – they shot several Croatans by mistake. Manteo, though, interceded for the white men again.

After this, the relationships between the native peoples and the Europeans seemed to run smoother. Governor White's daughter, Eleanor White Dare, gave birth to a girl, who was named Virginia. She was the first child of English descent born in North America.

Simon Fernando, amazingly, still rode at anchor off the Outer Banks, having spent nearly a month simply unloading colonists and supplies. As if he weren't already anxious to leave, storm season approached. The colonists insisted Governor White embark with Fernando and return to England. They needed more tools and edibles, not to mention a more obedient ship's captain, and they felt White was the only one with the authority to bring this about. White was reluctant to leave his duties and his family (especially his granddaughter, only a few days old), but he gave in.

It was agreed that, should the colonists leave Roanoke Island, they were to carve the name of their destination on some conspicuous tree. If they left due to an attack by natives, Spaniards, or others, they were to add a Maltese cross to the message.

Bad lucked plagued Governor White from the moment of his departure. Several of Fernando's men died in a freak accident even as they sailed; others were stricken with disease. Storms blew the expedition's two ships off course, fogs hid the sun, and the vessels ran out of beer, wine, and water. Somehow, they reached Ireland.

White returned to England in October 1587. At this time King Philip II of Spain was assembling the largest armada in history, his goal all out war with England. All English ships were needed for the island nation's defense. Despite this, White managed to secure two small ships, the Brave and the Roe, under Captain Arthur Facy, which set sail on April 27, 1588. Captain Facy, however, was even more determined to go looting than Captain Fernando. The following several weeks were spent chasing ships, boarding ships, and being chased by ships. The Brave and the Roe managed to lose sight of each other along the way.

A French vessel attacked the Brave, and most of the crew were killed or wounded. White himself was hit by sword, pike, and bullet. He watched helplessly as the French looted all the supplies meant for Roanoke.

Somehow the crippled and undermanned Brave limped back to England. John White felt ill in mind, spirit, and body. Yet soon afterwards the English navy defeated the Spanish Armada.

It was not until March 20, 1590, that another fleet sailed for the Roanoke colony. Among the vessels were the Hopewell, the Little John, and the Moonlight, and the man in charge of them, John Watts, was no captain but the representative of a board of merchants, his mission, to make a profit from the venture. He made no secret of his intent to go privateering. John White could only ride along as they boarded ships, raided Caribbean islands, and fled larger sea-borne forces. At one point the wind died, and the small fleet floated dead in the water for eleven days. The English raiders' take was unimpressive, so finally, in late July, Watts agreed to sail for Virginia.

Even now the forces of nature seemed to conspire against Governor White. The weather turned so bad the voyagers could not make landfall for two weeks.

It began to look to the crew of the expedition as if Roanoke were cursed. On August 16, Governor White finally stepped ashore in North

America again. He and his landing party spotted smoke in the distance, and they wasted the day trying unsuccessfully to locate the source. On August 17, high waves swamped one landing boat and overturned another. Seven men drowned. "The mischance did so much discomfort the saylors, that they were all of one mind not to goe any further to seeke the planters," wrote White. It took all the persuasiveness of White and Captain Cooke of the Hopewell to make the near-mutinous crew land on Roanoke Island.

A party finally beached near the settlement. "As we entered up the sandy banke upon a tree, in the very browe thereof were curiously carved these faire Roman letters CRO: which letters presently we knew to signifie the place, where I should find the planters seated."

At the colony proper White found new houses built, and the whole surrounded by a new palisade. Inside the walls they discovered more carvings on a post near the entrance: "5. Foote from the ground in fayre Capitall letters was graven CROATOAN without any cross or sign of distress."

Inside the fort bars of lead and iron, guns, shot, and other heavy items lay scattered in the high weeds. Several chests, buried for safekeeping, had been dug up, their contents scattered. White found his own belongings "rotten and spoyled with rayne." There was no trace of anyone, dead or alive.

It was August 18, 1590 – by an eerie coincidence, little Virginia Dare's third birthday. The landing party left. It seems odd that they searched only a few hours after trying three years to get there, but the tree carvings indicated the colony had left for Croatan Island.

More bad weather hit. The Hopewell was lifted onto a sandbank more than once. The men of the Moonlight gave up completely and sailed for the Caribbean. The Hopewell escaped the sand only to be blown out to sea. The crew's food and fresh water being low, they made for the Azores instead of Croatan.

At the Azores, amazingly, they found the Moonlight (which had not quite made it to the Caribbean) and the Little John (which had seen great success in privateering). It was all too much for the men of the Hopewell. They refused to sail back to Virginia. Governor White could only hope his people, his family, and his granddaughter were alive and safe on Croatan. But none of the Roanoke colonists were ever seen again.

No one attempted to learn more about the colony's fate for the next twenty years, not until after the founding of Jamestown in 1607. Native peoples all around the area passed on rumors of Roanoke soldiers being held prisoner somewhere, or of people seen far inland who carried crosses or dressed like Europeans, or of some tribe somewhere that had slaughtered all the colonists.

The seemingly obvious answer to the riddle was that the settlers did precisely what they agreed on: They picked a new location, carved the name on the post, and left. The problem is, no remains or artifacts pointing to English occupancy have been found on Croatan.

Others have suggested that Spaniards found the colony and slaughtered or enslaved the inhabitants. While it is true the Spanish resented the English presence in North America, according to David Stick, they had no luck finding the settlement: "[A]s late as 1600 the Spaniards were still looking for the English colony, which they believed to be on Chesapeake Bay, rather than Roanoke Island." [Stick, p. 238]

The late Wingina's people had no fond memories of the English intruders, and other tribes were outright hostile to Europeans. Inevitably, it was suggested that native peoples of the Carolina coast slew the colonists.

If the Roanoke settlers were slain, though, the deed was done elsewhere, since White found only deserted buildings and no corpses or graves. Melvin Robinson, in his book Riddle of the Lost Colony (1946), theorized that modern searchers cannot find any clues as to the fate of the colony because they never colonized Roanoke Island to begin with! The actual location of the fortified settlement, according to him, was on Cedar Island, far to the southwest; somehow, over the centuries, the names were confused. Few people accept this theory, because the remains of fortifications that would match the colony's have been found on Roanoke, while no such remains have been discovered on Cedar Island.

Some researchers claim that modern descendants of various tribes

– the Croatan, the Doeg, the Delaware, and the Shawnee, among others – share with the colonists family names, or physical characteristics (such as gray eyes), or linguistic features (native words that sound suspiciously like their Elizabethan English equivalents). Therefore the colonists must have been absorbed into native culture centuries ago. However, plenty of other English people, and certainly English words, were assimilated by the nations of the east coast as the generations passed.

In this writer's opinion, it is a mistake to think of the Roanoke colonists as a single entity. If they left the settlement willingly, they may have meant to travel to Croatan, but circumstances probably dictated that they split into two or more groups. If nothing else, finding food for one-hundred-plus people had been a major problem even during Ralph Lane's stay. Families with children, trying to sail small boats or hike through unfamiliar wilderness would find it even more difficult. Remnants of the colony may have ended up with the Croatan – and the Delaware, the Doeg, and others besides. Some might even have reached Tennessee and become the Melungeons.

Is a "general dispersion" of people the answer? "No one really knows – and very likely no one ever will. The fate of Raleigh's colonists remains as much a mystery as before." [Stick, p. 246]

Kupperman, Karen Ordahl. Roanoke: The Abandoned Colony (Savage, MD: Rowman & Littlefield Publishers, 1984).
Morfitt, Ian, "Meet the Melungeons," Fortean Times no. 106 (Feb. 1998), pp. 24-27.
Quinn, David Beers. Roanoke Voyages, 1584-1590, Vol. I (New York: Dover Publications, 1991).
Stick, David. Roanoke Island: The Beginnings of English America (Chapel Hill, NC: University of North Carolina Press, 1983).

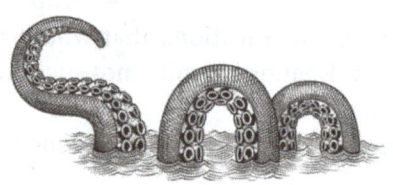

- Bierce, Ambrose – "Mysterious Disappearances"
- Leamington Spa, UK: Strange disappearance

The Running Man

Having mentioned Ambrose Bierce's "Mysterious Disappearances" under the entries for David Lang and Oliver Lerch, I might as well touch upon the third sub-story, "An Unfinished Race."

James Burne Worson, a shoemaker in Leamington Spa, Warwickshire, England, enjoyed his liquor. Sometimes, however, he would make bets of questionable wisdom. On September 3, 1873, he bet some acquaintances that he could run to Coventry and back at one go – a round-trip Bierce describes as 40 miles, but is closer to 23. Worson started out at once, followed by three men in a cart: Barham Wise, a draper, Hamerson Burns, a photographer, and a third man whose name has not been recorded.

Worson jogged along determinedly for several miles, because he actually was in good condition. The three men behind jeered him or cheered him as the whim struck them. Bierce writes:

"Suddenly — in the very middle of the roadway, not a dozen yards from them, and with their eyes full upon him — the man seemed to stumble, pitched headlong forward, uttered a terrible cry and vanished! He did not fall to the earth — he vanished before touching it. No trace of him was ever discovered." [Bierce, p. 88]

The three followers searched the ground for a while, but there had been no place for Worson to go. They returned to Leamington and reported the incident to the police – and they were promptly arrested. The men were of good standing, however, and, unlike Worson, sober at the time. The police could find no sign of foul play – nor could they find Worson. Eventually the three betting men were released. "If they had something to conceal, their choice of means is certainly one of the most amazing ever made by sane human beings," Bierce concludes.

Rodney Davies, who did extensive research on Mr. and Mrs.

Cumpston and other cases (see "Voids"), traveled to Leamington Spa to check out this account. He discovered that the records of the Leamington Spa Borough Police Force had long been destroyed. The local trade directories and postal directories for the 1870s mentioned no James Worson, Barham Wise, or Hamerson Burns – but Davies admits they may not have actually lived in Leamington. Neither the Royal Leamington Spa Courier nor the London Times carried the story. (Strangely enough, however, Davies ran into Mr. and Mrs. Cumpston again, in the papers for December 11 and beyond. Maybe 1873 was a year for disappearances.)

What Davies did learn, to his surprise, was that Ambrose Bierce lived in England in 1873 – and in Leamington itself from spring 1874 until August 1875.

Davies concludes that Bierce "might have heard about it by word of mouth when he lived at Leamington," and it is possible he changed the principle character's names for his story (as he was accused of doing in the David Lang case). Or perhaps "An Unfinished Race" was just a work of fiction; take your pick.

Bierce, Ambrose, "Mysterious Disappearances," in Ghost and Horror Stories of Ambrose Bierce (New York: Dover Books, 1964), pp. 86-91.

Davies, Rodney. Supernatural Vanishings (New York: Sterling Publishing Company, 1996), pp. 130-132.

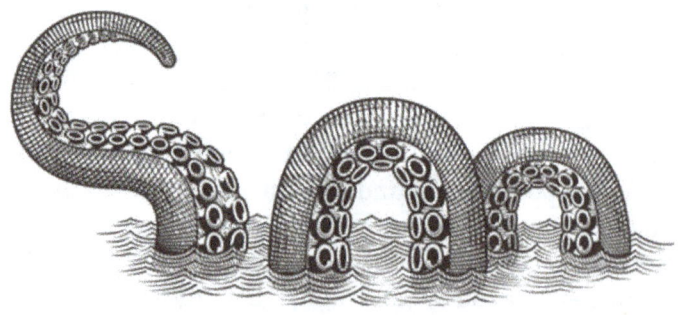

- Aliens dancing in road
- Dancing creatures in road
- Indiana: Dancing silver beings
- Silvery creatures dancing in road

Silver Dancing Flying . . . Things

Late in the evening of October 22, 1973, De Wayne and Donna Donathan were returning home from a visit to Mrs. Donathan's mother. As they drove around a hill only a block from their house in Hartford, Indiana, they spotted what they thought were two children in the road ahead. Donna Donathan, behind the wheel, brought their vehicle to a halt about 30 feet from the figures. They were not children, but thin, shiny-silver humanoid creatures about 4 feet tall.

"Their feet would come up slowly, one at a time and the arms would flop funny," she told APRO investigator Don Worley. "They moved slower than humans and their feet and arms would go up funny." The creatures' arms "flopped" and did not seem to end in hands. Their feet were "square", as if they wore silver boxes for shoes.

Donna screamed and swerved onto the shoulder to get around the things. De Wayne, who was holding the couple's baby, said he thought they were children wrapped up in aluminum foil at first. Despite the approaching car, they left the road leisurely, "in a slow, skipping motion with arms swinging slowly." Slow or not, when Mr. Donathan looked back a few seconds later, the beings had gotten behind a fence and into a nearby cornfield.

The couple turned around after a minute or two and drove back down the street (State Road 26). The creatures were gone, but the Donathans proceeded to the Hartford City sheriff's office to report the matter.

A state trooper (who wished to remain anonymous) drove out to the area. Deputy Sheriff Ed Townsend and a wrecker driver, Gary Flattner, soon followed in Townsend's patrol car. At the site of the encounter, the latter two heard a "high frequency sound." Eventually they all returned to the sheriff's office, but the state trooper drove out again, and Flattner followed alone, driving his wrecker. Some miles to the southeast of the initial encounter, Flattner stopped as a strange migration of rabbits, housecats, a raccoon, and an opossum flowed across the road. He grew aware of the high frequency sound again, and he spotted the silver beings.

The entities were in a field north of the road. Flattner stopped and turned his spotlight on the creatures; the reflection from their suits (if they were wearing suits) was so bright he had to shut the light off again. The creatures' heads were oval, without ears or facial features, the chin areas drawing out into gas-mask-type hoses that ran down to their lower chests. Theirs arms "just seemed to end," without hands. Their feet or shoes were indeed like boxes, about 3 x 6 x 2 inches. After being hit by the light, the creatures jumped in place in slow motion, as if skipping rope. On the fourth jump, the creatures kept going. They sailed off into the night, never to be seen again.

Both Flattner and the Donathans also saw tiny, flashing red lights to the north but did not know if they were significant. Despite the lights and despite the fact that one of the biggest UFO flaps of all time took place in October 1973, there was no indication that the silver dancers were UFO occupants.

Lorenzen, Coral and Jim. Encounters with UFO Occupants (New York: Berkeley Medallion Books, 1976), pp. 219-222.

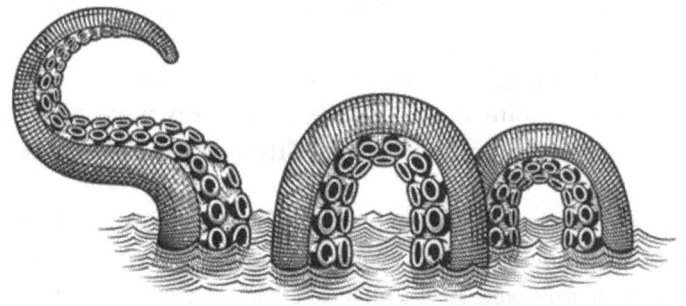

- Dinosaur in Irish lake?
- Ireland: Lake monster
- Lake monster resembles Theropod dinosaur
- Sraheens Lough, Ireland -- monster

The Sraheens Lough "Dinosaur"

A series of encounters often shelved with Loch Ness-type monsters took place at Sraheens Lough, a lake on Achill Island, which almost touches the west coast of Ireland. On May 1, 1968, sheep farmer Michael McNulty and football player John Cooney were driving past the Lough from the tiny village of Keel to the town of Achill Sound. Suddenly something lurched across the road in front of their car. "The remarkable thing," writes Swedish author Jan-Ove Sundberg in The INFO Journal, "was that the two men gave an exact description of a supposedly extinct, prehistoric animal -- a flesh-eating dinosaur by the name of Coelophysis!"

The Coelophysis (Greek for "hollow form", referring to its birdlike bones) was a bipedal carnivorous dinosaur -- a theropod -- of moderate size, extinct since the Triassic era, 225 million years ago. [1]

Sundberg read about the monster in John Keel's Strange Creatures from Time and Space and took the trouble to fly to Ireland and track down more witnesses. Gay Dever of Keel had been only fifteen years of age in June 1968 when he went bicycling past Sraheens Lough. "Crawling out of the water came the strangest animal I have ever seen," he told the Swedish writer. "It was much bigger than a horse, black in color with a long, slender, sheep-looking head, long neck and tail. It moved like a kangaroo and its hind legs were bigger than its front ones. When the nasty looking thing entered the beach, I left the area as fast as I could."

Only two nights later, two young women, Bernie Sweeney and Mary Callaghan, were hitchhiking home from a dance. Their route took them along the road by the lake. Just as a car stopped for them, Bernie glanced toward the lake and saw "a big, shiny and black 'something' that raced forward with speed from the south side and towards her." She screamed and ran. The driver jumped out and grabbed Mary's arm, asking what was wrong. Mary also spotted the monster and could do nothing but point in shock. The driver only saw something vanish back into the water.

A group of geological students from Australia visited the Lough in 1969. They didn't find the monster, but they discovered, significantly, that the lake is actually the crater of an extinct volcano (with an entrance, perhaps, to hidden caves?). To this day the surrounding farmers claim that three or four sheep a week vanish from the mountains near Sraheens Lough. [2]

1. Lambert, David, Ultimate Dinosaur Book (New York: Dorling Kindersley, 1993), pp. 46-47.
2. Sundberg, Jan-Ove, "Monster of Sraheens Lough," in INFO Journal Vol. 5, no. 6 (March 1977), pp. 2-9.

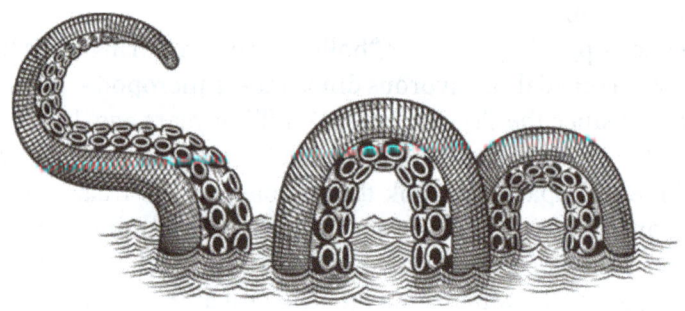

- Cherokee Indians – legendary creature
- North Carolina: Living UFO
- UFO as living being

Star-Creatures of the Cherokee

Unidentified Flying Objects possess a mobility other phenomena lack. Ghosts normally haunt a fairly small area. A Sasquatch can hike over the land, and a sea monster can swim across the ocean, but UFOs can potentially visit any point on the globe. It should come as no surprise that other cultures in other times have spotted strange things in the air.

Anthropologist and ethnologist James Mooney was famous for his works preserving the traditions of Native Americans. His book Myths of the Cherokee could not have been produced without the help of A'yun'ini, or "Swimmer", a "genuine aboriginal antiquarian and patriot," from whom nearly three-fourths of the Cherokee folktales were obtained. [p. 236] One of Swimmer's tales concerned Star-Creatures, another species of living UFO to accompany Nevada's "Flying Clam."

"One night a hunting party camping in the mountains noticed two lights like large stars moving along the top of a distant ridge." The lights eventually disappeared over the summit. They appeared for the next two nights as well, following the same path, and on the morning of the fourth day the hunters climbed the ridge:

"[A]fter searching for some time, they found two strange creatures about so large (making a circle with outstretched arms), with round bodies covered with fine fur or downy feathers, from which small heads stuck out like the heads of terrapins. As the breeze played upon these feathers showers of sparks flew out."

The hunters carried the creatures to their camp, intending to take them back to their village. At night, the strange beings glowed brightly. They caused no trouble and kept quiet, but on the seventh night of captivity "they suddenly rose from the ground like balls of fire and were soon above the tops of the trees." The Cherokee hunters realized they were stars come to earth. [p. 257-258]

Mooney, James. Myths of the Cherokee (Nashville, TN: Charles and Randy Elder, 1982). Originally published in the Nineteenth Annual Report of the Bureau of American Ethnology (1900).

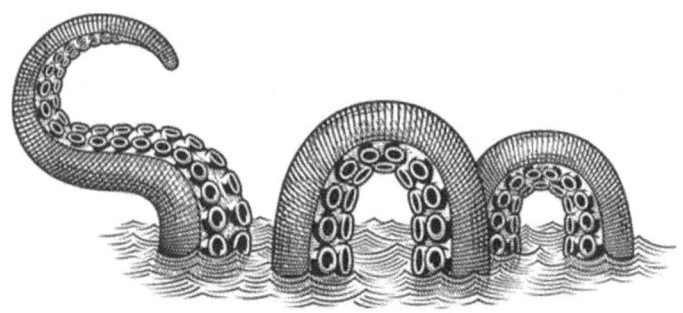

- Animals, talking
- Argentina: Bear-like creature
- Liverpool (UK): Talking cat-like creature
- Michigan: Strange animal abducts girl
- Scotland: Foxlike apparition
- Talking animals
- Washington state: Talking bear
- Zooforms (animal-like entities)

The Talking Bear and Other Animals not Acting like Animals

"It was told in the New York World, July 29, 1908 -- many petty robberies, in the neighborhood of Lincoln Avenue, Pittsburgh --

detectives detailed to catch the thief. Early in the morning of July 26th, a big, black dog sauntered past them. 'Good morning!' said the dog. He disappeared in a thin, greenish vapor."
 --Charles Fort, Wild Talents

Over the past several years, former law enforcement officer David Paulides has documented hundreds of missing person cases in wild areas and national parks in a series of books called Missing 411. Critics argue that it is only natural for the occasional hiker, hunter, or camper to get lost or die in the wilderness, but Paulides outlines specific criteria that place these missing person accounts beyond the norm. One of the signs of an extraordinary disappearance has to do with animals.

I don't know whether to think of this aspect of disappearances as amusing in a Disney-ish way or as exceptionally creepy. I refer to the subset of missing people (mostly children) who, when located, describe seeing -- or who were seen by witnesses in the vicinity of -- animals that do not act like normal animals. As a matter of fact, witnesses often have trouble identifying the species of the creature in question, though they are usually described as dog, wolf, or bear-like. The poster girl for this phenomenon was Katie Flynn of Wallaha, Michigan.

Henry Flynn ran a lumber mill near Wallaha, and a large part of the operation consisted of hauling logs up to the sawmill at the top of a hill, depositing the load, then going back down for more logs. Three-year-old Katie would ride one of the horses on the way up, and as the men unloaded the lumber, she would trot down a separate trail through the trees and pop out at the base of the hill, ready to ride up again.

One day in June 1868, Katie ran down the trail but didn't appear at the other end. Henry Flynn assumed she had gone home, so the alarm that she was missing did not go out until late evening. Henry, his workmen, and two hunters who happened to be passing by searched the woods with torches well into the night.

The next day the hunt began again. At about 4:00 pm the searchers heard a couple of faint cries coming from the underbrush near a local river. As the men neared the river, a huge black hairy "bear" plunged into the water and swam furiously for the other bank. It disappeared into the woods before anyone could get a better look at it.

In the underbrush they found Katie standing on a dead tree that had fallen partially across the river.

The Flynns asked their daughter what had happened. According to the Ludington Daily News, the three-year-old replied, "Big dog came up to me, took me in his arms and walked away with me." One of Katie's shoes was missing; "Big dog ate it," was her explanation.

Another Ludington Daily News article expanded on the event. The black creature – whatever it was – had come out of the woods and played with Katie. It "held out its paw and she caught hold of it and it had walked away with her." It picked berries, which it brought back to her in its paw, and it lay next to her all night to keep her warm.

As David Paulides points out, "Bears are not nurturing warm creatures that cuddle children." Some accounts called the unknown animal a wolf, but "A wolf cannot pick berries, place them in its paw and carry them back in that paw." We can only say, with Paulides, that "Katie Flynn had something very unusual happen to her in the summer of 1868."

So here for your perusal are some more very unusual animals.

The Talking Bear

The Fortean Times no. 45 reported on a vociferous bruin. It seems that Greg and Stephanie McKay of Enumclaw were camping near Greenwater, Washington, in July 1985. On the morning of the 6th, their camp was invaded by "a bear-like animal" eight feet tall.

"'You may think this sounds crazy, but the bear talked to us,' Stephanie, 35, said in a telephone interview. In a very high-pitched voice that didn't sound human it asked them their names and whether they had permission to use the campsite. They said they had permission, but the bear told them to get off the property immediately." [p. 34]

As the couple packed, the bear started throwing stones at them. Understandably, they fled at top speed. Greenwater Fire Department officials visiting the site found only the paw prints "of a large dog," though saying the creature was an eight-foot-tall talking dog isn't much better. "The case was eventually dismissed as a product of overactive imagination."

I remember seeing this story in The Weekly World News, which did not help its credibility. However, the Fortean Times' sources were the Boston Globe, Houston Chronicle, San Francisco Chronicle, San Diego Union, and the Seattle Times of July 10, 1985, among other newspapers.

A Ted with a 'Tude

Latino cryptozoologist Scott Corrales describes a bizarre ursine creature in "Monster Hunting in Latin America and Spain" (Fate April 2004). In April 1997 two sisters were walking beside the AO-12 highway near Roldan, Argentina. They were near a silo factory when they suddenly noticed "a diminutive creature, entirely covered with hair and with shiny eyes" (p. 38). The younger sister felt a sudden unshakable urge to walk toward the being. The older sister grabbed her arm and yelled at her to keep her from going to it.

For a time, the creature simply stared at the women, but eventually it made an amazing leap entirely across the road (about forty feet) and disappeared into a soybean field.

A few nights later, a Mrs. Coronel, in her house in the country, felt a "strange compulsion" to open the door and step outside. She did so and spotted a small "bear", about 65 feet away, staring intently at her. She described herself as being "mesmerized", only snapping out of the spell when her husband yelled for her from the house. Mrs. Coronel described the creature as having a bear's face, but it stood upright.

Several other people (all women) also saw the creature, which author Corrales calls "A Teddy Bear with a bad attitude." One can only wonder what would have happened if the first two witnesses had been alone. Maybe they would have simply wandered off with their little ursine friend, like Christopher Robin with Winnie-the-Pooh...

Semeel the Guardian

Dawn Collinson, in the Liverpool Echo of Feb. 9, 2008, uncovered an old story of a mystery animal that may have actually prevented a tragic disappearance. Early in November 1953, two boys, David, age 12, and Alan, age 11 (last names withheld), were playing Cowboys and Indians south of Liverpool in a section of forest called Little Woods. At about 4:20 pm they built a campfire. As Alan (with questionable wisdom) fired flaming arrows into the trees, David spotted an enormous tabby-colored cat, 4 feet tall (presumably while on all fours) only 20 feet away. The creature said "Hello, children," "in a clear, well-spoken voice," according to Collinson. The boys ran away in terror and stumbled out onto a nearby street, where they were almost hit by a bus. Predictably, their parents did not believe the story.

The boys girded up their courage and ventured out to the woods the very next day, lighting a fire at about 4:20 again. "The enormous cat came slinking out of the woods, arched its back and sat by the fire opposite the boys." It gave its name as "Semeel" and said it was something called a "Guardian". It warned the boys to stay out of the forest because a local man (whose name they recognized) was lurking there, waiting to kill them. Then it padded off into the trees.

The boys' parents were still unimpressed, because the man "Semeel" accused was in Wales at that time. However, several days later the police discovered that the man had returned secretly from Wales. He had built a rough dwelling in Little Woods and was living there while the boys played nearby, unknowing. Furthermore, the man had unsuccessfully tried to abduct a child five years earlier. He confessed that he had been planning to abduct David and Alan.

The boys encountered the Guardian Semeel three more times, but the giant feline apparently did not like the way the forest was being cleared for a housing project, for after its fifth manifestation it never appeared again.

The Vulpine Visitor

Adventure/travel writer Richard Curle lived in Scotland, "on the Borders," when he was a boy. One winter night in the 1890s, "over forty years" before the publication of his autobiography Caravansary and Conversation (1937), at about 2:00 am, young Richard Curle woke and watched the swirling snow and waving tree branches outside his window. "I was wide awake, as wide awake as I am now." He became aware of "steady, unhurried" footsteps approaching the house. They appeared to pass through the back yard gate and cross the courtyard to the kitchen door. They then entered the house and climbed the stairs. Familiar with the layout of the house, Curle mentally marked their passage as they reached the top of the stairs, turned left, left again, took a few steps down, passed through the room next to Curle's, and finally stopped before the boy's door. The boy watched in horror as the handle turned and the door opened, revealing "a creature with the face of a fox, which walked on its hind legs. It was dressed in some sort of way and, would you credit it, wore a top hat, which added to its appearance an indescribably macabre touch."

The creature was larger than a normal fox. It possessed a bushy vulpine tail, but Curle detected no foxlike odor. It stared at him silently for several moments. Curle yelled "Go away!", and the entity obediently turned and marched off. Its footsteps followed the same path they had in approach, leisurely but steadily, "until at last they died out on the road leading to the woods."

The episode bears some resemblance to "hag assaults" and "night terrors" as described in David Hufford's The Terror that Comes in the Night. Some night terror cases include the loud, approaching footsteps as well as the appearance of a bizarre, usually evil creature. People being "hagged" usually suffer from temporary paralysis, however, and Curle maintains that he sat up in his bed and shouted at the fox-thing. A similar phenomenon called "false awakening" can lead one to believe one is awake, when in fact one is still dreaming. Curle writes that "if one does not know when one is wide awake, what does one know?" He dismisses the idea of a hoax, because the creature's legs were too small in proportion to be a human's. He concedes that he might have had a once-in-a-lifetime hallucination.

A new class of humanoids with animal heads, usually those of dogs but sometimes with those of wolves or foxes, has been the subject of much discussion on the Fortean Times Message Board in recent years. Jonathan Downes, Director of Great Britain's Centre for Fortean Zoology, has dubbed these animal-like entities "zooforms". A fox with a top hat, though, is like something out of a cartoon. It is tempting to dismiss Curle's childhood memory as a hypnogogic dream, but perhaps it bears some relationship to the modern "dogmen" and other creatures. Poor thing made a long trip for nothing, though . . .

Corrales, Scott, "Monster Hunting in Latin America and Spain," Fate Magazine Vol. 57 no. 4 (Apr. 2004), pp. 32-39.

Curle, Richard. Caravansary and Conversation (New York: Frederick A. Stokes Co., 1937), pp. 271-274.

Paulides, David. Missing 411: Eastern United States (North Charleston, SC: CreateSpace, 2011), pp. 54-57.

"Talking Bear," Fortean Times no. 45 (Winter 1985), p. 34.

"Uncanny Encounters," Fortean Times no. 237 (special issue 2008), p. 23.

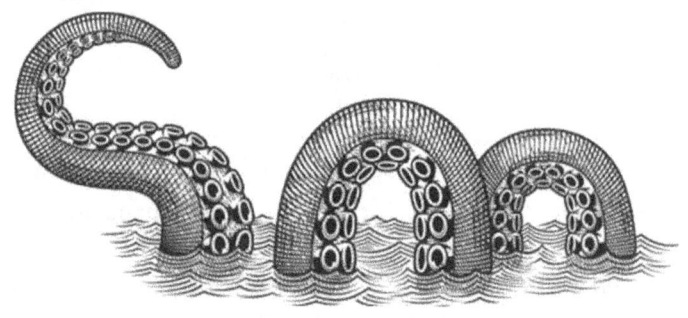

- Dragon report – Texas
- Modern-day dragon sightings
- Texas: Dragon-like entity plus paranormal phenomena

The Texas Dragon

Susie Mills owned ten acres of land on the eastern edge of Denton, Texas, off Mills Road. She promoted the fourteen houses on her land as a "Writers' and Artists' Retreat." She ended up renting to anyone she found amiable, although most of the forty-seven residents did work in the university town of Denton. The land, once the property of her ex-in-laws, was rumored to have been an ancient Indian burial ground. It did play host to a number of paranormal events.

The young people living in the retreat began reporting strange things. They would be speaking to someone, glance aside, and see the person they were speaking to exit through a doorway. When they glanced back, of course, the other person was still present. Some residents, including Nancy Guesman, reported hearing people talk when no one else was around. "I've seen my dogs chase things in my house when there seems to be nothing there," she told investigative reporter Arthur Myers. "They'll be running full tilt and then suddenly stop, dumbfounded." Men who hunted in the area rarely came again, reportedly feeling "uncomfortable" on Mills' land. Conversely, people of Native American descent felt a "need" for the place, and emotionally troubled people felt more at peace on the land.

Susie Mills herself believed she was being visited by her late grandmother, especially in times of stress. She would smell her grandmother's distinctive perfume at night. "Horses born here often have blue eyes. They are invariably paint or Appaloosa, despite the breeding," Ms. Mills claims. Even dogs born in the area often have one blue eye. The most intriguing manifestation at the retreat, however, is a long, lanky "dragon".

The dragon first showed up in 1984. Sometimes it appeared on a huge scale, up in the sky, its body formed from clouds, but at other times a smaller version would materialize on the ground. One evening Ms. Mills took a photo of her tenants as they sat around the back yard. The picture showed a wispy arc with a curving "tail" over the young people, although none of them were smoking. Perhaps it was the dragon.

The creature, fortunately, exudes an aura of friendliness. "It's something that comes near us in time of trouble," as Susie Mills says. Ms. Guesman claimed to see it three or four times, once in its monstrous "cloud" form, sailing north to south high in the sky.

A Chinese friend of Susie Mills identified the entity as a "Ming" dragon, bringer of good fortune. Mills thought it more resembled the dragon on the Welsh flag, so she called it Argynr. Sometimes people split the difference and called it Argynr/Ming.

There was some evidence of old Native American rituals found on a cliff overlooking the commune, but no one can say how that would relate to a dragon, Chinese or Welsh. The phenomena – and the dragon – were still manifesting themselves at the time of Myers' visit in late 1985.

This charming account puts me in mind of a short story by John Wyndham called "Chinese Puzzle," in which a Chinese dragon, brought to Wales as an egg, ends up being courted by a Welsh dragon. Perhaps Angynr/Ming was their offspring...

Dragons should be found in ancient myths and fairy-tales, not in Texas, or so one would think. There are modern dragon reports, but the incredulity factor suppresses them, even in works on the paranormal. In 1966 parapsychologist Raymond Bayless visited the home of "Mrs. N." and her family (which included three children). They reported phantasmal footsteps, spontaneous fires, a doll that flew off a shelf by itself, and other typical poltergeist events. While he and the whole family were seated in the living room Bayless himself heard dishes and pans being rattled and banged in the kitchen, which was an open area within his view.

Bayless interviewed family members, including the second oldest child. "He discussed these events logically and apparently factually," the investigator wrote in Animal Ghosts, "but at the end of his story he detailed a fantastic scene which was purely imaginary. He said that after one outburst of phenomena he saw the tail of a mysterious dragonlike beast drag across the floor." Bayless could accept poltergeists but not dragons, it seems.

Bayless, Raymond. Animal Ghosts (New York: University Books, 1970) pp. 148-149.
Myers, Arthur. Ghostly Register (New York: McGraw-Hill, 1986), pp. 328-331.

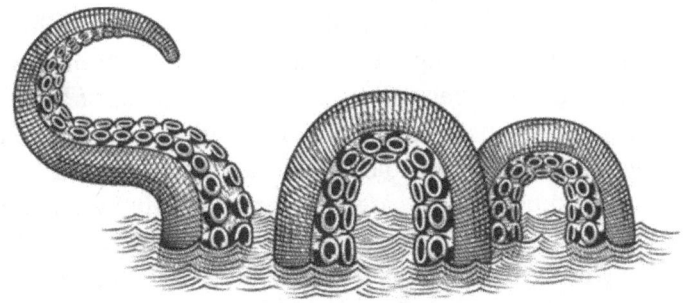

- Modern artifact in archeological site
- Time travel hoax

The Time Travel Story that Folded Itself

In 1986, archeologists at a dig near New Delhi were astonished to discover a Coca-Cola bottle "hundreds of feet" underground, amid pottery fragments and bones dating back ten thousand years. There was no sign of tampering with the site, so the implication was that some thirsty but careless time traveler dropped the modern artifact in ancient India. "It is the most baffling thing I have ever seen," declared dig leader Ramar Kashim. ["Two Unearthed Enigmas," p. 9.]

Or was it? Twenty years later, Fortean Times editor Bob Rickard admitted that the source of this amazing story was a notorious tabloid, the Sunday Sport of September 21, 1986. In these more technologically advanced times, Rickard was able to check out the tale on the World Wide Web. "Googling failed to locate any trace of the Indian archeologist who vouched for the site, or the European archeologist, quoted, who blamed time-traveling UFO tourists." Nor was there any other trace of this amazing find, which would have created, one would think, quite a stir in the academic world.

As in the case of Rudolph Fentz (see "The Chronokinesis of . . ."), this tale of a cola out of time was probably based on a work of science fiction, to be specific, David Gerrold's classic The Man Who Folded Himself. In this novel, young Daniel Eakins inherits a "time belt" from his late Uncle Jim. The belt allows Daniel to travel back and forth in time, creating numerous alternate histories and paradoxes. He tries to keep the secret of time travel to himself, but occasionally he slips:

"I thought I'd been more careful, but apparently I wasn't. Or one of me wasn't. One of the Pompeiian artifacts in the British Museum has definitely been identified as a fossilized Coca-Cola bottle from the Atlanta, Georgia, bottling plant." [Gerrold, p. 71]

It is interesting that two supposedly real accounts of time travel were based on specific works of fiction, as opposed to simply making up a story from whole cloth. Will this trend continue? I seem to recall a letter to the Fortean Times in which the writer claimed to be walking along one day when he spotted an old-fashioned British Police Call Box sitting on a street corner. Glancing back only moments later, the witness saw that the box had vanished. I'm going to look for that, some rainy day when I've nothing better to do . . .

Gerrold, David. Man Who Folded Himself (Dallas, TX: BenBella Books, 2002 [1972]).

Rickard, Bob, "Tales from the Vault," Fortean Times no. 214 (Oct 2006), p. 80.

"Two Unearthed Enigmas," Fortean Times no. 48 (Spring 1987), p. 9.

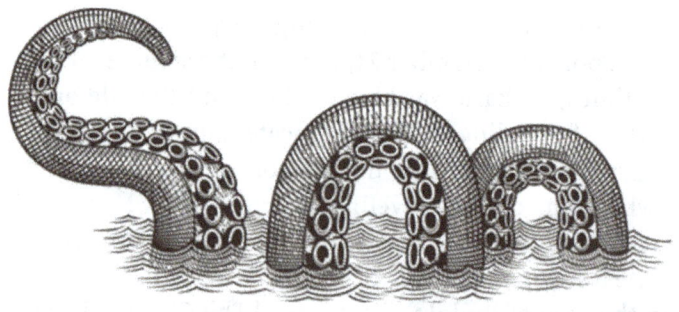

- Indiana: Creatures develop in toxic waste pit
- Spontaneous life?
- Squid-like creatures seen in toxic waste, Indiana
- Toxic dump – creatures seen dwelling in

Toxic Waste Creatures

To celebrate forty years of publishing, Fortean Times no. 308 asked its resident paranormal experts to choose the top forty strange stories appearing in that magazine. The choices ranged from the Angels of Mons to Nikola Tesla to a faded Willie Nelson poster mistaken for a miraculous picture of Jesus.

A few favorites eluded all the staff's efforts at locating them, however. Robert Damon Schneck declared that he'd read a story about "small, squid-like creatures swimming around inside barrels of toxic waste."

"The idea of little monsters evolving to fill the toxic waste niche appealed to my B-movie sensibilities," wrote Schneck. [1]

There is a brief mention of the affair in Fortean Times no. 108, but Mr. Schneck was probably thinking of another magazine entirely: Strange Magazine no. 18, to be precise, and the article "Mystery of the Oil Pit Squids" by Tim Swartz. [2]

GMC Delphi Interior and Lighting, Anderson, Indiana, manufactured plastic automotive components such as bumpers, grills, and headlight casings. In November, 1996, at Plant number 9, workmen were cleaning out a sludge pit when they noticed something moving in the waste chemicals. A General Motors employee – a thirty-year veteran who wished to remain anonymous – said the creatures were six to eight inches long, about an inch in diameter, the reddish-gray color of earthworms, and possessed of tentacles and apparently eyes. "The pit was full of these things, all swimming around," said the workman. "These were definitely living animals."

The pit contained antifreeze, stripper, oil, and a chemical called Polyal, used in the "formation of plastic bumpers."

On November 15, a Delphi employee caught one of the creatures in a jar. The jar was kept in the office of Paul McConnell, of General Motors Worldwide Facilities Group. At the same time, an anonymous complaint was lodged against Plant 9 with the Indiana Department of Environmental Management (IDEM). Aside from "unusual growth" in the waste pit, the complaint charged that open canisters of toxic waste were to be found in the area, that waste had been buried beneath a newly-created walking trail, and that employees suffered from persistent coughs, rashes, and fatigue.

IDEM sent investigators Mike Randall and Don Stilz to the plant in March, 1997. They investigated the numerous complaints and learned that in December someone had stolen the jar with the "creature" in it. Men-in-Black? A corporate conspiracy? Or did the janitorial staff just not understand the significance of the "stuff" in the jar? Despite this, both IDEM and the Environmental Protection Agency admitted that a "creature of an unknown origin or type" had been seen in the pit. [3]

Delphi spokesperson Sharon Morton announced that water leaking from the sprinkler system into the waste pit had promoted "a bacterial growth." Plant employees were unimpressed. "A bacterial growth doesn't swim around on its own," said one. "These things looked like small squids with thin tentacles and eyelike attachments," said another. "It was quite a shock to see these things surviving in the toxic waste."

IDEM investigators checked the emulsion pit as it was being drained completely on March 12, 1997. No living creatures were found. Jo Lynn Ewing of IDEM admitted, "If there were any living things, bacterial or otherwise in that pit, any evidence of their existence was destroyed when the pit was originally cleaned in November of 1996."

In 2006, the Indiana Economic Digest announced that the Anderson Delphi plant was closing. [4]

1. Emerson, Hunt, "Fortean Top 40," in Fortean Times no.308 (Jan. 2014), p. 31.

2. Swartz, Tim, "Mystery of the Oil Pit Squids," in Strange Magazine no. 18 (Summer 1997), pp. 28-30.

3. "Toxic Sludge Mutant," Fortean Times no. 108 (April 1998), p. 19.

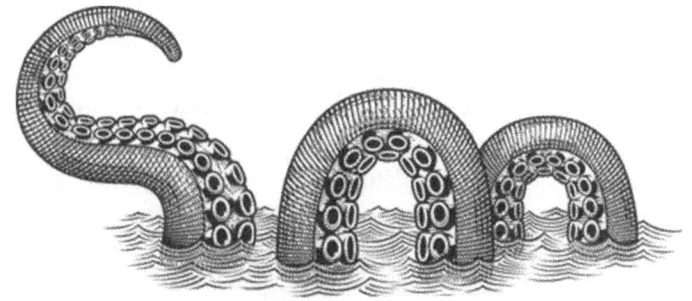

- Farmer picks up tiny UFO
- Ireland: Tiny UFO, 1956
- Man "wrestles" UFO
- "Mini-UFO" in Ireland
- Object falls from sky, Ireland

UFO Wrestling Federation

"To see a flying saucer is no longer unusual. There have been those persons who claim to have ridden in them and talked to their occupants. But to wrestle, even if the match was a losing one, this is a new twist."
Riverside [CA] Enterprise, Sept. 11, 1956

Argosy, True, Saga, and other "Magazines for Men" were a common sight on magazine racks from the 1940s into the 1980s. Less genre-specific than hunting, war, or crime publications, Saga and its fellows contained articles on movies and movie stars, politics, sports, and somewhat stranger subjects like Bigfoot, UFOs, Jack the Ripper, and sea monsters. Saga even produced a spin-off publication, Saga's UFO Report, beginning in 1974.

In an era where finding even an occasional Fate Magazine was a rarity, UFO Report was a boon to teenagers interested in the paranormal and unexplained. On the other hand, the present writer has traced numerous stories that "I heard about somewhere" to this source, only to be disappointed by running into a dead end.

That seemed to be the case for an odd tale mentioned in UFO Report Vol. 1, no. 5, concerning an encounter between a son of the ould sod and a strange object from the sky.

On Friday, September 7, 1956, near Moneymore, Northern Ireland, a farmer, Thomas Hutchinson, and his wife watched a strange object drop from the rainy skies into a field about 250 yards away. Hutchinson decided to investigate but maneuvering around hedges and rain-swollen streams slowed him down.

The thing was still present when he reached the field: an upright, elongated object, thick in the middle and tapering at the top and bottom, with a knob at the top and a plate-like base. It was mostly red, except for four white stripes around the midsection. The farmer kicked it over, but it sprang back up like a punching-bag toy.

The object looked and felt to be made of canvas, with the material gathered at the lower end "like the neck of a bag," but very uniformly. Hutchinson decided to take the thing in to show the police at Loup, a nearby town, so he picked it up by the base. It weighed only a few pounds. He started back through the rain with his strange prize, fighting his way through rushing water, marshy ground, and thick hedges. The body of the object began spinning, rotating above the base he held in one hand, first counterclockwise, then clockwise.

The farmer set the spinning thing down to force open a wall of shrubbery. The moment he released it, the mysterious construct shot up into the sky, spinning faster and now glowing. [1]

That was how things stood from the mid-seventies onward – until Fortean Times no. 317 (Sept 2016). Shane Cochrane, a freelance Irish writer, dug up the original newspaper reports concerning Hutchinson and his flying friend.

A few details differed from the old account in Saga: Maud Hutchinson (the farmer's wife) accompanied Thomas at least part of the way. The object was about three feet tall and eighteen inches thick at its thickest point (UFO Report stated it was three and a half feet in diameter, perhaps mistaking height for width). It was pale red with dark red stripes. The most interesting difference – it fought Hutchinson every inch of the way across the marshy field. "Then all of a sudden the monster rose and it nearly pulled my husband off his feet when he tried to hold it," Maud Hutchinson said later. "I started to panic and then I ran home and prayed."

An RAF officer and the Royal Ulster Constabulary said the object was probably just a weather balloon. The desk sergeant at Loup sprang to the farmer's defense: "Thomas Hutchinson is a level-headed, God fearing chap. He's not the sort of man who would imagine he seized a flying saucer if, in fact, he didn't have one."

Sometimes when one chases down old stories, they evaporate into exaggeration and rumor. Other times they expand in significance – and wackiness. Carrying a weird object to the authorities does not sound that strange – fighting it all the way as you might an angry housecat is another matter. So the later report (which ought to suffer from exaggeration) was actually the tamer. Also, according to Cochrane, the Hutchinson incident was the last major event in a two-year UFO "flap" that engulfed all of Ireland.

1. Farish, Lucius, and Dave Titler, "UFOs – Touching is Believing," Saga's UFO Report Vol. 1 no. 5 (Spring 1974), p. 68.
2. Cochrane, Shane, "Ireland vs. the Flying Saucers," Fortean Times no. 317 (Sept. 2014), pp. 54-55.

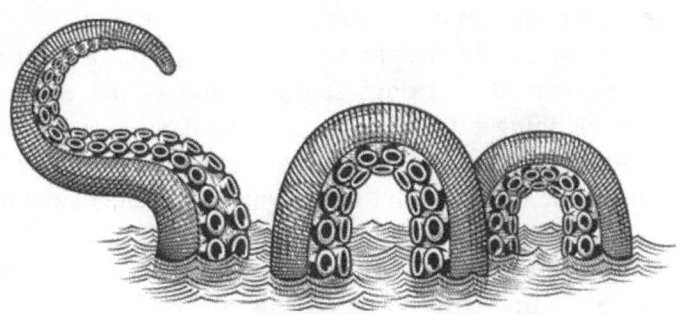

- Angikuni, Lake: Disappearance
- Crocker Land/Crocker Mountains, Arctic
- Disappearance: Inuit/Eskimo village
- Eskimo village disappears
- Inuit village disappears
- Mysterious lands, Arctic
- Northwest Territories, Canada: Disappearance

The Vanishing Village

"The northern lights have seen queer sights -- as the much-quoted Robert W. Service remarks -- and the everlasting silence of the regions under the Arctic Circle cloaks some strange mysteries. But the northern lights do not tell of the queer sights, nor does the Arctic silence get vocal about its mysteries. There is nothing to do, usually, but guess."
--Emmett E. Kelleher, Halifax Herald, Nov. 29, 1930

In late summer 1930, trapper Joe Labelle drew his canoe onto the shore of Lake Angikuni, about 500 miles northwest of Churchill, in Canada's Northwest Territories. He had come upon a small Inuit village (six caribou-skin tents that housed about 25 people), and he was desperate for human company in that frozen, rocky land.

He was to be greatly disappointed. He called out a greeting, but only two half-starved sled dogs staggered out of the encampment toward him, whining piteously. Labelle soon discovered the dead bodies of seven other dogs scattered around the area. The lack of activity and noise (beyond that of the surviving dogs) gave him the creeps. He finally entered a tent.

"I could see the place hadn't known any human life for months, and I expected to find corpses inside," he explained later. "But there was nothing there but the personal belongings of a family. A couple of deer parkas (skin coats) were in one corner. Fish and deer bones were scattered about. There were a few pairs of boots, and an iron pot, greasy and black. Under one of the parkas I found a rifle. It had been there so long it was all rusty."

It looked to Labelle as if the tent owners had stepped out, expecting to return in a moment – but they did not return. He examined the rest of the encampment.

"I figured there had been about 25 people in the camp but all signs showed the place hadn't been lived in for nearly 12 months. As I strolled about, with those two walking skeletons of dogs following me, I found the other tents in a similar state."

One might think that six tents hardly qualifies as a village; perhaps the Inuit folk had merely moved on.

The villagers, however, had left behind hides, clothing, cooking utensils, and, of course, their huskies. Inside one tent, more exposed to the wind that the others, Labelle found fox skins, ruined by rain and mud. Under the skins was another rusty rifle. "Those two rifles seemed strange -- the last thing an Eskimo ever parts with is his rifle," the trapper told authorities.

Labelle wandered down to the water in search of clues only to find the strangest mystery yet. Here was an Eskimo grave, with a cairn built of stones over it – except that the stones had been removed, one by one, and placed to one side. The body the grave had contained was missing. Joe Labelle could not imagine why a corpse would be removed in such a fashion: this sort of desecration was unheard of among the northern peoples.

Labelle caught a few fish for the surviving dogs but then moved on. There had been no signs of a struggle; in fact, the whole scene looked peaceful. But he refused to sleep in the deserted encampment.

The trapper visited several other Inuit communities over the next few months, but no one knew anything about the missing villagers (or if they did, they did not reveal the fact to Labelle). Finally, rather late in the day, he returned to the white men's outposts and reported the incident to the Royal Northwest Mounted Police (now the Royal Canadian Mounted Police). According to journalist Emmett Kelleher, the Mounties dutifully went out to the area and on the way asked white trappers to watch for clues, but nothing was ever found of the missing villagers. [Kelleher, p. 7]

Missing Metropolis of the North

Six skin tents flapping in the sub-arctic wind ... the disappearance of two dozen people is a mystery, yes, but just as mysterious is how the story of the vanishing Inuit village snowballed over the years into a bloated, lunatic mass abduction.

The case came to general knowledge in Fate Magazine (August 1955), in "The Eskimo Village Mystery," by Murray T. Pringle. Stranger than Science by Frank Edwards and Strangely Enough by C. B. Colby (both 1959) spread the village's fame even farther. Edwards put the village's population at about thirty, and even that was stretching the poor resources of Angikuni.

As the years passed, the size of the village and the efforts of Labelle and others to locate the inhabitants increased. By the Internet age the village had become a thriving city of 2,000 to 2,500 people (as one online commentator pointed out, the entire population of the Northwest Territories was probably less than 2,500 in 1930). There were permanent buildings, a trading post, shanties, huts, and shacks in this community (in reality there are no trees on the rocky tundra to provide wood). Rather than simply stumbling upon the site, Labelle was a frequent visitor. Food was still simmering in iron pots over cooking fires, as if everyone up and left mere minutes earlier. Another added touch: the investigating Mounties saw strange blue lights on the horizon while investigating the empty town – obviously aliens were involved.

The insanity reached critical mass on the Unexplained Mysteries website (and probably elsewhere by now). Labelle is described as making his "monthly" visit to the town, which now boasts a harbor where the white men chug along in diesel powered boats (Angikuni is best described as a glorified string of puddles). The trapper is shocked to find the 2,500 inhabitants missing, including his many "friends and acquaintances." He stumbles along for miles until he reaches the fish storehouse of his old friend Fran MacKenzie, a retired colonel. "Mack" and his customers are gone as well.

Labelle finds a series of strange items: Mack's diary, which tells of weird lights in the sky; the ex-colonel's crutches, smashed; the distinctive eyeglasses and silver cigarette case of the local Inuit leader – which had been buried with him when he died, a year earlier.

When the Mounties arrive, they find that all the graves in the local cemetery have been opened and all the bodies removed. They find a still-living husky near MacKenzie's storehouse. The dog has had cologne sprayed on it and lipstick smeared over its lips; it is wearing a woman's necklace and panties; its ears have been pierced as if for earrings, and someone had crammed a wedding ring onto its front paw.

Naturally, the Mounties see strange lights in the sky, and witnesses in the surrounding area report seeing a "cylindrical, bullet-shaped object" rocketing toward the lake earlier. Those lousy, corpse-stealing, dog-marrying aliens!

Will that Village Ever Vanish?

It seems as if somebody somewhere wants the missing village story to go away. The Royal Canadian Mounted Police National Home Page on Lake Anjikuni [sic], last updated 12/17/2014, states in part:

"An American author by the name of Frank Edwards is purported to have started this story in his book *Stranger than Science*. It has become a popular piece of journalism, repeatedly published and referred to in books and magazines. There is no evidence however to support such a story."

This shows that the RCMP are unaware of the 1930 newspaper story (and of their own investigation into the matter), just don't care, or are trying to erase it from the public memory for some reason.

Some of the points given against the Angikuni case are based on later exaggerations and mistakes, and they are easily answered even with only the one short original account.

Neither Labelle nor the villagers could have traveled by kayak in November, as the waters would be frozen: As Kelleher wrote, Labelle finished out the trapping season before arriving in Halifax, indicating that some time had passed. Kelleher also mentions an Inuit boy found wandering across the tundra "a few months ago" and wonders if he might have come from the lost village. This seems to set the trapper's adventure in August when the temperature is respectably high, even in subarctic regions.

The timeline might even be pushed farther back. Kelleher makes it sound in his article like the Mounties have been investigating for a while already, which means some time has passed since Labelle returned to inform them. (Some accounts say the trapper "rushed" to the nearest telegraph office for help as soon as he left the village. I have no statistics, but I suspect there wasn't a telegraph office within several hundred miles of Angikuni in 1930.)

Labelle himself, of course, estimated the scattering of tents had been abandoned as much as a year earlier.

There was no sealskin available in Angikuni to make traditional Inuit kayaks: a complaint based on some versions that have "wave-battered kayaks" down by the water. Labelle did not mention kayaks.

A permanent village could not have existed that far north: It was not permanent, but a temporary tent community.

Nelson of the Northwest

In 1976, writer Dwight Whalen investigated the story for Fate Magazine. He contacted the RCMP, who called the story a hoax, and whose files were unavailable to the public anyway. He appealed to the Federal Department of Indian and Northern Affairs, the Hudson's Bay Company, and the Manitoba Provincial Archives, to no avail. Finally, the Public Archives in Ottawa uncovered the Halifax Herald story and a report from a Sergeant J. Nelson.

On January 5, 1931, Sergeant Nelson sent his report to the Officer Commanding, R.C. Mounted Police, Prince Albert, Saskatchewan. It seems the good Sergeant spoke to a Mr. Simons, "who operates a trading post at Windy Lake, N.W.T., and has just returned from visiting his post by plane." Simons discounted the story because he would have surely heard of it from his trapper and Eskimo clientele.

Sergeant Nelson thought little of Joe Labelle, who "is considered a newcomer in this country. The Manitoba records show this to be his first season that he has taken out a trapping license." [Whalen, p. 69] I'm not sure how that is relevant. Did that mean he wasn't as observant or knowledgeable as a long-time resident of the Northwest Territories? He knew how important rifles and sled-dogs were, and how strange it was to leave clothes, cooking pots, furs, etc., behind.

The photograph of the "deserted village" accompanying the news story was a stock picture from the RCMP's own files. The implication was, if Kelleher passed this off falsely as the Angikuni village, then he might have misrepresented other facts as well. I can only wonder how difficult it would have been in 1930 to send a photographer several hundred miles into the wilderness (and it truly was subarctic winter by then) just to snap a few photos. If there was an appropriate photo on file...

There was also a stock photo of an Inuit family "like those of the tribe that vanished;" no one ever mistook it for a picture of Angikuni's actual inhabitants.

Nelson ends with a further jab at Emmett Kelleher: "From my own knowledge of the correspondent, I consider the whole story fiction. Mr. Kelleher is in the habit of writing colorful stories of the North and very little credence can be given to his articles." This despite the fact that Nelson had not yet interviewed Kelleher about the subject, and so far as anyone knows never did.

Some modern writers have taken Sergeant Nelson's ad hominem accusations as much to heart as others latch onto the uber-fantasized "Missing Metropolis." Whalen, for instance, concludes that "the case for the vanished village rests upon the story of an inexperienced trapper told to an imaginative and not too conscientious newsman."

John Robert Colombo, author of over seventy books on Canadian history, literature and folklore, calls Labelle's account a "tall tale" and Kelleher's news story a "journalistic hoax" right out of the gate in his Mysterious Canada (1988), though he provides no new information.

Brian Dunning's Skeptoid site reprinted part of a letter from RCMP historian S. W. Horrall: "Our files were carefully searched. No strange craft was ever reported. No one named Joe Labelle ever came to the RCMP in panic about Lake Anjikuni. The RCMP did not send out any search parties. The only records we have on the story are copies of letters to correspondents like yourself informing the writers that the story is entirely fictitious." In 2013 Dunning contacted Patrick Derksen of the Millennium Library in Winnipeg concerning Angikuni. According to the Millennium staff neither the Kelleher news story nor the Sergeant Nelson report ever even existed. "They also searched all other Manitoba newspapers from the day, and found no references to the story whatsoever, nor any record of an Emmett E. Kelleher. Certainly nothing like it appears in the microfilm copies I have on my desk right now," writes Dunning.

This convinced Skeptoid not only that Frank Edwards invented the original Angikuni story, but that Dwight Whalen in 1976 invented the 1930 news story and Sergeant Nelson's report! (The site has since been updated and corrected.)

In this writer's opinion, the Vanishing Eskimo Village is possibly the most exaggerated yet most condescendingly dismissed and most feebly "debunked" case in the realm of true life mysteries.

And the biting wind still howls over the lonely rocky shores of Angikuni.

The Enchanted Sky

When someone among the Bering Strait Eskimos disappears mysteriously, the people have a ready explanation: "Every one had thought that he had gone to the land of the Peeleuptuk, which is the land of missing men." [Snell, p. 74] The inhabitants of Siberia are well aware of an Other World, or Worlds, rather. "There are different views on how many worlds exist. The Chukchi believe in nine, the Yakut in seven and the Evenk in three. To the Chukchi the worlds are alternately peopled by men and spirits." [Riordan, p. 18] One such world is called the Land of Gloom, inhabited by keleks (evil spirits), as mentioned in the folktale, "The Eight Brothers."

Perhaps the three Inupiat seal hunters in the folktale "The Enchanted Sky" (from Lela Kiana Oman's Eskimo Legends) glimpsed Peeleuptuk. The hunters paddled seaward from what is now Kotzebue on their kayaks as they usually did, but the sea looked unnaturally smooth and glassy. The youngest man, out ahead, bumped into an expanse of solid – well – sky: "It was blue and impenetrable and like a ceiling it came down to meet the water."

The older hunters were reluctant to approach the barrier, but the young one skirted the strange wall of air. Soon he discovered an opening:

"There was a crack, and beyond, the sea tossed relentlessly, and, as if it were the proper thing to do, he stood up in his qayaq (kayak) and curiously looked up into what was above. The other two saw only the bottom half of the young man and his qayaq. They did not reach him, but turned their qayat (kayaks) around while yelling, 'Get down in your qayaq! Get down in your qayaq!'"

The older hunters paddled away, calling to their foolish companion to return. The adventuresome youth merely described what he saw through the opening: "Come back and see how beautiful it is. There are flowers in bloom and trees laden with fruit. Come back! I am going to climb up!"

The other two hunters kept calling to their young companion, but he did not answer, having climbed into the "crack" in the sky. They paddled back to their village and told the people what happened. Many other men in umiat (skin boats) paddled out to the spot of disappearance. All they ever found was the Inumiat youth's kayak and wooden paddle, thumping softly as the waves brought them together . . . [Oman, p. 115-116]

Not on the Map

In 1818 Commander John Ross of the Royal Navy sought the Northwest Passage. He discovered a landmass he named Baffin Island, and he thought that Lancaster Sound might be the Passage. However, he gave up after searching it a single day. The Sound, he reported, was cut off to the west by a vast mountain chain he named the "Crocker Mountains." A new expedition under William Parry, a year later, sailed farther west than the supposed mountains, so they were dismissed as an optical illusion.

In 1906, Robert E. Peary reached 86 degrees north. He spotted land in the distance beyond the pack ice, with towering peaks, northwest of

Ellesmere Land. He named it "Crocker Land." Donald MacMillan's 1914 expedition did not find them – but he spotted mountains 200 miles farther west. "Crocker Land" appears to exist as a shifting mirage – but where is the original of the mirage? [Ramsey, pp. 232-237]

The "Open Polar Sea" was a concept that appeared during the search for the Northwest Passage. In 1652, mapmaker Joseph Moxon was in exile in Amsterdam as a supporter of Charles II (during Cromwell's regime). He met a Dutch fisherman who had just returned from the Spitsbergen fishing grounds. The fisherman said they had not taken a sufficient haul, so their captain ordered them farther north. To their amazement, they kept sailing north, reaching the pole and two degrees beyond! It was as warm as Holland in summer. Moxon remarked that he believed the fisherman, "for he seem'd a plain, honest and unaffectatious Person, and one who could have no design upon me."

As late as 1850, Arctic explorer Elisha Kent Kane reached the northwestern tip of Greenland and saw from the cliffs "open water, with heavy breakers and no ice whatever." He believed that there were two "poles of cold" at 80 degrees north, and that at the pole it was actually warm! Such a concept might explain Hyperborea, the land beyond the North Wind, in Greek mythology. [Ramsey, pp 166-169]

Charles Fort, in New Lands, chapter 37, writes of several mysterious "cities" seen occasionally in the far north:

"In the English Mechanic, Sept. 10, 1897, a correspondent to the Weekly Times and Echo is quoted. He had just returned from the Yukon. Early in June 1897, he had seen a city pictured in the sky of Alaska. 'Not one of us could form the remotest idea in what part of the world this settlement could be . . . But whether this city exists in some unknown world on the other side of the North Pole, or not, it is a fact that this wonderful mirage occurs from time to time yearly, and we were not the only ones who witnessed the spectacle.'" [Fort, p. 491]

Perhaps people in the far north vanish into these strange Lands of Missing Men. On the other hand, perhaps colonists from the Other World are sent here sometimes. As ornithologist Katharine Scherman points out, the Inuit tribes of Baffin Island have no origin myth, and they had to come from somewhere:

"The Eskimos not only do not know who the old ones were, but they do not know where they themselves came from ... they came to this land, their background wiped from their minds as if it had never existed. Here they developed a specialized culture perfectly adapted to their frigid environment – and here they live today, the last survivors of an ancient, gentle race." [Scherman, p. 160]

Dunning, B. "The Vanishing Village of Angikuni Lake." Skeptoid Podcast. Skeptoid Media, 16 Jul 2013. Web: http://skeptoid.com/episodes/4371

Fort, Charles. Complete Books (New York: Dover Books, 1974 [1941]), p. 491.

Kelleher, Emmett E., "Vanished Eskimo Tribe Gives North Mystery Stranger than Fiction," from the Halifax Herald, reprinted in Danville (Virginia) Bee, Thursday, Nov. 27, 1930, p. 7.

Oman, Lela Kiana. Eskimo Legends (Anchorage, Alaska: Alaska Methodist University, 1975 [1959]).

Ramsey, Raymond H. No Longer on the Map (New York: Viking Press, 1972).

RCMP National Home Page concerning Lake Angikuni: http://www.rcmp-grc.gc.ca/en/fun-facts-and-urban-legends

Riordan, James. Sun Maiden and the Crescent Moon (Interlink Publishing Group, 1989).

Scherman, Katharine. Spring on an Arctic Island (Boston: Little, Brown and Co., 1956).

Snell, Roy J. Told Beneath the Northern Lights (Boston: Little. Brown & Co., 1925).

"Village of the Dead" at Unexplained Mysteries website: http://theunexplainedmysteries.com/Lake-Angikuni-Mystery.html

Whalen, Dwight, "Vanishing Village Revisited," in Fate Magazine Vol. 29 no. 11 (issue 320), Nov. 1976, pp. 67-70.

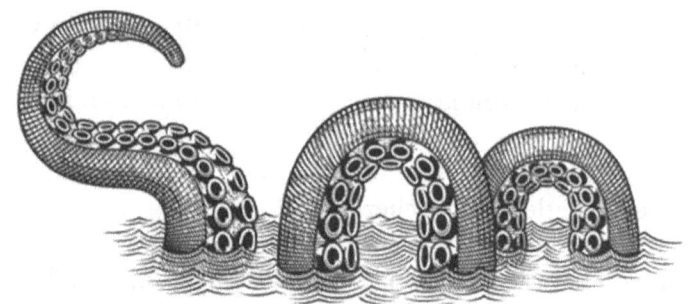

- Dimensional opening in bed/floor
- England (Bristol): Dimensional opening in hotel bedroom
- Hotel: Dimensional hole/portal

Voids

The Void in the Bed

On Monday, December 8, 1873, Thomas B. Cumpston and his wife, Ann Martha Cumpston, of Virginia Road, Leeds, were traveling from Clifton to Weston-super-Mare. They decided to stay overnight in Bristol, Avon, and continue to Weston-super-Mare in the morning. They checked into the Victoria Hotel, just across from the Bristol & Exeter Railway station, and went to bed about midnight.

At about 1:00 am the Cumpstons sought out the landlady, Mrs. Tongue, and complained of voices that seemed to be emanating from the next room. Naturally, there was nothing to hear when Mrs. Tongue entered their suite. The traveling couple went back to bed, but sometime between 3:00 and 4:00, according to the usually conservative London Times, they were disturbed "by terrible noises which they could not explain, and which frightened them very much." The bed seemed to open beneath them "and did all sorts of strange things" that are not elaborated on. According to the Bristol Mercury of December 13, Ann Cumpston testified later that "[t]he floor seemed to be giving way, and the bed also seemed to open. They heard voices, and what they said was repeated after them. Her husband wished her to get out of the way. The floor certainly seemed to open, and her husband fell down some distance, and she tried to get him up."

After helping her husband out of the black void in the bed and floor, Mrs. Cumpston asked him to fire his pistol. He shot into the ceiling, but the terrifying noises continued. The frightened couple climbed out the window and dropped twelve feet to the yard below. Mr. Cumpston fired off his pistol again, then the couple fled to the railway station in their nightclothes.

The Times account continues: "Mr. T. Harker, the night superintendent on the Bristol and Exeter Railway, said the parties rushed into his office partly dressed, crying out 'Murder,' and they were in a terrible state of excitement. They told him they had escaped from a den of rogues and thieves, and they had to defend themselves." They asked Harker to search the waiting room to make sure no one was following them.

Harker called for a constable, who searched Mr. Cumpston and found, not only the pistol, but three knives on his person. The Cumpstons were promptly taken into custody and brought up before the Bristol Police Court later that same Tuesday.

The Cumpstons told their story to an incredulous court. Mr. Cumpston, who possessed a speech impediment, could barely talk due to his distraught state. Fortunately, a telegram had been sent to a Mr. Butt, presumably at the Cumpstons' request. Mr. Butt appeared at the hearing and "in reply to the Bench said the parties occupied a very good position in Leeds. He offered to take proper charge of them if they were handed over to him, which was ultimately done, the defendants being discharged from custody [Times article]."

The prosaic London Times concludes: "No explanation can be given of this strange affair, and the belief is that it was an hallucination." The Bristol Mercury concurs: "There is little doubt that the whole was an hallucination." The Bristol Daily Post of December 10 mentions that police scoured the hotel room and found nothing out of the ordinary, so they echoed the general sentiment. In the century and a half since, others have speculated that the Cumpstons barely escaped falling into some sort of opening into another dimension.

Some writers have wondered why Mr. Cumpston carried a revolver and three knives with him on this excursion. The fact is that Victorian England was not all that safe a place, and it was still legal in Great Britain to buy handguns over the counter in 1873.

British author Rodney Davies, with help from Elizabeth Shaw of the Bristol Central Library, uncovered a few facts about the Cumpston case. The Victoria Hotel (Josiah Brown, proprietor) was located at 140 Thomas Street and became the Bute Arms in 1876. It was torn down in the 1920s. The railway station across the street is now called Temple Meads.

Charles Fort, in Chapter 18 of LO!, calls the Cumpstons "an elderly couple." Thomas Cumpston, however, was only twenty-five at the time of the incident. He and his wife lived at Number 35, Virginia Road, Leeds. According to the 1881 census Thomas was a "linen manufacturer employing about 90 persons" -- the "very good position" alluded to by Mr. Butt. Ann Cumpston gave birth to two boys and a girl in the years between 1876 and 1879.

Hallucination or Void?

D. J. West's "A Pilot Census of Hallucinations" (from Proceedings of the Society for Psychical Research Vol. 57, Part 215, April 1990), carries the following account from a twenty-one year old student nurse. It is entitled, prosaically, "Case 0878":

"It was roughly 8.0 a.m. I was sat in my room having a cup of tea . . . Suddenly a large hole appeared in the floor -- it took up most of the floor and the edges looked as if it were a rocky formation. Although I couldn't see to the bottom of the hole I knew it was very deep. A voice [said] to me to 'jump in'. The hole and the voice disappeared. I've not had this experience again."

Like the Cumpstons a century earlier, the young nurse heard a mysterious voice from the opening and, as the English couple's experience was dismissed as a hallucination, so too did the woman send her account to the Census of Hallucinations. What if these events were not illusions? Suppose Mr. Cumpston or the nurse jumped or fell into their respective openings? What would have happened? One can only wonder.

The Hole in the Path

University professor and folklorist Theo Brown spent most of her life in Devonshire, where she spent a great deal of time collecting tales of ghosts, fairies, and psychic events. In 1982 she published Devon Ghosts, a book of stories legendary and true.

In her Introduction, Ms. Brown informs us that most people of Devon will not speak of strange events, for the fear of ridicule is strong in the southwest of England. One of the delightful aspects of Devon Ghosts, however, is reading of Ms. Brown's ability not only to convince her informants to speak, but to get them to write out sizable personal accounts for her. One such account came from the Reverend Dr. A. T. P. Byles, who told her in 1974 of a strange event that occurred years earlier.

In 1946 Dr. Byles became the vicar of St. Bartholomew's Church in Yealmpton, "a rather remote village to the south of the A38, on a road between Totnes and Plymouth," in southern Devonshire. Yealmpton's main claim to fame was that "Old Mother Hubbard" once lived there. She was the housekeeper for a local family who inspired Miss Sarah Martin to write a poem about an old woman whose cupboard was bare.

Anyway, there was a door in the south side of St. Bartholomew's that opened onto a path that led to a wider lane. One Saturday afternoon near sunset, Dr. Byles walked up the path to meet his wife, who was arranging flowers within the church. He writes:

"In the middle of the path I saw a hole, of irregular shape, about a yard in width. I thought it was a subsidence, and went into the church and told my wife about it. Coming out shortly afterwards, I found that the hole was very much larger, and asked my wife to come out and see it. We both looked into it, and I suggested lowering myself into it. However, it was of uncertain depth, and when I threw a stone it bumped against stonework which we could see, and which looked like part of a wall."

The hole had grown to about nine feet in diameter, and the vicar worried that someone might fall in. He headed into the village to look for planks to cover it. While there he ran into Mr. Knight, "the local builder and undertaker," and invited him to the church to see the opening.

Upon returning to the path, Dr. Byles was astonished to see no sign of the hole -- the narrow lane and the grassy turf to either side were exactly as they had been before. After listening to the vicar voice his confusion, Mr. Knight simply said "That's all right, sir" and never mentioned the "Hole" again.

The Byles moved to London in 1950. Dr. Byles admitted to telling a few people about the Hole over the years. After receiving his manuscript, Theo Brown visited Yealmpton personally. The story of the "Hole" was well known to the villagers, but no one had ever seen such a thing themselves, before or after Byles' experience. They frowned upon her suggestion that the grounds around the church be excavated to search for underground cavities or structures. Ms. Brown concludes: "It may have been quite a unique event with a significance that must for the present remain obscure."

Here again, one can only wonder what would have happened if the vicar actually had descended into the opening. And what was the "stonework" the Byles saw, which looked like part of a wall?

Writer and TV producer Paul Chambers scoured nineteenth century newspapers for strange disappearances and found a hundred cases reported in the London Times alone, noting that "for some reason, vicars seem particularly adept at vanishing without trace." Dr. Byles may have had a narrow escape.

Brown, Theo. Devon Ghosts (Norwich: Jarrold & Sons Ltd., 1982), pp. 24-26.

Chambers, Paul, "The Vanishing," Fortean Times no. 194 (April 2005), p. 42.

Davies, Rodney. Supernatural Vanishings (New York: Sterling Publishing Company, 1996), pp. 116-119.

"Extraordinary Hallucination." London Times, December 11, 1873, p. 11.

"Extraordinary Occurrence at a Bristol Hotel." Bristol Mercury, December 13, 1873.

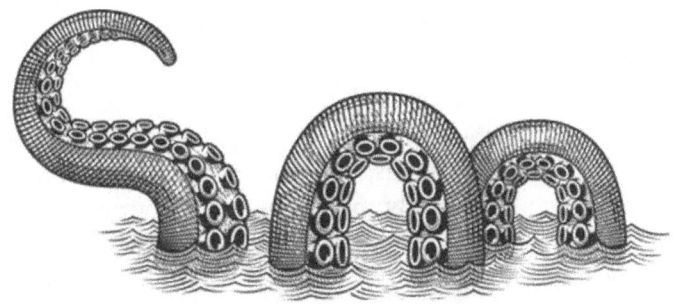

- Colorado: Red-eyed monster
- Wazooey Man (unidentified creature)

The Wazooey Man

"The Wazooey Man" is a bizarre entity that haunts an arroyo off Red Creek Road, several miles southwest of Pueblo, Colorado. Jim Brandon writes:
 "Around May 15, 1973, two boys who were plinking with an air pistol in the arroyo one evening gradually became aware, in the fading light, of two huge red eyes. They looked like bicycle reflectors, and with a jolt of youthful ebullience, one of the boys took a shot at them."
 This act proved to be ill-advised, because a poltergeist-like force lifted the young men from the ground and dumped them into a shallow gulch nearby. As if this weren't enough punishment, a wooden fencepost uprooted itself from the earth and hit one of them on the head (presumably the one who shot "it"). The boys ran for their truck but lost the keys somewhere along the way. They started home along Red Creek Road, trying to hitch a ride. Any time they tried to head west -- the direction of the canyon -- something like a "mobile haystack" with big red eyes would appear and frighten them away.
 The red eyes, like bicycle reflectors, put one in mind of Mothman. The "mobile haystack" is a little stranger, but perhaps, if West Virginia's famous bogey, with its peepers set into its shoulder-area, were to spread its batlike wings, the silhouette might look from straight

on like a haystack with red eyes. At any rate, this is all we're told of the Wazooey Man.

In 2011, a pair of men crossed America visiting sites mentioned in Brandon's book. On May 15, they entered the arroyo. They found dozens of spent shotgun shells, old couch cushions, various stuffed animals, and large, apparently man-made, stone structures – but no Wazooey Man. Their adventures have appeared on YouTube, uploaded by "mandate33".

Brandon, Jim. Weird America (New York: E. P. Dutton, 1978), pp. 49-50.

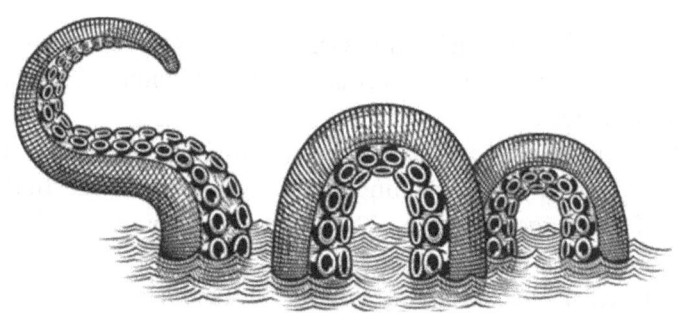

AFTERWORD

I still have a list of rumors, familiar and obscure, old and new, that many people have heard about, but the details have faded with time or were never given in the first place. There are plenty of rumors I've heard myself that I have never tracked down to my satisfaction, concerning events psychical, cryptozoological, and just plain weird. Maybe you, the reader, can seek out one of these rumors yourself. Maybe you even know someone who was involved in the original event. Rumors like:

* A military transport plane, sometime in the 1940s or '50s, crashes somewhere on the west coast. The skin of the fuselage is full of punctures, the windscreens are all shattered. The pilots and crew – all dead – their bodies are covered with puncture wounds that seem to have burst from within. All the men's firearms have been emptied, as if they had shot futilely at some invincible foe at 10,000 feet.

* An expedition enters a cave system somewhere in Asia or the Middle East, led by geologists and archeologists. Somewhere in the dark tunnels giant humanoids covered with white hair attack the expedition, and at least one scientist is killed ...

* Vehicles drive down the back roads of the USA, vehicles resembling no known make or model of car or truck – some not even possessing wheels. Unidentified Driving Objects, no less.

* All sorts of strange voices, some claiming to be of extraterrestrial origin, echo out of radios, amplifiers, and walkie-talkies, even ones that are switched off or unplugged.

* And perhaps the strangest story of all: When I attended good old Hoover Elementary School, I ate lunch occasionally with a boy whose father was a police detective (at least, that's what he said). The boy would gleefully outline the seedy and gory details of major crimes committed in the Tulsa area. There was one case, however, that stumped him, his detective dad, and the whole police department.

Essentially, a young woman had been found murdered in her house or apartment. Her throat had been cut, her wrists bound together, and her body had been hung from a coat hook on a closet door.

The crime was a classic locked-room mystery. As I recall (and it has been many years since I heard the story), the circumstances precluded suicide, all the doors (and windows, if there were any) had been secured from the inside, and, of course, no one but the dead woman was to be found when the police entered.

The capper was this: Something – I would assume flakes of skin – had been found on the underside of the door that didn't come from the victim. According to my lunchtime pal, it looked to all involved as if the killer had entered the room under the door like some kind of huge slug. This was supposed to be a deep, dark secret lest the populace fly into a panic, but the old man just had to blab it to his son, who blabbed it to me (and no telling who else).

And how did the killer get out? My friend paused in eating his ham and cheese sandwich and shrugged.

"He went down the toilet for all they know."

Watch for "I Heard of that Somewhere, Too" Coming Soon!

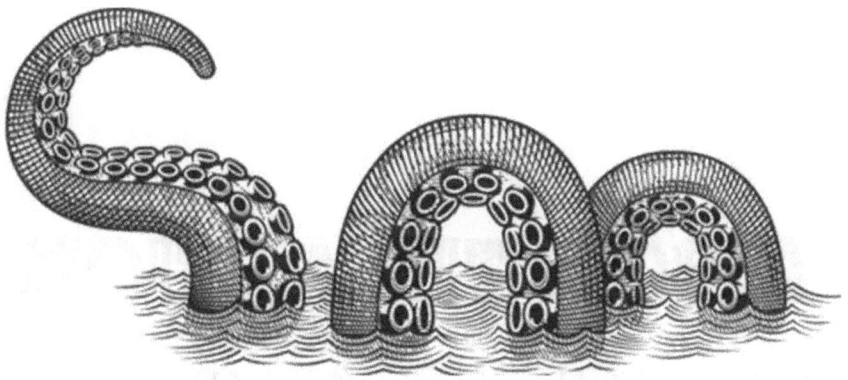

To Carroll B. Colby, Ivan Sanderson, Charles Fort, John Keel and other pursuers of monsters and mysteries. Their books always reached me at just the right time and in just the right order to guide me down the paranormal super-highway.

ABOUT THE AUTHOR

Michael D. Winkle was born in Tulsa, Oklahoma into what he thought was a serene and logical world. When he was eight years old, however, he picked up a little paperback called Strangely Enough! and read about ghosts, flying saucers, people bursting into flame, and planes and ships vanishing into thin air, after which logic fell by the wayside.

He has worked in many professions over the years, from librarian to postal worker to bookkeeper, as writers are wont to do, but he pursues supposedly true stories of the weird and paranormal in his spare time. Michael is the author of some thirty short stories and of several articles on various subjects. He resides in the small town of Owasso, Oklahoma.

www.ingramcontent.com/pod-product-compliance
Lightning Source LLC
Chambersburg PA
CBHW070140100426
42743CB00013B/2775